PARABLE AND STORY
IN JUDAISM AND CHRISTIANITY

Studies in Judaism and Christianity

Exploration of Issues in the Contemporary Dialogue Between Christians and Jews

Editor in Chief for
Stimulus Books
Helga Croner

Editors
Lawrence Boadt, C.S.P.
Helga Croner
Leon Klenicki
John Koenig
Kevin A. Lynch, C.S.P.

 A STIMULUS BOOK

PARABLE AND STORY
IN JUDAISM AND CHRISTIANITY

Clemens Thoma and Michael Wyschogrod, Editors

63502

A STIMULUS BOOK

PAULIST PRESS ◆ NEW YORK ◆ MAHWAH

Library of Congress Cataloging-in-Publication Data

Parable and story in Judaism and Christianity / Clemens Thoma and
  Michael Wyschogrod, editors.
      p.   cm. — (A Stimulus book)
  Includes bibliographies and index.
    Articles grew out of a consultation on Parable and story as
  sources of Jewish and Christian theology held in Lucerne,
  Switzerland, June 2–4, 1986 and sponsored by the Institute for
  Jewish-Christian Relations of the American Jewish Congress and the
  Institute for Jewish-Christian Research of the Theological Faculty
  of Lucerne (Catholic)
    ISBN 0-8091-3087-4 : $8.95 (est.)
    1. Jesus Christ—Parables—Congresses. 2. Parables in rabbinical
  literature—Congresses. 3. Parables—Congresses. 4. Storytelling—
  Religious aspects—Congresses.   I. Thoma, Clemens, 1932–
  II. Wyschogrod, Michael, 1928– .   III. American Jewish Congress.
  Institute for Jewish-Christian Relations.   IV. Theologische Fakultät
  Luzern (Switzerland). Institut für Jüdisch-Christliche Forschung.
  BT375.2.P36   1989
  261.5′8—dc20   89-8865
                                                                        CIP

Published by Paulist Press
997 Macarthur Boulevard
Mahwah, N.J. 07430

Printed and bound in the
United States of America

Contents

Introduction

Clemens Thoma and Michael Wyschogrod

Stories are at the heart of both Judaism and Christianity. This is true of the Hebrew Bible and the New Testament, both of which—whatever else they may contain—tell some remarkably interesting stories. But the telling of stories did not end with the biblical period. A rich story literature continued through subsequent centuries, though not at a steady rate. Because stories and parables invite interpretation, there were periods when the interpretive spirit almost overwhelmed the story-generating one. During such periods, it almost appeared as if Judaism and Christianity were philosophical systems in which stories played a secondary role at best. Yet, the power of the Jewish and Christian story-telling genius was such that it could never be suppressed for long. Interpretations come and go, but the great stories are told forever, and sooner or later they are rediscovered, like Abraham's wells that the Philistines had stopped up and which Isaac reopened (Gen 26:18).

The essays in this book do not tell stories (though they quote many), and in that sense they are acts of interpretation. But they attempt to interpret stories without losing sight of the primacy of story and parable, as expressing truths that cannot be expressed in any other way.

It is natural that after a story is told, questions about its meaning arise. This is particularly so in the case of parables which generally have a "point" that the listener is supposed to fathom. This is also true of non-parable narratives, especially when they occur in a religious context. The believer knows that there is something he is supposed to learn from the stories, and he therefore searches for an authorized interpretation.

What is there about religious experience that makes it so natural to express it in the story medium? And what is there about the story medium that it so often has religious implications, even when the story,

1

as in parables, does not explicitly deal with religious issues? These are the questions that draw theologians to literary issues, and literary critics to religious issues.

When Jewish and Christian literary scholars and theologians begin to speak to one another, they bring to the dialogue not only the different perspectives of their disciplines, but also the complexities that have characterized the relationship between Judaism and Christianity, the faiths that grew out of the Hebrew Bible and the New Testament, respectively.

In the development of strategies to deal with such questions, attention must be paid to a number of hermeneutical issues. One of these is the dimension of time. It is improper to lift the Jewish and Christian scriptures, and subsequent Jewish and Christian literature, out of their origins within the verbal culture of their times. We are dealing here with "transformative revelations" (an expression used by Michael Fishbane in his *Biblical Interpretation in Ancient Israel,* Oxford, 1985, p. 18) by means of which one generation infuses with life what it had received from earlier generations. From the very beginning, revelation did not appear in fixed and unyielding formulas but rather as material to be worked on and developed by human beings who defined their humanity and their relation to God in the process.

Ever since the second century CE, Jewish and Christian literature has been subjected to contradictory interpretations because of tensions between the two communities. It is therefore particularly important for Jewish and Christian scholars in our time to work together on contested texts, especially parables and narratives which tend to have an unusually wide influence.

Stories and parables deal mainly with human affairs but their overtones reach into many directions, drawing human affairs into mysterious realms where the human and what is more than human interact. Above all, stories and parables preserve the mystery without which explanation becomes lethal to the human spirit because it loses respect for the inexplicable behind that which is explained.

This book is divided into three sections. Part I (with essays by David Flusser, Clemens Thoma, David Stern and Aaron Milavec) refers to "Ancient Parables and the Gospel." These essays deal with New Testament and Rabbinic parables, both separately and in relation to one another.

Flusser compares Aesop's Fable of the Miser with the Rabbinic Parable of Wheat and Flax and Jesus' Parable of the Talents. The Greek parable recommends that man use his abilities to better his life, while the other two parables see life as a loan from God which has to be repaid with interest. Flusser demonstrates that the changes which occurred during the development of the fable brought it close to a central component of the parable. This essay contributes to an understanding of the relation of fable to parable.

Thoma reports on the project of the Lucerne team which is editing, translating and analyzing approximately 1,300 Rabbinic parables. He speaks of the mashal/nimshal (narrative/normative instruction) structure which always wishes to elicit a new point (hiddush) that constitutes the lesson of the parable. After analyzing the structures of several selected parables, Thoma discusses the theological aspects of Rabbinic parables.

Stern discusses Jesus' Parable of the Wicked Husbandmen. He first surveys previous interpretations and examines the distinction between simile and metaphor, with the former associated with parable and the latter with allegory. He does not accept the distinction between sacred and secular parables and concludes by relating the Parable of the Wicked Husbandmen to the question of the nature of Jesus' authority and acceptance of him as the messiah. Throughout the essay, Stern deals with both theological and literary issues.

Milavec also deals with the Parable of the Wicked Husbandmen. He points out that, traditionally, this Parable has been interpreted to teach that God has rejected the Jews because they killed God's Son. The Parable has thus become one of the pillars of supersessionist Christianity (the view that Christianity has replaced Judaism). But, according to Milavec, a careful reading of the Parable in its various versions does not bear out such an interpretation. The resurrection theme, for instance, is missing from the Parable, which makes it harder to identify the son of the Parable with Jesus. Finally, those who will inherit the vineyard are also Jews. The anti-Jewish image that this Parable has acquired is therefore undeserved.

Part II of this volume (with essays by Frank Kermode, Paul Michel and Lawrence Boadt) deals with "Literary-Critical Reflections on Parable and Story." Here, the emphasis is on literary and linguistic issues that arise in the interpretation of biblical stories and parables.

Kermode points out that recent literary studies of biblical narratives approach the subject from rather different angles than those pursued in Erich Auerbach's *Mimesis*. Nowadays, some come to the text with the Formalist criteria of the 1960s, some with various kinds of "reader response" theories, while others rely on the style of narratological analysis developed in Israel. Kermode discusses Sternberg's notion of "gaps and blanks" which seem to form an essential component of biblical narrative. Kermode concludes that in their manner of writing stories, there was much in common between the authors of the two bibles.

Michel approaches parables as a form of figurative speech. After discussing the function of figurative speech, he investigates its formal structure. He identifies four exegetical paths that lead from the text to the communicative point of the parable. Drawing on numerous rabbinic parables, Michel places the parable midway between direct communicative speech and lyrical poetry because, like communicative speech, the parable has a meaning beyond itself but, like lyrical poetry, parables have their own linguistic integrity.

Boadt starts with a survey of the literature, paying particular attention to the work of Dan O. Via and John Dominic Crossan. He then comments on the contributions to this volume by Stern, Flusser and Milavec, finding some points on which he differs. He devotes the rest of his paper to a discussion of the power of narrative, including the example of a narrative Christology. He concludes that the Catholic interest in narrative theology should help stimulate Christian interest in Jewish origins.

Part III (with essays from Romano Penna, Kathryn Hellerstein and Alan Mintz) is titled "Story: Ancient and Modern" and juxtaposes an essay on St. Paul with treatments of modern Yiddish and Hebrew literature.

Penna argues that even in St. Paul's Epistle to the Romans—one of the most theological documents of the New Testament—significant narrative aspects can be found. After defining more closely what he does and does not mean by narration, he states that the genre of narration is found on six levels in the Epistle. Paul narrates stories from the Hebrew Bible, and he deals with the narrative dimension of the Christological kerygma. We are also given autobiographical information about Paul, the Epistle's author, who, in turn, comments about the theological biographies of the Epistle's readers. The Epistle is replete with instances of theological narration and abundant use of similes. Penna helps us read Romans from a new perspective.

Hellerstein starts by exploring the complex interaction between narrative and prayer in classic rabbinical prayer and in medieval *piyyutim*. She then turns to the role of prayer in modern Yiddish poetry. Just as prayer replaced sacrifices after the destruction of the Jerusalem Temple, so in the modern period many Yiddish poets substituted narration about prayer for actual prayer. Based on a careful analysis of a number of Yiddish prayer poems, Hellerstein documents the deep religious tensions that are reflected in these works. She concludes that the modern Yiddish poet is unable to relinquish entirely the form of Jewish prayer but at the same time sometimes finds it necessary to subvert the prayer form.

Mintz concludes this volume by maintaining that modern Hebrew literature became the modernist medium through which Jewish writers explored their uprootedness and dislocation. Over against the Rebirth and Catastrophe models, he interprets Hebrew literature in a more distinctly literary mode since, he argues, in literature the grip of non-literary history is partly held at bay. After exploring such issues as the quasi-canonization of literary texts and the contribution of secular literary criticism to the understanding of the Bible, Mintz concludes that modern Hebrew literature can tell us where God is not, somewhat in the spirit of the negative theology of medieval Jewish philosophy.

The articles in this volume grew out of a consultation on "Parable and Story as Sources of Jewish and Christian Theology" held in Lucerne, Switzerland, June 2–4, 1986. Some participants in that consultation delivered preliminary papers which they revised in light of the discussion for publication in this volume. Others, stimulated by the discussion, wrote papers after the consultation on themes that emerged during the consultation. The result is a volume that combines originality with openness to influence from others working on related topics.

The 1986 consultation followed an earlier one held January 16–18, 1984, also in Lucerne, on "Understanding Scripture: Explorations of Jewish and Christian Traditions of Interpretation," published under the same title as a Stimulus Book in 1987. Both the 1984 and 1986 consultations were sponsored by the Institute for Jewish-Christian Relations of the American Jewish Congress and the Institute for Jewish-Christian Research of the Theological Faculty of Lucerne (Catholic), the latter acting in consultation and collaboration with the Vatican Commission for Religious Relations with the Jews.

In our Introduction to the 1987 volume, we explained the genesis of the collaboration whose second fruit is now in the hands of the reader. We spoke of our conviction that a forum was needed where Jews and Catholics—and Jews and Christians—could deal with scholarly and theological issues in a non-political atmosphere. "We were convinced," we wrote in the 1987 Introduction, that, important as social and political issues are, the center of Jewish-Catholic relations had to be located in an exchange of views about issues of common scholarly concern, conducted in an atmosphere of respect for the views of all concerned and dedication to the standards of historical and theological research. Genuine scholarship cannot thrive in an emotional atmosphere, whether of mutual suspicion or uncritical affection.

This is the conviction that continues to guide our work and which the reader will find reflected in the pages of this volume. The editors are grateful to the American Jewish Congress, responsible Church authorities, and Helga Croner, President of the Stimulus Foundation, for their support of the scholarly enterprise that resulted in this volume.

I.
ANCIENT PARABLES
AND THE GOSPEL

Aesop's Miser and
the Parable of the Talents

David Flusser

I. INTRODUCTION TO THE LITERARY ASPECTS

In a previous study,[1] I have demonstrated that the parables of Jesus belong to the older type of rabbinic parables, namely the non-exegetical "ethical" type. I also discussed there the affinity between the parables and the Aesop fable and even suggested that one of the roots for the *Gattung* of the Jewish parables can possibly be found in Greek philosophy, which contains stories similar to rabbinic parables. In any case, the transition between these kindred *Gattungen* is evidently fluid.

Here we want to cite a concrete example of such a tendency of fluidity by describing the process of advance from an Aesop fable through its new form in a Greek philosophical text, and finally to a similar motif in the Parable of the Talents (Mt 25:14–30; cf. Lk 19:11–12).[2] But before we examine the interaction between these texts, it is important to make some remarks about the parable itself.

1. The Meaning of "Talent"

In European languages the word "talent" has the meaning of ability, and a talented person is described as being gifted. Evidently it is mostly unknown that the term itself actually stems from our parable.[3] Indeed, the definition of the modern word "talent" is very close to the central meaning of the parable itself. We have to understand Matthew 25:14–15 along these lines: "A man going on a journey[4] called his servants and entrusted to them his property; to one he gave five talents, to another two, to another one, to each *according to his ability*.[5] Then he

9

went away." Thus when distributing the talents, the master took into careful consideration what he knew about each servant's aptitude.

The meaning of the text is that God has bestowed upon each one of us our individual abilities and everyone is obligated to fully develop his special talent which has been graciously granted to him, in order that it may be productive. It seems that the metaphoric use of talents in the parable is derived from an ingenious interpretation of Proverbs 3:9: "Honor the LORD with (literally: from) your substance." The point of departure for this understanding of the verse is a pun, based on the contemporary Hebrew pronunciation: Honor the Lord from your substance (mehonecho)—from what He has graciously granted to you (mima shechononcho). This creative interpretation of Proverbs 3:9 quite possibly existed already in Jesus' time and is certainly earlier than the beginning of the third century C.E.[6] Hence it is not difficult to assume that Jesus had this proverbial sentence in mind when he invented the Parable of the Talents. Anyhow, the content of the aphoristic rabbinic saying fits admirably the moral teaching of the parable.

Yet there is another decisive element in the plot of this parable which conveys a moral and religious stringency, so that it can express the message proper in the spirit of Judaism and Christianity. The Parable of the Talents belongs to a type of Jewish parables the object of which is a property entrusted by the proprietor to others. That property must be returned to its owner in at least the same state as it had been before or, if conditions permit, even augmented and improved. The third servant thought that the original state would be sufficient, and he did not grasp that his duty should have been to repay the sum to the owner with interest, and his failure to do so brought the punishment upon him.

There is no doubt obviously that the servants are obliged to repay the sum to their master, although that final obligation is neither mentioned in Matthew nor in Luke in their elaborate wording. That final repayment is in fact a significant point in the deep meaning of the parable. In all those Jewish parables having human life as their theme—and the Parable of the Talents forming an example of that theme—the proprietor symbolizes God, and the entrustment of property means a gracious loan from Him, being entrusted yet never a possession of ours at our discretion.

In this sense, it was told of Rabban Johanan ben Zakkai, that his disciples tried in vain to console him when his son died. At last R. Eleazar came and sat before him and said, "Let me tell you a parable. To what is the matter like? To a man with whom a king has deposited an article of value. Daily the man wept and exclaimed, 'Woe is me! when will I be free from the responsibility of this trust?' You too, my master, had a son versed in the Torah, who had studied the Pentateuch, Prophets and Hagiographs, Mishnah, halakoth and 'aggadoth. He has departed sinless from this world. Surely you should derive comfort from having returned your trust intact!' Rabban Johanan said to him, 'Eleazar my son, you have comforted me as men can comfort' " (ARN, version A, chapter 14, p. 3).

The theological point of departure of Jesus' Parable of the Talents will become even more understandable when comparing it with the famous dictum of Rabbi Akiba. He used to say, "All is given against a pledge . . . the shop stands open and the shopkeeper gives credit and the account-book lies open and the hand writes and every one that wishes to borrow let him come and borrow; but the collectors go their round continually every day and exact payment of men with their consent or without their consent, for they have that on which they can rely; and the judgement is a judgement of truth" (Sayings of the Fathers, 3–17).

In all these sayings, the deep meaning of Jesus' Parable of the Talents comes to light: Man is obliged to fully develop his own self in accordance with Him, whose unworthy servant he is.[6a]

2. The Typical Pattern of Rabbinic and Jesus' Parables

The parable appears in Matthew (25:14–30) and also in Luke (19:11–27), in a rewritten form. The two variants have in common the following formal features which need some clarification: (a) In both versions of the parable the number of the servants to whom the master entrusts a sum of money is larger[7] than the three servants who play a major role in the message of the parable. (b) The number three is a typical pattern in parables and similar literary forms, e.g., the fairy tales. Often this number is used in order to create a gradation. In both forms of our parable there is a descending gradation.[8] (c) In our case both the number three and the descending gradation are meaningful only in the Matthean variant, because three different persons represent in the simplest way the variety of human abilities.

In Luke the descending gradation is a "blind motif" and this confirms again the priority of the Matthean version. But even there one can recognize that the plot of the parable itself is built upon the contrast of only two protagonists, the positive and the negative hero. This pattern is also typical for parables and for other literary forms, e.g. the fairy tales.

Among Jesus' parables the most famous one of this type is the Parable of the Two Sons (Mt 20:9–10). The contrasting figures represent in such cases the right and wrong behavior, and in the parables emphasis is placed upon a warning against improper conduct. In our parable, the first two servants belong together: both are "good and faithful" servants and have done "well" (Mt 25:21, 23); the third servant is "wicked and slothful" (Mt 25:26; cf. Lk 19:22), and he acted wrongly. As we have seen, all three components—the larger number of servants, the three who play a major role in the story, and the twofold division between well-doers and wrong-doers—are common to both versions of the parable as they have been preserved in Matthew and in Luke.

It is evident that behind the tripartite structure of the Parable of the Talents there is a basic contrast between only two opposites. This is confirmed by a parallel rabbinic parable in which only two servants appear, one clever and the other foolish.[9] In the passage, the Hebrew author answers an opponent who does not believe in the heavenly origin of the Oral Law: "My son, were not both Scriptures and Mishnah given by the Almighty? Does the fact that they are different from each other mean that both cannot have been given by Him? By what parable may the question be answered? By the one of a mortal king who had two servants whom he loved with utter love. To one he gave a measure of wheat and to the other he gave a measure of wheat, to one a bundle of flax and to the other a bundle of flax. What did the clever one of the two do? He took the flax and wove it into a tablecloth. He took the wheat and made it into fine flour by sifting the grain first and grinding it. Then he kneaded the dough and baked it, set the loaf upon the table, spread the tablecloth over it and kept it to await the coming of the king. But the foolish one did not do anything.

"After a while the king came into the house and said to the two servants: My sons, bring me what I gave you. One brought out the table with [the loaf baked of] fine flour on it, and with the tablecloth spread over it. And the other brought out his wheat in a basket with the bundle of flax over the wheat grains.—What a shame! What a disgrace! Need it be said which of the two servants was the more beloved? He of course who laid out the table with [the loaf baked of] fine flour upon it. The truth is that when the Holy one gave the Torah to Israel, he gave it to them as wheat out of which the fine flour of Mishnah was to be produced, and as a flax of which the fine linen cloth of Mishnah was to be produced."

A. Jülicher[10] already learned from a Jewish predecessor about the existence of this rabbinic parallel to the Parable of the Talents. He considered the importance of the rabbinic parable negligible because the similarity between them is not great enough to assume a common source and the parable of Jesus is much more simple and less sophisticated. In reality, one does not need to be well versed in the various branches of popular literature in order to be able to recognize the striking similarity between the Parable of the Talents and its rabbinic parallel. The skeleton of the two parables is identical: A master gave to his servants a part of his property. The one (or: the first two of them) dealt with what was entrusted to him (or: to them) and made improvements. The other servant did not do anything with his master's property. When the master returned home, he said to his servants: "Bring me what I gave you." The one servant (or: the first two) brought the entrusted property amended and improved while the other servant brought it in the same state as he had received it. Thus there is no doubt that the first one (or: ones) became more beloved by the master than the foolish servant.

This kind of similarity and such a degree of parallelism does not occur very often in the case of parables. More often one encounters such a close kinship with the whole shape of the story among fairy tales. If one could distinguish such common features in two fairy tales, one would not hesitate to speak about two variants of one common model. Why should a similar conclusion not be permitted in the case of two parables, one rabbinic and the other by Jesus? In such cases, it is not unusual for the various motifs to be interchangeable while the main structure remains more or less intact. In our case, one discovers a difference in the two parables between the kind of property which the master entrusted to his servants (talents or pounds—a measure of wheat and a bundle of flax) and therefore naturally there is also a difference between the kind of profit involved with the entrusted property.

As to the parables, we are also obliged to pay attention to the message which the story has to transmit. The teaching[11] of the Parable of the Talents is that we have to develop the gifts which God has granted us, in the optimal way and not allowing them to become an unused capital or a hidden treasure which lies dormant.[12] On the other hand, the author of the rabbinic parallel wanted to show that although the Torah and the Mishnah are different, they were both given by the Almighty.

However the real purpose of the parable has a far deeper significance. In dealing with the Written Law, the refinement and improvement result in the Oral Law. But even so, the two parables, the rabbinic and that of Jesus, are so similar that one would probably not perceive any serious disharmony if the rabbinic parable were to be used as an illustration for the message of the Parable of the Talents. The opposite experiment might not be as successful, although the result of such a transplantation should not seem too far-fetched to an open-minded reader.

There are two somewhat apologetic alternative explanations that would plead for the "splendid isolation" of Jesus' Parable of the Talents. The first is to deny any genetic connection between the two parables and to declare that the rabbinic parable is of negligible meaning and importance. The second alternative seems less popular today, namely to assume that the later rabbinic parallel is a reshuffled version of Jesus' parable. The first alternative is, in my eyes, unrealistic because the similarity is too evident. The second alternative cannot be dismissed without further consideration, although the apologetic background of this explanation is very obvious. The assumption of a dependence of rabbinic parables upon those of Jesus is, of course, always open to serious objections.

Against those who are prone to assume that the Parable of the Talents is a distant forefather of the rabbinic parable about the wheat and the flax, it must be observed that while the two parables are built according to the same structure, the data employed to fill this structure in each parable are entirely different. This is in accordance with the general rules, typical for the whole *Gattung* of parables. In our case the two similar parables are products of the same laws which regulate the various mutations within a single model. We should also not forget that the Parable of the Talents itself already was not created in a literary void. The impact of the creative forces which gave birth to so many rabbinic parables as well as the parables of Jesus produced both varieties which developed from the same structure.

II. REPAYMENT WITHOUT INTEREST

Now we want to see what happened to the third servant who received only one talent. He dug in the ground and hid his master's money (Mt 25:18).[13] He did this because he was afraid of his master whom he believed[14] to be a hard man, reaping where he did not sow and gathering where he did not winnow (Mt 25:24–25; Lk 19:20–21). The natural precaution of the third servant was exaggerated and dictated by misplaced fear. He was afraid that if he did not hide the money he would run the risk of losing it and then he could not return the entire sum to his hard master. The two other servants traded with their master's money and invested it with the bankers. Because of their wise investments, when their master returned he was able to receive what was his own with interest.

The third servant did not dare act in like manner. Evidently he was afraid, and he wrongly reasoned that the safest way to keep the sum intact was to hide it burying it in the ground. The sum indeed remained intact, but it did not produce any additional profit either. Hence the servant's precautionary measure turned out to be a much more risky course of action for which he suffered. When the master returned, he gave the order to have the talent taken away from the third foolish servant and given to his first servant, and to punish this foolish slave severely.[15]

1. Similarity with Aesop's Fable "The Miser"

An untimely precaution which leads to an opposite result (a loss) is, according to modern terminology, a current *motifeme*.[16] The same *motifeme* is e.g. behind the plot of the famous comedy of Beáumarchais, *The Barber of Seville* (1775), whose subtitle is significantly *La précaution inutile* (*The Unnecessary Precaution*). The same *motifeme* of an exaggerated precaution is also found in the Aesop fable,[17] "The Miser," whose secondary variant will be meaningful for the Parable of the Talents. The similarity between the parable and the fable is not exhausted by this common *motifeme* because both also have in common the motif of the danger of hiding a treasure in the earth.

The story of the fable is as follows: "A miser turned into cash all his property and bought a mass of gold and buried it somewhere. By acting thus he buried his own soul and his mind. He went there day after day and inspected it. But it happened that one of the workers watched him and perceived what had happened. He dug up the nugget and carried it off. Later on the miser returned, and as he found the place empty, he began to lament and tear out his hair. Someone who saw him wailing, after having learned the cause, said to him: 'Do not grieve like this, my friend, because when you possessed the gold you did not possess it. So put a stone instead of the gold and deem that it is your gold, and the stone will surely fulfill the same task. For as I see, when the gold was yours, you did make no use of it.' " The story teaches that property has no value if you do not enjoy it.

The last sentence of the Aesop fable was added to the story to teach its moral doctrine, but this commonly happens with the concluding sentence of a fable.[18] We must recognize however that this conclusion does not fully express all the implications latent in the plot. The plot itself teaches us much more than that unused property has no value. Indeed, it has a broader application. The practical issue of the Aesop story is simply that if a sum is hidden in the earth, it is unproductive.

By the way, the same advice can be gleaned from what happened to the third servant in the Parable of the Talents. In both stories, the basic development of the plots is similar, while the difference between them is based upon the various characters of the two heroes. The Aesop miser is a kind of Moliere's Harpagon; he buried his property in the ground because he was madly in love with his gold. So even before it was stolen, he did not really possess it, because in his obsession he was not able to use the gold for his own pleasure. His foolishness turned his property into idle capital.

However the reason why the talent of the third servant in the parable also became unproductive is different. The servant did not bury the talent in the earth for the same concerns that motivated the miser in the fable. The talent was not the servant's property; it was only entrusted to him and he did not feel any emotional attachment to it. He buried the talent in the earth because he was afraid of his master whom he thought to be a hard man, reaping where he did not sow and gathering where he did not winnow (Mt 25:24–25; Lk 19:21).[19] By hiding the talent, he hoped to avoid the danger that it would get lost,[20] but he did not take into consideration that he could have increased the value of his master's money by wise investment.

This simple consideration is valid both for the third servant of the parable and for the miser in the Aesop fable: if he would not have been so madly fascinated with the very possession of the property, his innate greediness would have led him, not to bury the property in the earth, but to invest it in order to receive it with increment. Thus the alternatives for the miser were to use his property for his own pleasure, or to satisfy his greediness by investing the gold.

2. Similarity Enhanced by Antiphon's Version of the Fable

The second alternative became a part of the Aesop fable in another version of the story, as it was adapted by the Greek sophist Antiphon (fifth century B.C.E.),[21] and this ingenious change made the similarity between the parable and the fable really significant.

It is a story about a man who saw another earning a great deal of money, and begged him to loan him a sum with interest. The other refused and, being of a distrustful nature, unwilling to help anyone, he carried the money off and hid it somewhere. Another man, observing him, filched it. Later, the man who had hidden the money returned and could not find it. Being very grieved at the disaster—especially that he had not lent to the man who had asked him, because then the money would have been safe and would have earned interest—he met the man who had asked for a loan. He bewailed his misfortune, saying that he had done wrong and was sorry not to have granted the other's request, as now his money was completely lost.

The other man told him not to worry but to hide a stone in the same place and think of his money as his and not lost: "For even when you had it, you completely failed to use it; so that now too you can think you have lost nothing."

When a person does not use a possession and will not use it in the future, what difference does it make whether he actually owns it or not? Moreover, any damage incurred would be of no consequence. When God does not wish to give a person complete good fortune—when He has given him material wealth but made him poor in right thinking—in taking away one, He has deprived him of both.

In the first variant of the Aesop fable it is said that the miser, by hiding his property in the earth, buried there also his own soul and his mind. This idea was enlarged upon by Antiphon the Sophist and developed into a philosophical resumé of the fable. The message of the revised fable teaches the Sophists' utilitarian dogma of the need for right thinking in order to possess worldly gain.

Right thinking is an indispensable prerequisite for a person trying to attain riches; if he is deficient in right thinking, he will also lose his material wealth. If some are inclined to interpret this practical morality in light of the economic changes current in Athens during the fifth century B.C.E., they will also have to examine the other numerous fragments of Antiphon the Sophist.[22]

In any case, it is not without interest that a similar pragmatic view about wisdom and riches appears in the message of a German *Volksbuch* named *Fortunatus*[23] which was printed in Augsburg in 1509. It was recognized that the popular book, composed in the period of the rise of the middle class, reflects the *Weltanschauung* of early capitalism. According to *Fortunatus*, it is only with the help of wisdom that one can acquire worldly property and riches. The author, moreover, makes reference to the example of Solomon (1 Kgs 3:5–14) who chose wisdom and became the richest king on earth.

But let us now forget the sociological approach to literature, because we actually want to answer the question concerning which version preserves the more original moral conclusion of the story. Is the first lesson taught in the Aesop fable closer to the original or is the second version of Antiphon more suitable for the whole plot of the fable itself? We do not dare give an unequivocal answer. In our opinion the two moral teachings complement each other: the story of the miser shows both that the property has no value if one does not enjoy it, and also that if one is deficient in right thinking one is in danger of losing one's natural wealth. Even so, the two moral applications do not exhaust all the meanings inherent in the fable,[24] but we cannot touch here on the broader problems of literary criticism.

For our purpose, it will suffice to note that fables commonly are not merely simple stories. Their goal is to teach a message, although fables are not metaphorical in the same degree as parables are. This is also valid for the Parable of the Talents and for our fable about the Miser. While the miser's property is nothing more than a nugget of gold, the servant's talent which also was buried in the ground actually means a person's abilities, which are useless if they are not cultivated.

Now we want to show that the variation of our fable from the Aesop corpus is earlier than that recounted by Antiphon. In this later stage of development two substantial changes were made. The first adaptation was that Antiphon added the observation about the importance of right thinking for the possession of material wealth. Apparently this change was made by Antiphon himself because it represents the ideology of the Sophists. The other modification, where the man begs the miser to lend him a sum of money with interest, quite possibly antedates Antiphon.

In Antiphon's version, this is the man who is later identified with the anonymous passer-by who met the miser after the theft and consoled him.[25] Of course this was not a very convincing adaptation because it is not very probable that a man whom the miser had refused to give a loan would have become so kind and help him solve his problem. I do not say that such a sudden change of mind cannot appear in a story, but the other version of the fable does not suffer from such an improbability. Hence it is logical to conclude that both, the motif of the man who asked for a loan and his identification with the accidental passer-by, were added to the more original story only in a later stage.

Nonetheless it was precisely this additional motif of a loan request with interest, in the secondary form of the story, and not the theme of the futility of a sum of money hidden in the ground, which made the comparison of the fable about the Miser with the Parable of the Talents so meaningful. Here one has occasion to observe how the forces, latent in the plot of the Aesop fable, pushed it into the vicinity of a parable of Jesus. In both stories an untimely precaution seduces a man to bury his own property in a hiding place in the ground, and in both cases the action results in disaster. In the fable the sad consequence of the false precaution was a theft, whereas in the parable the servant is punished by his master because by hiding the talent in the earth he missed the opportunity to loan it with interest and so to multiply it.

Antiphon, or already his predecessor, became aware of one of the creative faculties latent in his story: he understood that hiding a treasure is stupid not only because the very act invites thieves, but also because a hidden treasure becomes idle capital unable to earn profit. With the aim of introducing the result of his observation into the plot itself, the writer partially changed the nature of the miser. In the earlier version of the fable, the miser was a kind of Harpagon, fascinated by the very possession of the property. In order to become the only living creature privileged to see it, he buried the gold in the earth and day by day went to visit the place and to take delight at the sight of the gold. In Antiphon's version, it is not said in so many words that the miser buried the gold and came to view it. Antiphon says only that the miser was "of a mistrustful nature unwilling to help anyone" and that therefore he carried his property off and hid it somewhere.

The miser resembles to a certain extent the master in the parable who is characterized by the third servant as "of a mistrustful nature, unwilling to help anyone." In addition and as a final touch, the author of the revised fable introduced a new *dramatis persona,* namely the man who begged the miser to lend him a sum of money with interest. Being misled by an exaggerated concern for dramatic impact, the writer identified the man who asked for the loan with the anonymous passer-by of the original story. Thus the author shifted the thrust of the Aesop fable because he discovered in the theme itself an inherent new application, and I believe that the revised fable became richer and more interesting.[26]

We have seen that Antiphon's version of the Aesop fable came closer to the Parable of the Talents, and I believe that we have learned a valuable lesson in literary analysis. Even non-essential movements within a plot sometimes lead to significant changes in the structure of the story, and the "small forms" are such that the boundaries between them are not hermetically sealed. Thus our case exemplifies again this truism and shows the similarity between fables and parables.[27]

3. Parables More Than Fables

In order to understand literature in its formative stages, we should be allowed to perform an experiment. Therefore I dare ask whether or not the Aesop story about the Miser could have been used as the basis of a good parable. I am not so sure that such a parable would have been successful because the story lacks sufficient motifs which could lend themselves to a metaphoric meaning. As we have seen from the Parable of the Talents—and as it follows from the Parable of the Hidden Treasure (Mt 13:34)—the mass of gold buried in the ground can fulfill an important or even a central task in a good parable. Yet it seems to me that rewriting the story of the Miser so that it may become a good parable is not a very promising enterprise.

On the other hand, the plot of the Parable of the Talents makes the story more or less appropriate for inclusion in the Aesop corpus without great difficulties, as long as the financial transactions described in the parable are taken at face value. Then the moral of the story would be a banal commonplace: Do not be overly cautious when dealing with the sum entrusted to you!

But how would it be possible to prevent the hearers from ascribing metaphoric meaning to the plot of the parable? Some of its elements clearly belong to the unequivocal literary conventions characteristic of parables, which would be instinctively recognized by all who are accustomed to hearing them. The schematic number of servants and the sums entrusted to them reveal the high stylization of the parable. Outside the parables, these components would fit only the European fairy tales.

Practically all the *motifemes* of the Parable of the Talents are conventional and have a metaphoric meaning within the *Gattung* of the parables. The function of the master is that of God, and the servants symbolize men. Here it is superfluous to explain the function of the departure of the master, his return, and the final recompense and punishment of the servants because Jesus' hearers were acquainted with rabbinic parables and easily recognized what Jesus meant. The cruelty of the second punishment (Mt 25:30; cf. Lk 19:27)[28] is a typical feature of the parables[29] and heightens their unreal atmosphere. When all these traits are considered together, they demonstrate that the story about the talents is beyond all doubt a parable. One indirect consequence of the comparison between the fable of the Miser and the Parable of the Talents is that in the overwhelming number of cases the *Gattung* parable is far more discernible than that of the fables.

Conclusion

The principal aim of the present study was not to fully comment and analyze the Parable of the Talents, although in the first part we tried with the help of rabbinic sources to elucidate at least partially the meaning of the parable. We cited a midrash on Proverbs 3:9 which explains how the property became a metaphor for a personal talent. We also quoted a pertinent parallel Jewish parable in order to show that the Parable of the Talents belongs to the *Gattung* of rabbinic parables. I hope that the two rabbinic passages convinced my readers not to overemphasize the eschatological meaning of the parable.

All this however was only the first step to accomplish our primary aim: to make a careful comparative study of the Aesop fable about the Miser and its relationship to the Parable of the Talents. We have seen how the changes which occurred during the development of the fable brought it close to a central component of the parable. This could only happen because the forces inherent in the fable began to work in this direction, and thus a new aspect of the plot became patent. In its more original version, the fable and the parable possessed only one important common element, namely the untimely precaution of hiding the treasure in the ground.

Yet in the version of Antiphon another important element was added, because by burying the treasure in the earth, it became idle capital, incapable of producing further revenue. We must also note the second element common both to this version of the fable and to the parable—the interest. While the motif of lending money with interest is no more than a by-product of the fable, it is a decisive element in the New Testament parable.

I hope that the results of the present study will be useful, not only for the particular case we have examined but also for the study of literary criticism in general. In addition, as a result of our investigation, I hope that I have made a modest contribution toward a better understanding of the parables.

NOTES

1. D. Flusser, *Die rabbinischen Gleichnisse und der Gleichniserzähler Jesu*, 1. Teil, Das Wesen der Gleichnisse (Bern: Lang, 1981). See also my review of C. Thoma and S. Lauer, *Die Gleichnisse der Rabbinen*, 1. Teil (Bern: Lang, 1986). The review appeared in *Judaica* 42 (Zurich, 1987), 103–109.

2. We will not refer to Luke's version of the parable very often because it was thoroughly rewritten. Although Matthew's version is not completely free from secondary redaction, his text of the parable is more or less faithful. See now especially the doctoral thesis of Bradford Humes Young, *The Parables as a Literary Genre in Rabbinic Literature and in the Gospels* (Jerusalem: Hebrew University, 1986), pp. 190–196, 214–216.

3. See e.g. Georg Büchmann, *Geflügelte Worte* (Berlin: Ullstein, 1986), pp. 34–35 and 39.

4. In Luke (19:11), the parallel Parable of the Pounds is preceded by the following remark: "He proceeded to tell a parable, because he was near to Jerusalem, and because they supposed that the Kingdom of God was to appear immediately." Luke already viewed the departure and the late return of the master as a symbol for the delay of Christ's Second Advent. In reality, the departure of the master in the parables of Jesus and in those of the other Jews was a technical means to describe how human beings would behave if they believed that God is not present. I hope that this aspect of the story will be more evident from the following rabbinic parable. See also my book (above note 1), pp. 63 and 123–124, and the rabbinic parable quoted there, p. 24 (*SemH* III, 3).

5. This motif is lacking in the parallel parable in Luke, but it is meaningful for the teaching of the parable.

6. It is attested in a saying of Bar Kappara. Rabbi Hayya bar Adda, the son of Bar Kappara's sister, had a good voice, and Bar Kappara used to say to him: "My son, when you take your stand before the reader's desk, recite the Shema in a ringing voice, as to comply with the teaching: Honor the Lord with (or: from) your substance (Prov. 3:9). From your substance, i.e. from what he has graciously granted you (mehonecho-mima shechononcho). The translation is taken from *Pesikta de Rab Kahana,* Piska 10:3, trans. W.G. Braude and Israel J. Kapstein (London, 1975), pp. 188–189. The Hebrew text is in *Pesikta de Rab Kahana,* ed. Bernhard Mandelbaum (New York, 1962), vol. 1, pp. 164–165, and see there the parallel texts. See also W. Bacher, *Die Agada der Tannaiten,* vol. 2 (Strassburg, 1890), p. 513, note 9. About the identity of Bar Kappara see there, p. 503, and *Encyclopedia Judaica,* vol. 4 (Jerusalem, 1972), p. 227 (Isaak Dov Gilat about Bar Kappara who lived at the beginning of the third century C.E.), and vol. 6 (Jerusalem, 1971), p. 602 (Sh. Safrai about Eleazar Ha-Kappar, late second century). It is occasionally difficult to distinguish between the statements of Eleazar and those of Bar Kappara who was probably his son. In our case the author is evidently the son, as W. Bacher has suggested.

6a. With regard to the parable, refer to: Paul Michel, *Alieniloquium,* Elemente einer Grammatik der Bildrede (Bern, Frankfurt, New York: Lang, 1987), p. 335. In my book, mentioned in note 1, pp. 23–24, I quoted rabbinic parables that are also built upon the motif of an entrusted property, namely TB *Shab* 152b, TB *Shab* 153a and *SemH* III, 3.

7. In Luke (19:13) their number is ten; in Matthew (25:14–15) the precise number is not indicated.

8. Although in Luke all ten servants received the same amount of one pound, the first servant gained ten more pounds, the second five pounds, and the third gained nothing. In Matthew already one discovers a descending grada- tion in the sums which each of the three servants received. This is in accordance with the intention of the parable: each servant received the sum which corre- sponded to his ability. In Matthew the descending gradation is expressed by the different amounts received by the three servants. The first and second servants doubled the sums of money entrusted to them while the third one did not make a profit. The last servant acted the same way in both synoptic versions of the parable, the only difference between them being that according to Luke (19:20) the third servant put the sum in a napkin, and in Matthew 25:18, "he who received the one talent went and dug in the ground and hid his master's money." Also here Matthew is evidently more original.

9. *Tana de be Eliyahu,* trans. from the Hebrew by W. Braude and I. Kapstein (Philadelphia, 1981), *Eliyyahu Zuta,* chapter 2, pp. 408–409. The Hebrew text is printed in Friedmann's edition, pp. 171–172.

10. See A. Jülicher, *Die Gleichnisse Jesu,* vol. 2 (Darmstadt, 1963), p. 485. He mentions Levi-Seligmann, p. 65, and says, "Die Verwandschaft mit Mt 25:11 ff. ist doch nicht gross genug, um die Annahme gleicher Quelle zu fordern, ausserdem ist Mt 25 viel naiver, weniger reflektierend."

11. The other message of the New Testament parable is expressed in Matthew 25:29 and Luke 19:26.

12. See also my book, note 1, p. 169.

13. According to Luke 19:20, he hid his master's money in a napkin.

14. This is how the servant describes the character of his master. The master himself repeats this description in his answer (Mt 25:26 and Lk 19:22). I person- ally believe that his reply and these characteristics are ironical. In any case, it seems to me that we cannot know anything certain about the real character of the master.

15. The punishment of the third servant is described in Matthew 25:28–30 and Luke 19:25–27. The original parable already contained the three compo- nents of his punishment. (1) First the sum of money is taken from the third servant and is given to the first one (Mt 25:28; Lk 19:24–25). (2) Next we find the saying: "To everyone who has more will be given, but from him who has not, even what he has will be taken away" (Mt 25:29; Lk 19:26)—I believe that this logion fits the parable and that its parallel saying in Matthew 13:12, Mark 4:25, and Luke 8:18 was taken from the context of our parable. (3) Finally we see the severe punishment itself (Mt 25:30; Lk 19:27). Both forms of punishment are not what Jesus actually said. In Luke this is a final part of the secondary "politi- cal" motif of the parable, and in Matthew the whole verse (25:26) is a redac-

tionary work, as noted by others. The original context of it is apparently Luke 13:28 and Matthew 8:12.

16. See especially Max Lühti, "Motiv, Zug, Thema aus der Sicht der Volks-erzählungsforschung," in *Elemente der Literatur* (Stuttgart, 1980), pp. 12 and 19, and C. Thoma and S. Lauer, *op. cit.*, p. 27.

17. C. Hahn, *Corpus fabularum Aesopicarum* (Leipzig: 1875), no. 412, 412b (pp. 198–199); *Fabeln der Antike*, ed. Harry C. Schnur (Munich: Tusculum, Heimeran, 1978) pp. 148–150. See the summary in *Babrius and Phaedrus*, ed. Ben Edwin Perry (London: 1965), p. 465, no. 225. The fable is also the subject of a fable by Jean de la Fontaine (IV, 20): "L'avare qui a perdu son trésor."

18. "The Miser" is not a pure classical fable, but what is called in German a *Schwank*. About the impossibility of finding an unequivocal definition of the *Gattung* fable, see the introduction to fables which appears in Perry's book (see above, note 17) and Schnur (below, note 24), pp. 7–10.

19. See above, note 14.

20. In the case of the Aesop miser, the burying of the treasure did not prevent its theft. As one reflects upon the story, it is clear that the miser himself invited this disaster by his own folly, because he went daily to feast his eyes upon his treasure.

21. See H. Diels and W. Kranz, *Die Fragmente der Vorsokratiker* (Berlin, 1971), vol. 2, pp. 361–363. The English translation is taken from Kathleen Freeman, *Ancilla to the Pre-Socratic Philosophers* (Oxford, 1948), pp. 151–152 (with corrections).

22. The spirit and even the literary form of Antiphon's "About the Concord" basically resembles the biblical book of Ecclesiastes.

23. *Fortunatus*, Studienausgabe, ed. Hans-Gert Roloff (Stuttgart: Reclam, 1981). See especially the conclusion of the text on pp. 194–195, and also pp. 256–269.

24. As an example for unexpected perspectives which one can discover in an Aesop fable, I would like to refer to what John Fielding, *Tom Jones* (Book 12, Chapter 2), writes concerning the latent meaning embedded in the fable of "The Weasel as Bride" (Aesop 50 and Babrius 32). About the fable, see also D. Flusser, "Abraham and the Upanishads," *Immanuel* 20, 1986, pp. 56–57 and note 56 there, as well as the text of Babrius with the German translation in H.C. Schnur and E. Keller, *Fabeln der Antike* (Munich: Tusculum, 1982), pp. 164–267 and the note there.

25. In the English translation of Antiphon (see note 21 above) the difficulty is clarified somewhat. The translator writes that the miser, after being very grieved by the theft, *"went to see* the man who had asked for a loan." This means that the man was not an accidental passer-by, but that the miser went to see the man on his own initiative. But in Greek the verb does not mean "to go to see" but it means "to meet." Diels translated the verb in this way and his rendering of the text is in accordance with the content of the first version of the fable.

26. Fables and parables (and other similar "small forms" as e.g. fairy tales and anecdotes) are, so to say, living organisms which are, even if they are put in writing, open to additional changes. I am tempted also to propose the following change in our Aesop fable; The miser marked the place where he buried the gold with a stone which precisely indicated to the thief where the gold was buried. Finally the passer-by, seeing the miser weeping, advised him to put the same stone in the earth instead of the gold.

27. In my book (see above, note 1), I tried to show the difference between parables properly speaking and *exempla*. The so-called Parable of the Rich Fool (Lk 12:13–20) is surely not a parable properly speaking, although in Luke 12:16 it is called a parable. Should it be considered as an *exemplum,* or could it be included without difficulty in the Aesop corpus? The parable is thoroughly stylized in Greek, and as far as I can see, it contains few real Hebraisms. Can it be that it was developed by Luke or by his Greek predecessor from an authentic text?

28. See above, note 15.

29. See my book, quoted above in note 1, pp. 42–43.

Literary and Theological Aspects of the Rabbinic Parables

Clemens Thoma

1. REMARKS CONCERNING THE RESEARCH SITUATION

There are many unresolved questions and several deficiencies in contemporary research concerning rabbinic parables. For example, many scholars deplore the fact that the study of the rabbinic parables takes place in the shadow of midrashic research and, even more so, in that of Christian and Jewish ideological presuppositions. Also, a very selective, short-sighted and apologetic comparison between rabbinic parables and the parables of Jesus is an example of unprofessional and overly ideological communication. No one seems to know, moreover, how many rabbinic parables exist in the midrashic compendia and in the Talmudim. Not even the editors of rabbinic texts and parables seem to realize which of the parables are unique and which are parallel enlargements of another earlier and simpler *mashal*. As a result of these factors, we do not have a form history, a redaction history, or a theological history of the parable.

Fortunately several excellent works have appeared in recent years shedding light on this problematic parable research and its relationship to various literary and theological questions. Some catchwords of a new wave of midrash and parable research are "inner-biblical exegesis,"[1] "literality," "(open-)textuality"[2] and "post-structuralist thought."[3] Literary coherence is stressed over against a tendency to isolate the smallest possible literary form which dissolves any literality in the rabbinic compendia. Midrashic research continues to prevail, and parable research is overshadowed by midrashic studies.

Especially in Europe, relations are strained between scholars with historical-critical approaches to both the parables of Jesus and those of the rabbis,[4] others who prefer a structuralist viewpoint,[5] and again others who (over-)stress hermeneutical and theological factors.[6] Jewish-Christian ideological differences place still further stress on the mashal-research. On the one hand, exegetical supersessionists are polemicizing against the allegedly inferior rabbinic parables;[7] on the other, some Jewish halakhic scholars underestimate the rabbinic parables because of their non-halakhic and supposedly inexact character.[8]

In order to make all of the rabbinic parables available (in the two talmudim and in the diverse tannaitic and amoraic midrash compendia there may be approximately 1,300 parables), we in Lucerne are attempting to edit, translate and comment upon *all* of the rabbinic parables and to shed light on the literary, historical and theological contexts of these parables.[9] Until now the rabbinic parables (or similes) have been commented on only selectively, for the purpose of comparison with New Testament parables, for illustrating some aspects of rabbinic literality, or for demonstrating that the rabbis, as well as the Christian authors, had a narrative theology. Only when the whole corpus of these parables is made available to the scientific and religious world will an accurate evaluation be possible.

Our work as a team in Lucerne is truly Jewish-Christian. My friend and research colleague is an orthodox Jew and a philologist. Every word in our work on the parables is written with a common, shared responsibility. Thus, we seek to create a climate of mutual confidence, removed from apologetic and supersessionist tendencies, for scholars and religiously-minded persons. We need an ideologically well-balanced and historically reliable approach to the rabbinic parables.

2. DEFINITIONS AND CIRCUMSCRIPTIONS

Within the rabbinic compendia, the parable is the most clearly shaped micro-structural unit. It is more clear in delineation and content than, for instance, the *petikhah* (proem), the *petirah,* the midrash in general, as well as the parables of the New Testament. In that light, it seems ludicrous that the present state of research concerning the rabbinic *mashal* is so underdeveloped.

Rabbinic parables are simple, secular, mono-episodic, fictional narrative units that serve to explain the rabbinic understanding of the Torah. They owe their *raison d'être* to the religious needs of the rabbinic communities. The rabbis needed rhetorical and argumentative forms for preaching and to defend the rabbinic identity as well as to provide practical guidance in the daily life of the rabbinic audience. All rabbinic parables have a bipartite structure composed of narrative (*mashal* proper) and normative instruction (*nimshal*) which can be easily identified from a form-critical perspective. The beginning and ending of these two sections are well marked. The *mashal* contains opening formulae, e.g. *le-melekh*. The *nimshal* can be identified by its introductory formulae as well, e.g. *kakh*. The end of the mashal-nimshal is indicated by a scriptural *lemma,* often the same one that begins the "motivation" (see below).

This initial description of the structure is reflected throughout the large body of rabbinic parables. What creates methodological problems is the overlapping of the parables with other micro- and macro-structures of rabbinic literature. This raises several questions: What rank does the *mashal* hold within the partially overlapping forms of haggadah, midrash, halakhah and scriptural lemmata? How can we determine the content and goal of the parables? The following schema of the mashal/nimshal structure may provide some initial answers to these and other questions.

The various elements of this schema require some elaboration.

Motivation

The *darshan* may have had to preach on Shabbat about a given pericope. There may have been discussions among rabbinic scholars that had to be addressed. There may have been a situation in the rabbinic communities that demanded an apologetic clarification. These and similar circumstances motivated a religious, rabbinic-minded narrator, and later a rabbinic writer, to create a complete rabbinic parable. This creative act consisted of the invention of a metaphorical tale that opens an insight into the Torah, as it was understood by the rabbis.

Ḥiddush

The rabbinic parable is of a religious-evocative nature, but rather than being primarily emotional in its appeal, it is highly dialectical-rational. To understand its content and its goal we have to explore what the *ḥiddush* of the narrator-writer was. *Ḥiddush* is a keyword in all rabbinic preaching and discussion (see *TBHag* 3a, par.) and a theological concept central to all rabbinic literature. The teller of the parable has a clear religious strategy, i.e. an idea how to make the light of the old biblical revelation shine for a new audience and how to bring forth a new

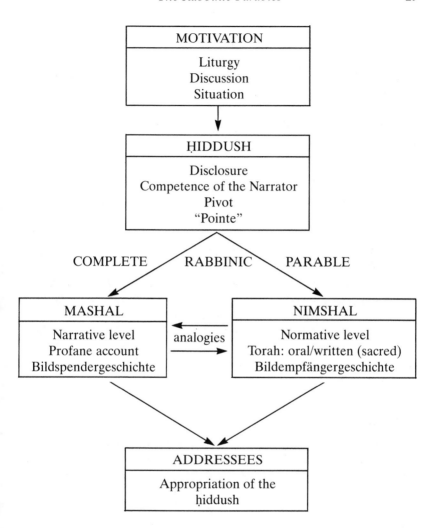

illuminative aspect of the rabbinic understanding of the biblical message (*tora šebeʿal pe.*).

Sometimes the *ḥiddush* goes beyond the reach of the biblical message itself. *Ḥiddush* reveals the literary, homiletic, and apologetic competence, as well as the contemporaneity, of the narrator. It is not possible to explain a rabbinic parable without knowing the *ḥiddush*. Modern authors speak in nearly the same sense about disclosure, pivot/point, critical twist, etc.[10] The primary *ḥiddush,* i.e. the creative idea of the mashal teller, may not be completely identifiable. However, the secondary *ḥiddush,* namely, the understanding of the aim of the *mashal-nimshal* by the addressees, can be traced or reconstructed fairly well, even in our own time. In our edition of the parables in *Pesiqta deRav Kahana* (*PesK*), we describe the *ḥiddush* prior to the presentation of the complete parable as a sort of explanatory introduction. This introduction reproduces to a certain extent the message intended by the original teller as well as the form in which it was received by his audience.

The Mashal *Proper*

This is an ordinary account with a simple plot. Something must actually occur in it. It represents a simple dramatic happening; otherwise it would remain only a comparison. This simple dramatic character is the result of the creative imagination of the narrator. The narrative utilizes archetypal figures and situations in life and is artificially constructed. It is not the result of observations within history, of the palaces of Roman emperors or of vineyards, banquets or family struggles.[11] It is composed, or possibly modified from an already existing story, in order to fit into the normative preaching of the *nimshal.* In short, the *mashal* is essentially referential. Only after *all* the references between the *mashal* and the *nimshal* have been identified is an understanding of the rabbinic parable possible.

The Nimshal

The *nimshal* is introduced by *kakh* ("so; in a similar way") and consists of biblical quotations and rabbinical expressions that reveal the self-understanding of the parable-teller as willing and able to give an authoritative and authentically rabbinic explanation of the Torah. From a form-critical perspective a *mashal* is not necessarily connected to a certain *nimshal.* There is, however, always a strong connection between the *nimshal* and the motivation of the parable. *Nimshalim* are often midrashic drafts which are also found elsewhere, and here only secondarily connected with the *mashal* proper.

The Addressees

The addressees are always a community, not individual persons (as is David in 2 Samuel 12:1–14). The intention of the parable is to influence the community in a sapiential manner, i.e. the hearers of the parable should receive a message which is not intended merely for the present or for themselves, but rather one that is also valid for all future Jewish generations. As a result, the specific addressees are situated within the realm of all Jewish history and expectations. It is the story-teller himself who deliberately places the addressees within this context.

3. LITERARY ASPECTS OF RABBINIC PARABLES

It is significant that the methods employed in the rabbinic parables which stimulate their hearers and readers toward the decisive disclosure (*ḥiddush*) are similar to those, for example, adopted and applied in American short stories in our own time. The German editors of a commentary on American short stories ask how these stories can gain a "measure of depth" despite their brevity. They arrive at the following conclusions. In order to gain depth it is important that the action is restricted to one meaningful moment noteworthy enough to arouse the interest of the reader and, at the same time, have an application generalized enough to point beyond itself in its significance. This type of distillation is particularly observable in the short stories of the twentieth century, in which an "unexpected turn of events" is introduced, i.e. an occurrence which is decisive for later life, or an "epiphany" (an intuitive grasp of reality), which is a sudden disclosure of important matters in life.[12]

Edgar Allan Poe wrote that "in the whole composition there should be no word written, of which the tendency, direct or indirect, is not to the one pre-established design." Henry James speaks of a "shock of recognition" as a characteristic feature of the short story which reveals the depth of the soul.[13] David Flusser stresses the literary relationship of the parables of Jesus and of the rabbis with the European "Volksmärchen": "Die drastischen Züge der Gleichnisse haben ihre Entsprechung in den europäischen Märchen."[14]

These references concerning the American short story and the European folktales highlight the mastery of the rabbinic authors in applying these same methods many centuries earlier. We must consider however that the rabbinic parables contain their own specific subjects and characteristics, and we must keep in mind the distance of centuries and the difference in religious aims and theological needs.

As illustrations of the literary, and especially rhetorical, character of many rabbinic parables and their application to the rabbinic Torah, I will now quote the parable of the "two luminaries" and the triple parable of the "rewarded waiting."

4. PARABLE OF THE TWO LUMINARIES: PESK 5:14 (MB I 104)

Parallels: BerR 6:3 (ThA 42f.); PesR 15 (p. 78a); YalqBer 8 (p.30); YalqJes 500 (II 809a)

Motivation

"This month will be for you" (Exod. 12:2). You calculate by it, but the people of the world do not calculate by it. Rabbi Lewî in the name of Rabbi Yôse bar Leʿay: Usually, the great calculates by the great and the small by the small. Esau, who is great, calculates by the sun, which is great. Jacob, who is small, calculates by the moon, which is small. Rabbi Nahman said: This is a good sign: Just as the great rules the day and not at night, so wicked Esau rules in this world and not in the world to come. Just as the small rules during the day and at night, so Jacob rules in this world and in the world to come.

Ḥiddush

The teller of the parable fastens onto the "for you" in Exod. 12:2 and in both of the subsequent midrashim in order to be able to portray that Israel is the heir of the ultimate promise despite its historical insignificance and oppression.

Mashal	*Nimshal*
Rabbi Nahman said:	
	So:
As long as the light	As long as the light
of the great	of wicked Esau
shines in the world,	shines in the world,
the light	the light
of the small	of Jacob
is not noticed.	is not noticed.
When the light	When the light
of the great	of wicked Esau
has set,	has set,
the light	the light
of the small	of Jacob
will be noticed.	will be noticed.
	"Arise, give light,
	for your light will come" (Is 60:1).

The following analogies exist: Light of the great (sun) → Predominance of anti-Jewish powers within historical time. Light of the small (moon) → unrecognized dominance of Israel in history and recognized dominance of Israel in the eschaton. To shine in the world → to exercise wicked dominance in history. Not be noticed → not to come to dominance in history. To set → to be rejected by God in the eschaton. To be noticed → to be united with God's dominance in the eschaton.

This is a parable, not just a comparison, because something actually occurs. The course of the narrative is stamped by a series of situations which are intrinsically bound together: 1. The light of the great shines. 2. The light of the small is not noticed. 3. The light of the great will set. 4. The light of the small will finally shine alone. The references from *mashal* to *nimshal* are completely in harmony. This harmony itself has important theological implications. The Esau-Jacob motif is employed in order to give hope that Israel will finally be predominant in relation to the peoples of the world who are presently oppressing Israel. Here we have a very subtle and concise rhetorical unit employing the simplest possible literary means. There is no dramatic element or complicated plot in it. May I add here that we did not find any ornamental adjectives, only qualifying ones, in all the parables of *PesK* and *BerR*.

Now we proceed to the second example: the triple parable of the "rewarded waiting." In *PesK* we have four double (or twofold) parables and six triple (or threefold) parables. The figure "three" is used very often for redactional (rhetorical) purposes and as a genre to delineate the progression of the *mashal* proper.

5. THE TRIPLE PARABLE OF THE REWARDED WAITING: PESK 21:3 (MB I 320f.)

Parallels: MHG Shem 27:21 (p. 614f.); MTeh 36:10 (p. 85; I and II); YalqJes 499 (II 808a: I); YalqPs 727 (II 909b: I and II).

Motivation

"Arise, give light, for your light will come!" (Is 60:1) "For the fountain of life is with you, in your light we will see light" (Ps 36:10).

Ḥiddush

The "light" in Is 60:1 and Ps 36:10 is interpreted as the special election of Israel. Since the symbolism of meal and marriage

also indicate election, the symbolism of light does not appear in
II and III.

Rabbi Yôhanan and Rêsh Laqîsh. Rabbi Yôhanan told one (parable),
and Rêsh Laqîsh told two.

Mashal	*Nimshal*
I	
Rabbi Yôhanan told one (parable):	
Like a man	So the Israelites:
who was on his way,	
as the sun was setting.	
	Before the Holy One, praised
	be he:
	they said:
	Lord of the worlds:
Someone came	In the days of Moses we made
and lit the lamp for him,	a lamp for you
but it went out.	but it went out,
Then someone else came	in the days of Solomon
and lit the lamp for him,	we made ten lamps,
but it went out.	but they went out.
Then the man said:	
From now on	From now on
I will wait only	we will wait only
for the light of the morning!	for your light
	"In your light
	we will see light" (Ps 36:10).
II	
Rêsh Laqîsh told two parables:	
Rêsh Laqîsh said:	
Like a king,	So:
who had a son	
and invited guests.	
The king said to his son:	the Holy One praised be he,
	said to the Israelites:
My son,	My sons,
do you wish to dine	Do you not wish to dine
with the guests?	with the peoples of the world?

He said to him:
No!

Before him they said:
Lord of the worlds!
"Turn not my heart to evil,
nor to evil courses" (Ps 141:4).
He said to them:
Do you wish to dine with them
because they are gleanings!?
Before him they said:
Lord of the worlds!
"I do not wish to partake
(even) of their delicacies"
    (Ps 141:4).
We do not desire
their enticing and beautiful gifts!

He said to him:
With whom, then
do you wish to dine?
He said to him:
With you!

What, then
do we desire?

Your enticing and beautiful gifts!

III
Rêsh Laqîsh told another parable. Rêsh Laqîsh said:

Like a king,
who had a daughter.
A man came
and asked for her hand.
But, he was not of her standing.
A second came
and asked for her hand.
But, he was not of her standing.
But when a third man came,
who was of her standing
and asked for her hand,
the king said:

So the Holy One, praised be he:

He said to the Israelites:
My sons!
Since my light is your light,
and your light is my light,
let us go, you and I,
and make a light for Zion!

Rise, give light,   "Arise, give light,
for your light will come!   for your light will come"
                                              (Is 60:1).

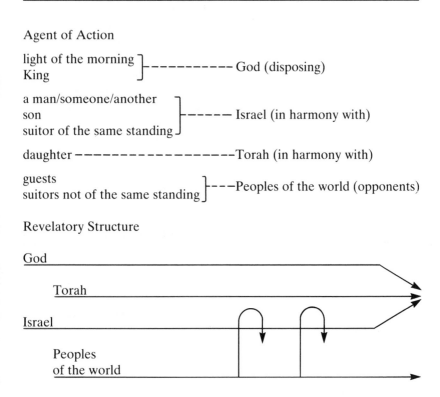

Agent of Action

light of the morning ⎤
King   ⎦ ─ ─ ─ ─ ─ ─ ─ ─ ─ God (disposing)

a man/someone/another ⎤
son   ⎬─ ─ ─ ─ ─ Israel (in harmony with)
suitor of the same standing ⎦

daughter ─ ─ ─ ─ ─ ─ ─ ─ ─ ─ ─ ─ ─ ─ Torah (in harmony with)

guests   ⎤
suitors not of the same standing ⎦─ ─ ─ Peoples of the world (opponents)

Revelatory Structure

This triple parable shows that there were redactors, not only copyists or "Vertexter," at work. There are elements of tension, complementarity and intensification between the first, the second and the third parables. In the first parable, the Jews are disappointed with any kind of salvation in history made by humans. They will wait for God, the final savior. This final salvation is the only fulfilling and enduring salvation. In the second parable, the Jews seek consolation in their historical troubles, which are caused by the peoples of the world, by reconfirming their exclusive spiritual relationship with the God of Israel. They are dining partners of God. God cares for them. The third parable is a sort of synthesis of the first and second parables. The sons of Israel are the only ones who accept and observe the Torah. The peoples of the world are not able or willing to observe the requirements demanded of Israel. Therefore God will lead Israel alone to find salvation and bliss.

All three parables express the faith and hope that Israel can find its identity and reach its goal only by intimate adherence to God. The peoples of the world try to do so as well, but they fail.

The rhetorical and even poetic character of this triple parable is revealed by some features at the periphery of the parables. In the first parable we can see, for instance, that there are no slavish analogies between *mashal* and *nimshal*. In the *mashal* proper there is, for aesthetical reasons, only a *second* lamp. But the *nimshal* records the *ten* lamps of the temple of Solomon. The story-teller is not ready to give up on literary aesthetics, although according to the *nimshal* he should leave behind his literary-aesthetic aims. This freedom of the story-teller is also exhibited by his use of the various symbols of light, meal, and marriage, all to represent the same idea.

6. THEOLOGICAL ASPECTS OF RABBINIC PARABLES

The rabbinic parables offer the simplest and most enlightening literary form for achieving significant insights into rabbinic theologies. Within the midrashic medium the parables carry in themselves the force and multiplicity of rabbinic theological utterances; therefore, they are the best representatives of rabbinic theology. A complete edition of all rabbinic parables, combined with serious commentary, would deliver the best approach to rabbinic theological thinking. This assumption challenges future research.

It was David Stern who recently supported the exemplary nature of the rabbinic parables. According to Stern, the rabbinic parables are "a model of representation" within the midrashic utterances. Stern's observation indicates the first of several theological characteristics of rabbinic parables which I would like to indicate here briefly. "The sudden proliferation of parables in the homily suggests the paradoxical fact that God's *ḥavivût* with Israel can be dramatized only through human representation."[15] Relying on Erich Auerbach, Stern remarks that the language and the content of the *sermo humilis* of the Church Fathers is comparable to the language of *ḥavivût* of the rabbinic parables. "Like the language of *ḥavivût,* the *sermo humilis* consists in . . . a new eloquence that eschews rhetorical virtuosity for the use of language as an instrument of ethical persuasion. Like the language of *ḥavivût, sermo humilis* is a didactic, homiletical language; its singular power comes from the fact that it never loses sight of the urgency of the lesson it has to teach or of the task it must perform."[16]

I would like to stress and modify this thesis in a few points. In *PesK, WaR, MekhY* and *BerR* we observe great conscientiousness in the formulation of the parables. Although the identity of the parable-tellers is not important for the redactors and copyists, the contents of the parables are. In addition, it is not always the original location in which the parables are found; they were often transferred from one place to another within the midrashic environment. So we cannot say that the parable is always the culmination of the midrashic utterances of the rabbis. But in any case, the parable is a resting place in the midst of midrashic exegesis and interpretations. Its simplicity and clarity underline its importance.

The conception of the parables as special expressions of divine *havivût* opens a door to the central message of the parables. Parables with subjects such as Israel and the peoples of the world are, in the final analysis, not descriptions, judgments or rejections of the peoples of the world, but rather accentuations of the innermost *havivût* of God with Israel. This focus of the parables is of great theological importance which is evident, for example, in the so-called "king" parables. The king is the highest human representative. He is at the same time the most authoritative, the wisest and the most lovable father. His son and daughter (Israel) are the most beloved and the most protected human beings. David Flusser relies here on the sapiential tradition of the immediate post-biblical times.[17] Proverbs 8:30 may be illustrative for us: *"We'ehyeh 'ezlô 'amôn, wa'eheyeh sha'ashu'îm yôm yôm, meśaheqet lefanaw bekhol 'et."* Translation: "Then I was beside him, like an intimate; and I was daily his delight, rejoicing before him always." With Willy Biesold, a scholar at our Institute, we could say that all parables are *'abbatic- 'amonic*. In some parables the *'abba* (the beloved father-king) is in the foreground, in others the *'amon* (the exclusively beloved child); in others both are equally emphasized. The language of *havivût* in all homiletic rabbinic parables is at least as strong as in the parables of the New Testament. There is an unshakable communion between God and Israel in the face of grief and temptation.

Second, the rabbinic parables always have an ethical orientation. Their ethic is directed at religious communities as a whole rather than at individuals. According to the teaching of the parables, the rabbinic community should be trustful and obedient before God. It should exhibit restraint and caution in relation to the seductive and menacing peoples of the world. Particularly important here is the attitude of repentance (*teshuvah*). In all of these ethical demands, the collaboration of God with the Jews is stressed. This is illustrated in the parable of "the rock" (*PesK* 24,17). With respect to the human urge toward evil (*yezer ha-ra'*), which is compared to a rock at a crossroad, God says to the rabbinic Jewish community: "Keep chipping away at the rock until the time comes for me to have it removed entirely from its place."

Third, many more of the rabbinic parables deal directly with the salvation history of Israel than we originally thought. Among the 133 *PesK* parables, twenty-four have eschatological aims. They are important units of comparison with the New Testament parables and with Christian doctrine in general.

The parables, as a prominent form of narrative text, endeavor to gain access to God within the Israelite tradition by describing God in an affirmative (*via affirmativa*) or in a negative (*via negativa*) way. In *PesK*, the majority of parables have a *via affirmativa* tendency. Like a king of flesh and blood, God is an unlimited sovereign. Like a good father, God is a loving, provident guide of Israel, and much more (*via eminentiae*). The *via negativa meshalim* are antithetical in character. In *PesK* there are ten antithetical *meshalim*. These reflect the rabbinic experience that humans tend to reduce God and, thus, deform Him. As a result, we find formulations such as: God is *not* like a king of flesh and blood; or, God is *not* like . . . but rather . . .

There are rabbinic parables of nearly pure systematic, theological character. An example is the parable of the "pleasing gift" (*BerR* 34:9; parallels: *YalqBer* 60; *YalqPs* 697; *YalqMPs* 24:12). Genesis 8:21 serves as the "motivation": "And the Lord smelled the pleasing odor." The rabbi who is narrating ignores the biblical sense of this verse and uses it instead to stress the greatness of Abraham and of the three young men in Daniel 3 in their readiness for martyrdom. This parable presupposes that Abraham, like the three young men, had been thrown into the fiery furnace as a result of his adamant confession of the One God. For the rabbis the "odor" in Genesis 8:21 was in fact not an odor from the sacrifice of Noah, but rather a hint that Abraham, the young men, and all martyrs readily offered themselves as a pleasing gift to God: "Like the friend of a king who honored the king with a pleasing gift. Later, the son of the friend had no such gift. But the grandson of the friend of the king once again did have a gift for the king. The king said to the grandson: Your gift is like the gift of your grandfather. So: 'The Lord smelled the pleasing odor' (Gen 8:21)."

Here we have a spiritualization and transformation of the notion of sacrifice. Readiness for martyrdom is the true sacrifice. All animal sacrifices are but a hint of the true sacrifice which originates from the hearts of Abraham, the three young men, and the other Jewish martyrs. Since there was no persecution in the time between Abraham and the three young men (under Nebuchadnezzar), the son, representing Israel in this interval, has no gift for the king. Therefore, only martyrdom is the real sacrifice, and the time of martyrdom is a time of special sanctity. Here the sacrifice of Noah has no value of its own.

The narrative text of the rabbinic *meshalim* is the best garment for the theological utterances of the rabbis. It displays various textures and colors and points to the presence of God in His creation. This variety in itself is rich and must be taken seriously. We have to study the parables from literary and historical viewpoints, as well as from a theological one. The historical and literary perspectives permit us to attain many theological insights. This process is reciprocal, however. It is precisely from these insights that we find our way back to the literary aesthetics of the parables. Eugen Biser has correctly observed: "Nicht erst im Denken, sondern schon im Bild ist der Logos zu suchen."[18] The literary metaphor itself contains theology and religiosity, and these, in turn, are inextricably bound up with literality and history.

NOTES

1. Cf. Michael Fishbane, *Biblical Interpretation in Ancient Israel* (Oxford, 1985); Meir Sternberg, *The Poetics of Biblical Narratives* (Bloomington, 1985).

2. Cf. Geoffrey H. Hartmann, in Sanford Budick, *Midrash and Literature* (New Haven, 1986); David Stern, "Rhetoric and Midrash: The Case of Mashal," *Prooftexts*, vol. 1 (Baltimore, 1981), 261, 292.

3. Cf. Robert Alter, "Old Rabbis, New Critics (Reviews)," *New Republic,* vol. 2 (January 5 and 12) (New York, 1987), 27–33.

4. Survey by Wolfgang Harnisch, "Gleichnisse Jesu: Positionen der Auslegung von Adolf Juelicher bis zur Formgeschichte," *Wege der Forschung* (Darmstadt, 1982), 366.

5. Cf. Erhardt Guettgemanns, "Einleitende Bemerkungen zur strukturalen Erzaehlforschung," *LingBibl* (1973) vol. 23/24, 2, 47; Arnold Goldberg, "Das schriftauslegende Gleichnis im Midrasch," FJB (1981), vol. 5, 1–90.

6. Cf. Hans Weder, *Neutestamentliche Hermeneutik* (Zurich, 1986).

7. Representative of this attitude was the very influential book by Paul Fiebig, *Altjuedische Gleichnisse und die Gleichnisse Jesu* (Tuebingen, 1904). For Fiebig, the rabbinic parables are examples of a narrow-minded mentality.

8. Even in their time, the rabbinic authorities had to deal with tendencies to underestimate the parables. Cf. *ShirR* 1 on Cant 1:1.

9. Cf. Clemens Thoma, Simon Lauer (eds.), *Die Gleichnisse der Rabbinen*, Erster Teil: Pesiqta deRav Kahana (Pesk). Einleitung, Uebersetzung, Parallelen, Kommentar, Texte [Series Judaica et Christiana 10] (Bern: Peter Lang, 1986).

10. Cf. Paul Michel, *Alieniloquium: Elemente zu einer Grammatik der Bildrede* (Zurich, 1987), pp. 282, 400.

11. That the *mashals* are echoes of historical events was the error of Ignaz Ziegler, *Die Koenigsgleichnisse des Midrasch–beleuchtet durch die roemische Kaiserzeit* (Breslau, 1903).

12. Cf. Karl Heinz Goeller, Gerhard Hoffman (eds.), *Die amerikanische Kurzgeschichte* (Duesseldorf: August Bagel, 1972), p. 14.

13. *Ibid.*, pp. 10–11.

14. David Flusser, *Die rabbinischen Gleichnisse und der Gleichniserzaehler Jesus* [Series Judaica et Christiana 4] (Bern: Peter Lang, 1980), p. 43.

15. Hartman and Budick, *op. cit.*, p. 117.

16. *Ibid.*, p. 121.

17. *Ibid.*, pp. 141–160.

18. Eugen Biser, *Theologische Sprachtheorie und Hermeneutik* (Munich, 1970), p. 371.

Jesus' Parables from the Perspective of Rabbinic Literature: The Example of the Wicked Husbandmen

David Stern

THE QUESTION AND ITS HISTORY

The relationship of Jesus' parables to the *meshalim* or parables of the Rabbis has been a theme of modern New Testament scholarship since the nineteenth century. The history of that theme need not be rehearsed here.[1] For the most part, its burden has been the glorification of Jesus' parables at the expense of the Rabbis'. Where Jesus' parables are typically described as vivid and lifelike, "fresh as the air of the Galilean mountains," in the words of Adolph Jülicher, the first modern scholar to deal critically with the New Testament parables, the Rabbinic parables have been characterized as pedantic, forced, and artificial, laden with the sullen dust of the classroom.[2]

This aesthetic valuation, usually presented as objective fact, appears to have covered, however, a deeper anxiety among the scholars about the originality of their material—that is, the authenticity of Jesus' parables in comparison to those of the Rabbis—and to have concealed more worrisome concern over such questions as, Who invented the literary form of the parable, the Rabbis or Jesus? or, in the case of similar parables, Who borrowed what from whom? Here, again, New Testament scholars traditionally emphasized the singularity and incomparability of Jesus' compositions.[3] The few Jewish scholars who responded to the question tended, in turn, to deal with it apologetically, as though the religious and literary merit of the Rabbinic *meshalim* required justification.[4]

In the past several decades, a number of studies—by Christian and

Jewish scholars—have shown a new willingness to address the question of the relationship between the parables of Jesus and the Rabbinic *meshalim* without engaging in theological competition.[5] David Flusser in particular has advanced our understanding of the question by showing that both Jesus' parables and the Rabbinic *meshalim* share compositional similarities—formulaic elements of diction, stereotyped themes, and motifs—which indicate that they were both part of a common narrative tradition. Flusser has argued that the *mashal*—a generic name in Late Antique Jewish literature for all parables, fables, and the like—is a type of traditional literature which, like such other types as the folktale and the oral epic, can best be described by its use of traditional, virtually formulaic and stereotyped features.

In my own independent studies of the Rabbinic *mashal,* I have confirmed Flusser's claim by demonstrating the state of nearly complete stereotyping that the *mashal* reaches in the classical literature attributed to the Amoraic sages who lived in the land of Israel from the third through the fifth centuries, the high period of classical Rabbinic Judaism.[6] If Flusser's and my arguments are correct in regard to the common background shared by the New Testament and Rabbinic parables, then the compositions attributed to Jesus are our earliest datable evidence in Late Antiquity for the tradition of the *mashal* that attains its full maturity in Rabbinic literature.

The qualifications implied in this last sentence only begin to suggest the critical methodological caveats that face any attempt to work back from the literature of the Rabbis to the New Testament. In the first place, there is the obvious pitfall of importing into the gospels anachronistic ideas and assumptions from a period nearly two and a half centuries after the time of Jesus, that is, from the date of the earliest literary collections which preserve the traditions of Rabbinic Judaism.[7] Moreover, the task of recovering from the synoptic texts the sayings of the historical Jesus, in their original forms and settings, faces obstacles that are all too well-known to need repeating here, and these difficulties are only multiplied when the focus of discussion shifts from the task of recovery itself to the application of its results in comparative study. Finally, and no less importantly, all knowledge concerning the historical Rabbis and their literary activity must also be recovered from collections that, like the synoptic gospels, were edited a considerable period after the personages named in them lived; here, again, the job of recovering the original saying becomes only more problematic once it is pursued for a secondary purpose.

Despite these reasons for hesitation, though, the comparative study of Jesus' parables with the Rabbinic *meshalim* is still worth pursuing. The Rabbinic *meshalim* constitute the largest fund of parables from the ancient world. No matter how many centuries after Jesus they may date from, they are still our closest evidence for the literary form as Jesus may have used it. As a result, they offer invaluable information, available from no other source, about the *varieties* of parables that were composed by Jews within the demonstrable historical and geographical context of Palestine in Late Antiquity. If nothing else, the Rabbinic *meshalim* provide a perspective sufficiently different from that of the traditional sources for New Testament scholarship to suggest new approaches to old problems. Flusser has already treated the issue of traditional composition, and thus turned comparative study away from the matter of originality *per se* to the question of how a common literary tradition has been directed toward different ends. It is now possible for us to proceed further, and to ask if the parables of the Rabbis can also help understand the function of Jesus' parables: Why and for what purpose might Jesus have used the literary form? How are they to be interpreted as texts? Where do form and function in the parable meet, and how do their intersection determine the meaning of specific parables?

In this essay I wish to suggest some answers to these questions by using the Rabbinic material to analyze in detail one New Testament parable, the Wicked Husbandmen. I have chosen this parable not only on account of its significance in the history of interpretation of the parables, but also because it is in its own right an important document of the early Church's attitude toward Judaism. At stake in its analysis are not only scholarly questions of antiquarian interest but crucial theological matters relating to Jesus' view of himself, his mission, and his relationship to his fellow Jews. Significant as they are for Jewish-Christian relations, these issues, as we shall see, are also not without relevance to the ways in which the parable, as a literary form, has been conceived traditionally as well as by modern scholarship.

At the outset, however, I wish to emphasize to the reader that in pursuing this comparative project my intention is not to turn the Wicked Husbandmen or any other New Testament parable into a Rabbinic composition. Although I would not wish to claim that my study is theology-free (as though it were even possible at this point in time to imagine anyone studying the Hebrew Bible or the New Testament without having some theological interest invested in his or her work), the main critical advantage that the Rabbinic evidence promises is an intellectual one:

the possibility of gaining access to a historically viable literary context from which to view the parables as narrative, specifically as a form of ideological narrative, that is, narrative constructed by design and rhetoric to impress a certain world-view upon its audience.

As we shall see, this approach to the parable will differ significantly from other methods that have been used in modern New Testament studies to analyze the parables. On the one hand, it is unlike other historically-oriented scholarship in that my plan is not to reconstruct the "original" parables—neither those of Jesus nor of the Rabbis; as we shall see, the only viable comparison between them is between the texts of Jesus' parables *as preserved by the editors/authors of the synoptic gospels* and the *meshalim* of the Rabbis *as preserved by the editors/authors of the Rabbinic literary collections*. On the other hand, my analysis will also differ from the literary approaches which have dominated most recent parable-research in that it is fully historical in orientation.

The practical difference that my approach makes will, I hope, be sufficiently self-evident from my reading of the Wicked Husbandmen. From a theoretical—or theological—viewpoint, however, the change in perspective will be no less dramatic. Since its inception, modern parable-research has been decisively shaped by a number of literary preconceptions which are based upon implicit theological assumptions. In this paper I wish to challenge these preconceptions; indeed, their inadequacy on both literary and theological grounds is, in my view, the most powerful argument for turning to the Rabbinic *mashal* as the only truly valid context for understanding the New Testament parables. Before turning to the analysis of the Wicked Husbandmen, we must therefore begin by looking at these preconceptions, and in particular the one that more than any other has shaped modern scholarship about the parables: the view of the non-allegorical character of the parables.

ALLEGORY, PARABLE, AND THE SCHOLARS

Since Adolph Jülicher's seminal work, *Die Gleichnisreden Jesu* (1888), virtually all modern critical scholarship about the parables has proceeded from the nearly dogmatic position that the literary form of the parable is not allegorical. Jülicher, the first to set this position, argued decisively that the original parables of Jesus, like all "correct and correctly preserved" parables, "requires no explanatory word, did not even endure such, for everything in it is clear." According to Jülicher, Jesus' parables were, in their original form, simple and vivid stories which Jesus used to enhance "the distinctiveness and persuasive power of his thinking . . . to illustrate the unknown by the commonly known, to lead gently upwards from the easy to the difficult."[8] As such they were entirely non-allegorical in character.

Jülicher himself based his case against allegory upon a distinction derived from classical rhetoric that differentiated between metaphor and simile in respect to their claims to literalness. According to this distinction, metaphor operates through substitution, thereby disguising its meaning behind its imagery and becoming what Jülicher called "dishonest" or "inauthentic" speech; in contrast, simile, which makes its figurative status explicit, is honest and authentic. Jülicher extended this distinction by associating parable with simile and allegory with metaphor; where the former was honest and authentic, the latter was dishonest and inauthentic. Since Jesus obviously could never have spoken inauthentically, his original parables must have been utterly uncontaminated by allegory. Jülicher was adamant about the distinction and its logic: "So far as I see," he wrote, "once we have broken with Origen and his theory of the deeper meaning of the parables, we cannot stop half-way . . . either the parables are wholly figurative speech or wholly literal. . . ."[9]

As his reference to Origen suggests, Jülicher's antagonism to allegory was partly a reaction against the centuries-old tradition of the allegorical interpretation of the parables. His insistence upon the non-allegorical "authenticity" of the parables was also partly a product of Romantic biases, widely held throughout the nineteenth century, which impugned allegory as an inferior type of literary discourse. Like many of his contemporaries, Jülicher did not understand much about allegory, neither in its classical setting nor in its pervasive manifestations throughout nearly all literary discourse.

The more pressing matter for Jülicher to resolve was the following question: If the parables were not originally allegorical, how then did they come to be interpreted allegorically? Jülicher's answer was the famous "hardening" theory of parabolic speech, based on Mark 4:11–12: Under the influence of Hellenistic Judaism and its literature, the evangelists, like Mark, believed that Jesus used parables as a way of withholding his message of salvation from his opponents, the Pharisees.

The evangelists' conviction was, in turn, a product of a bitter rift between the early Church and their Jewish contemporaries—a result of the enmity that early on developed between Jews and Christians; it was not, in other words, an authentic reflection of Jesus' own teachings. The Markan passage was either fraudulent or incorrectly presented, as were the other allegorical interpretations that the evangelists and the early Church attached to the original narratives, sometimes even within the texts of the synoptic gospels themselves. The parables Jesus had told were actually far simpler than the ones preserved in the gospels. Jülicher never doubted, however, that the gospel parables preserved an "authentic kernel" of Jesus' speech. Indeed, for Jülicher the task of modern parable-research was to salvage those kernels, to rescue *ipsissima verba* from the corrupted allegorical texts of the evangelists.[10]

JÜLICHER'S SUCCESSORS

The influence of Jülicher's work on subsequent parable-research has been enormous. Until recently, virtually every important scholar engaged in parable-research has followed Jülicher in rejecting allegory from the parable even when the same scholar has disagreed with Jülicher over his definition of the parable. This has had several results. Because Jülicher claimed that allegorization had already contaminated the parables as preserved in the synoptic gospels, his approach called into question the received text and forced the scholar to reconstruct the "original" parable before interpreting it; inevitably, these reconstructions reflect the desires of the scholar-interpreter as much as they do the force of the parable itself.

At the same time, Jülicher's project of recovery effectively removed the parables from their most concrete context, the literary text in which they were preserved, and did not—indeed, could not—supply an adequate context to replace it. And as every modern student of interpretation knows, there is no interpretation outside of some context. The end result has been a kind of chaos of subjectivism; this was noted already by Jülicher's earliest critics, and has persisted down to this very day, so that even when contemporary scholars agree upon a general framework for a parable's meaning, the heralding of the eschaton for example, they often differ upon the exact meaning of Jesus' eschatological teachings and its precise wording in the parable.

The best example of this scholarly dilemma is the case of Joachim Jeremias, the most influential of all New Testament parable scholars in the last half-century. Jeremias consciously sought to complete Jülicher's project of "recovering" the "original" parables of Jesus by decontaminating them from the allegorizing corruption of the evangelists. To accomplish this, Jeremias formulated a number of laws to describe the ways in which the original parables were initially allegorized; he also proposed

original versions of the parables that accorded with what Jeremias believed must have been their messages, the "simple essential ideas" which
"Jesus was never tired of expressing."[11]

These ideas are essentially three in number: "the eschatological
nature of [Jesus'] preaching, the intensity of his summons to repentance,
and his conflict with Pharisaism."[12] Yet Jeremias' interpretations of the
parables' "original" meanings are no less subjective than the allegorical
interpretations he rejects out of hand.[13] As one scholar has commented,
Jeremias' mainly eschatological interpretation of the parables "looks
very much like a summary of a rather conservative Lutheran piety."[14]

In reaction against Jeremias and the tradition of parable-interpre-
tation he represents, several attempts have recently been made to reha-
bilitate the conception of the parables as allegorical compositions.[15] No
one, however, has questioned the very applicability of the allegory-
parable distinction in the first place, while most scholars have invested
their efforts in offering new definitions for the parable as alternatives
to the allegorical conception. These definitions, which might all be
subsumed under the title of the parable as not-allegory, begin, again,
with Jülicher's work. And not surprisingly, the initial reactions and
criticisms Jülicher's work received, particularly in Paul Fiebig's interesting comparative studies of Jesus' parables and Rabbinic *meshalim,* anticipate many of the methodological difficulties that have attended the
more recent attempts at definition.[16]

C.H. DODD AND HIS INFLUENCE

The specific approach to the parable that I wish to concentrate upon
here first appeared in the lectures C.H. Dodd originally delivered in
1935 and which were later published as *The Parables of the Kingdom.*
Dodd accepted Jülicher's basic parable-allegory opposition, and then
asked, "What then are the parables, if they are not allegories?"[17] In
response, he answered: The parables "are the natural expressions of a
mind that sees truth in concrete pictures rather than conceives it in
abstractions," and are used

> to enforce and illustrate the idea that the kingdom of God has come
> upon men there and then. . . . They use all the resources of dramatic
> illustration to help men see that in the events before their eyes . . .
> God is confronting them in His kingdom, power, and glory. This world
> has become the scene of a divine drama, in which the eternal issues
> are laid bare. It is the hour of decision.[18]

For Dodd, the parable is no mere similitude or narrative-scene. The "realism" of the parables' style arises, he writes, "from the conviction that there is no mere analogy, but an inward affinity, between the natural order and the spiritual order; or as we might put it in the language of the parables themselves, the Kingdom of God is intrinsically *like* the processes of nature and of the daily life of men."[19]

I have quoted from Dodd at length in order to convey an idea of the heightened and dramatic rhetoric of his language. While Dodd is most famous today for his contribution of the term "realized eschatology" to the vocabulary of parable-research, it may be that his most lasting achievement in the field will be recognized in retrospect to have been his view of the parable as what later scholars sometimes call a "language-event," that is, a performative act of language.

While scholars like Jülicher saw the parables mainly as didactic instruments that convey ideas to audiences unaccustomed to theological and metaphysical abstractions, Dodd and his successors conceive of the parables as virtual experiences in themselves, linguistic and poetic events that go beyond the merely discursive stretch of conventional metaphysics and theology. As one writer on parables has described such a "parabolic experience": it "is a way of believing and living that initially seems ordinary, yet is so dislocated and rent from its usual context that, if the parable 'works,' the spectators have become participants, not because they want to necessarily or simply have 'gotten the point' but because they have, for the moment, 'lost control' or as the new hermeneuts say, 'been interpreted.' "[20]

The inflated rhetoric that characterizes this passage indicates its author's desire to find in the parable an expression of language as pure, unmediated epiphany, as a language-event so immediately present to, and constitutive of, its audience that it no longer needs to be interpreted by them. Indeed, in scholarly writing of the sort that this passage typifies, the term allegory has become a kind of trope for interpretation; in this scholarship, to say that the parable is *not* allegorical means in effect that the parable is *beyond* interpretation—on the other side of purely intellectual or rational understanding. The parables of Jesus are endowed with the full presence of an originary voice, with the plenitude of a revelation that not only need not be interpreted, but instead itself "interprets" its audience and transfigures its hearers. This is, in short, the parable become the Logos—a timeless, hermeneutically inexhaustible and rhetorically irresistible entity. Not surprisingly, some scholars have associated this conception of Jesus' parables with the idea that the literary form of the parable is itself informed by a kind of open-ended polysemy, a capacity for sustaining an endless number of interpretations.[21]

PAUL RICOEUR ON THE PARABLE AS METAPHOR

Among scholars who have recently articulated this conception of parabolic language, Paul Ricoeur has been the most influential. In a number of works, Ricoeur has defined parable as a species of metaphor; according to Ricoeur, the parable, like metaphor, has the capacity literally to "re-define and re-describe reality."[22] Ricoeur has also described parabolic narrative as an extended metaphor, as "the conjunction between a *narrative form,* a *metaphorical process,* and an appropriate 'qualifier,' " by which Ricoeur means a key to the referent of the parable. In the case of the parables of Jesus, this referent is first the Kingdom of God and, ultimately, "the experience of the whole man and of all men."[23] For Ricoeur, in short, the parable is "a fiction capable of re-describing life."[24]

Ricoeur's interpretive project is characteristic of other recent attempts to apply a literary approach to the study of the Bible in general and the parables in particular. Although these approaches employ a number of different methodologies—among them the New Criticism, archetypal criticism, structuralism, semiotics, deconstruction—they may all be said to share a desire to direct attention to the exchanges and transactions that take place *within* the text, in this case the parable, rather than outside or "behind" it. Thus, Ricoeur is not essentially concerned either with recovering or reconstructing the "original" parable or even the parable's original meaning. The notion of an "original" or "historical" meaning is itself suspect for Ricoeur since, as he has written elsewhere, every text has a "two-fold historicity"—"of tradition, which transmits and sediments the interpretation, and of interpretation, which maintains and renews the tradition."[25]

While Ricoeur's approach does not exclude historical analysis, it is essentially ahistorical, not because Ricoeur privileges ahistoricism *per se* but because he hopes that by concentrating upon the "literary" aspects of the text he will be able to isolate its more permanent and abiding elements—in sum, the keys to the contemporary relevance of the Bible and its powers of transformation. For Ricoeur, that permanent and abiding element, the transformatory kernel of the parable, resides in its metaphoric character.

It is, of course, somewhat ironic that Ricoeur should identify parable with metaphor, when Jülicher had initiated the epoch of modern parable-research by explicitly rejecting metaphor as inauthentic discourse. In fact, Ricoeur acknowledges this irony, though not by disavowing Jülicher's rejection of allegory; rather, he argues that Jülicher thought of metaphor in the purely ornamental terms of Aristotelian rhetoric and therefore did not understand the inherently "productive" power of metaphoric language: the ways in which metaphor not only transfers meaning between the literal and the figurative spheres but actually creates and produces meaning.

For Ricoeur, the same productivity is true of parable. As he writes elsewhere, "the narrative-parable is itself an itinerary of meaning, a signifying dynamism. . . ."[26] Furthermore, the itinerary of meaning that the parables of Jesus encapsulate is a model for the way in which the gospels in their entirety function, as does even the life of Jesus. The narrative of Jesus' life is simply the parable writ large, the kingdom-to-come to which the individual narrative-parables Jesus delivered comprise its key.

To get a better grasp of Ricoeur's view of the parable, it will be helpful to summarize his analysis of The Wicked Husbandmen; after presenting Ricoeur's analysis, we will turn to the Rabbinic *mashal* and, on its basis, offer an alternative interpretation for the parable.

THE PARABLE OF THE WICKED HUSBANDMEN

The parable of the Wicked Husbandmen is one of two narrative parables that are preserved in all three synoptic gospels (Mk 12:1–12; Mt 21:33–46; Lk 20:9–19) as well as in the Gospel of Thomas (65).[27] [The other parable of this sort is the Sower (Mk 4:3–9; Mt 13:4–9; Lk 8:5–8.] Although present-day New Testament scholars still dispute the precise relationship between the different gospels, I will follow the conventional view assigning priority to the Markan version, and assume that Matthew and Luke were in one way or another using Mark's version. In any case, the differences in details between the three versions are relatively minor.[28] The following is Mark's version of the parable:

> And he began to speak to them in parables: "A man planted a vineyard, and set a hedge around it, and dug a pit for the wine-press, and built a tower, and let it out to tenants, and went into another country. When the time came, he sent a servant to the tenants, to get from them some of the fruit of the vineyard. And they took him and beat

him, and sent him away empty-handed. Again he sent to them another servant, and they wounded him in the head, and treated him
shamefully. And he sent another, and him they killed; and so with
many others; some they beat, and some they killed. He had still one
other, a beloved son; finally he sent him to them, saying 'They will
respect my son.' But those tenants said to one another, 'This is the
heir; come, let us kill him, and the inheritance will be ours.' And they
took him and killed him, and cast him out of the vineyard. What will
the owner of the vineyard do? He will come and destroy the tenants,
and give the vineyard to others."

At the outset it should be said that within the synoptic tradition
itself there already exists evidence for the interpretation of this parable
as an allegory. Thus, at the conclusion of the parable's narrative (in all
three synoptic versions), Jesus asks his audience of Jewish priests,
scribes, and elders:

"Have you not read this scripture: 'The very stone which the builders
rejected has become the head of the corner; this was the Lord's doing,
and it is marvelous in our eyes'?" (Ps. 118:22–23)[29]

And in Matthew the following statement is added to the scriptural
quotation:

"Therefore I tell you, the kingdom of God will be taken away from
you and given to a nation producing the fruits of it. And he who falls
on this stone will be broken to pieces; but when it falls on anyone, it
will crush him."

This statement, in effect an anti-Jewish interpretation of the psalm
verse, requires that the son in the parable be understood as Jesus; according to Matthew's interpretation, Jesus' death will be the cause for God's
rejection of the Jews and the election of the Church as the New Israel.
And indeed, this Christological interpretation early on became the standard reading of the parable's meaning. Thus, the second century Church
father Irenaeus writes: "For inasmuch as the former [the Jews] have
rejected the Son of God, and cast Him out of the vineyard when they
slew Him, God has justly rejected them, and given to the Gentiles
outside the vineyard the fruits of cultivation."[30]

Significantly, when Jülicher came to study the parable seventeen
hundred years later, it was precisely this allegorized presentation of its

meaning in the gospel text that led him to dismiss the entire passage as an invention of the early Church, falsely attributed to Jesus.[31] Yet even a traditional historico-critical scholar like Jeremias, who affirms its authenticity, admits that the text of the parable of the Wicked Husbandmen is problematic because it "exhibits an allegorical character which is unique among the parables of Jesus."[32] As Jeremias notes, the opening description of the Vineyard is drawn from Isaiah 5:1–7; the image of the vineyard symbolizes Israel, the tenants Israel's leaders, the owner God, the messengers the prophets, and the son Christ. The punishment of the tenants is a symbol of the ruin of Israel, while "the others" to whom the owner will give the vineyard are the Gentile Church. While Jeremias goes on to reconstruct a text of the "original" parable, which ends up closely resembling the version now extant in the Gospel of Thomas, this highly simplified version of the narrative still "tells of a single messenger repeatedly dismissed by the tenants empty-handed, and driven out with contumely and injury."[33]

According to Jeremias, "there can be no doubt that in the sending of the son Jesus himself had his own sending in mind" (although Jeremais concedes that it cannot be assumed that Jesus' Jewish audience would have recognized the symbolism).[34] From this undoubted assumption follows Jeremias' proposal for the "original" meaning of the parable: "Like so many other parables of Jesus, it vindicates the offer of the gospel to the poor. You, it says, you tenants of the vineyard, you leaders of the people! you have opposed, have multiplied rebellion against God. Your cup is full! Therefore shall the vineyard of God be given to 'others' (Mk 12:9)."[35] Indeed, Jeremias believes that this original tale reflects the historical resentment felt by Galilean tenant farmers toward their absentee foreign landlords.

As Frank Kermode notes, Jeremias' interpretation is simply a "more rationalistic allegory" than the other interpretations, even "a somewhat ridiculous fable about current affairs."[36]

RICOEUR ON THE WICKED HUSBANDMEN

In contrast, Paul Ricoeur's interpretation of the parable is anything but a fable of current affairs. The specific aim of Ricoeur's analysis of the parables is "to reconstruct the codes that govern the transformations at work in the narrative."[37] Borrowing from A.J. Greimas' narratology, Ricoeur defines those transformations in terms of what Greimas calls isotopies, that is, dynamic but repeating (and redundant) semantic categories which make a uniform reading of the narrative possible and are derived from recurring interactions between characters, images, places, and so on.[38] In the Wicked Husbandmen, for example, the first isotopy centers on vegetation, as in the image of the vineyard. A second one concerns the body and death, as epitomized in the fates of the various messengers whom the vineyard's owner sends to the wicked tenants.

For Ricoeur, the process of metaphorization in the narrative actually begins with the tension or clash between two isotopies. In the Wicked Husbandmen, this occurs when the vineyard's owner sends the messengers to the husbandmen to request fruit; but instead of sending back fruit, the tenants return the beaten body of the servant. "In this way," Ricoeur writes, "the dying body [of the servant] becomes the substituted and inverted sign of the refused object-value, the fruits of the vineyard."[39] This "metaphorization"—the identification which Ricoeur sees between the dying body and the refused fruit—is the parabolic kernel of the narrative's overall meaning: "So that the fruit may increase, life must decrease."[40] And this metaphorization reoccurs in the narrative of the gospels, most clearly in the parable of the Sower. For Ricoeur, this parable is the companion to the Wicked Husbandmen because it explicitly deals with the fecundity of the Word. Indeed, in Ricoeur's reading, the real process of metaphorization in the gospels is to be found in the conjunction between these two parables: ". . . the great metaphor encompassing these two parables" is that "if the word is to increase the body must decrease. . . ."[41]

This "criss-crossing between the euphoric process of the word and the dysphoric process of the body's march toward death" is, of course, the metaphor conveyed by the life of the speaker of the parables: Jesus.[42] "In effect," Ricoeur concludes,

> what progressively happens in the Gospel is the *recognition* of Jesus as being the Christ. We can say in this regard that the Gospel is not a simple account of the life, teaching, work, death, and the resurrection of Jesus, but the communicating of an act of confession, a communication by means of which the reader in turn is rendered capable of performing the same recognition which occurs inside the text.[43]

Which is to say that the entire process of metaphorization contained in the gospel is to be understood by the reader as a parable of the religious process—the act of conversion—he or she is to undergo.

Parable here is no longer a mere literary form, but rather a kind of infinitely repeating and self-engendering transformation which recurs any number of times inside and outside the text we have looked at. It occurs inside the narrative of the Wicked Husbandmen, between its isotopies; within the gospel text, between the parables of the Wicked Husbandmen and the Sower; between the two parables and their larger narrative context, that is, the gospel-narrative of the life and teachings of Jesus; and, finally, between that larger narrative and all the sub-narratives it frames, and the religious existence of the text's reader. All these criss-crossing relations Ricoeur ultimately subsumes under the literary rubric of intertextuality. Contrary to its name, though, this intertextuality is not primarily textual; rather, it describes the process of metaphorization that, "more than any other, is what exercises the reader's productive imagination."[44]

For Ricoeur, then, the meaning of the parable lies in the process of metaphorization, in the exchange of the body for the word. Powerful as this reading may be, however, there are difficulties with it. In the first place, it will be recalled that, for Ricoeur, the process of metaphorization proceeds from the clash between the two isotopies of the narrative, from the semantic opposition between the image of the fruit of the vineyard which the husbandmen refuse to send back to the owner and the other the image of the beaten, dying body of the messenger which they do send back in place of the fruit; from this clash of images issues the metaphoric meaning that in order for the fruit, the Word, to increase, the body must decrease. Yet the narrative does not relate that metaphor so much as its opposite: just as the requested fruit is refused, so too the body must suffer.

A second, more serious difficulty with the reading lies in the vast integrative ambition of Ricoeur's project: his wish to integrate the parable into the larger context of the gospel narrative, and, beyond that, into the experience of the text's reader—and to subsume all of it under the category of intertextuality. Our difficulty here is not with the unity Ricoeur presupposes in the gospel text—the textual unity between the parable-narrative and the larger narrative context—which perhaps is simply not there, as a traditional historical-critical scholar might argue. Rather, our hesitations concerning Ricoeur's project lie in the unbroken thread of intertextuality that he claims to stretch all the way from the parable within its literary-narrative context (perhaps even from the tension between the two isotopies in the single narrative of the Wicked Husbandmen, the point which for Ricoeur constitutes the very beginning of his process of metaphorization) to the outer limits where the text inspirits the "productive imagination" of its audience. While some members of the gospel's audience may subscribe to this article of belief in intertextual coherence, it is hardly the rule of faith that Ricoeur assumes it to be for everyone.

It is certainly questionable to claim that such intertextuality directly proceeds from the literary form of the parable—that narrative itself, or *in* itself, is a guarantee of such theological meaning. For what is that seamless, endless, all-encompassing web of intertextuality that Ricoeur adduces if not a theological datum, a trope for Christ as Logos? As the distinguished literary critic J. Hillis Miller has written, "Christ as the Logos is not only the basis of the analogies, echoes, and resemblances among things of the world created in his name and between things created in his name and things hidden since the creation of the world. Christ as Logos is also the basis of the correspondences within the realm of language, for example the correspondence between visible vehicle and invisible and unnamed tenor in a parable."[45] The impulse here is deeply logocentric in the classical Johannine sense, if not also in the more contemporary deconstructionist one. Students of literature will easily recognize in Ricoeur's notion of metaphor the lineaments of the Romantic notion of the symbol.[46]

Yet the impulse to attribute such power to the parables of Jesus seems to be nearly irresistible. In the essay from which the quote just cited was taken, even Hillis Miller adopts it. In distinguishing between sacred parables (Jesus' in particular) and secular ones (like Kafka's), he writes:

> The parables of Jesus are spoken by the Word, the Logos, in person. . . . The fact that the Messiah speaks the parables guarantees the correspondence between the homely stories he tells of farming, fishing, and domestic economy on the one hand, and the spiritual or transcendent meaning on the other, the meaning that tells of things beyond the threshold of the domestic and visible, the meaning that nevertheless can be spoken only in parable, that is, indirectly. . . . Believing in the validity of the parables of the New Testament and believing that Jesus is the Son of God are the same thing.[47]

It is not clear what Miller means by "believing in the validity of the parables"—validity as *ipsissima verba?* as literary narratives? as historical documents? Nor does he explain what the alternative view of Jesus' parables (or of other sacred parables) might be for someone who does not believe that Jesus is the Son of God. Would Jesus' parables then have the same status as the secular parables Miller discusses—Kafka's, for example? These parables, Miller writes, are "not spoken by the Word itself translating itself to human ears and human understanding but [are] spoken by some all-too-human person casting out figurative language toward something across the border from any direct seeing, hearing, or understanding."[48]

Even for someone who does not believe Jesus was the Son of God, this characterization ill suits the New Testament parables. Instead of sacred and secular, it would be preferable to use other categories to differentiate between parables. Such a distinction might be as simple as one between ancients and moderns, a corrolary perhaps to what Walter Benjamin had in mind when he wrote that "Kafka's work presents a sickness of tradition." For Benjamin, Kafka's parables, like those of Jesus or the Rabbis, were part of the tradition of wisdom literature. But where Jesus' or the Rabbis' parables actually conveyed wisdom, communicated some kind of teaching, Kafka's sole instruction was that the path to wisdom had been lost, that "only the products of its decay remain."[49]

What is weakest about Miller's essay, though, is not solely the distinction between sacred and secular parables. Rather, it is the failure even to acknowledge that there may be readers who will wish to read Jesus' parables and to accept their literary validity *without*, however, necessarily believing in their sacrality, or the divinity of their presumed author. The same criticism can be applied to Ricoeur's interpretation of the Wicked Husbandmen (and, for that matter, to many of the other recent literary approaches to the parables which yoke the sophisticated techniques of contemporary literary criticism to obvious, though not always explicit, theological presuppositions about the parables' authority and authorship). Ricoeur's interpretation of the Wicked Husbandmen is predicated upon the belief that Jesus intended the figure of the son in the parable's narrative to refer to himself. This assumes, first, that Jesus possessed knowledge of his eventual death, and that such knowledge must have been either literally or figuratively prophetic; second, that Jesus understood his eventual death as part of a larger schema, either the drama of the election of the Church (as in the medieval view) or of Christian salvation (as in Ricoeur); and third, that we today can know these facts about Jesus from the evidence of the gospels. But what are those of us who do not share these suppositions to do with the parable? How are we to understand the Wicked Husbandmen? Or are we doomed to be the proverbial outsiders in Mark's famous hardening theory of parabolic discourse—those who, even if they see and hear, will never understand?

To ask these questions is, in effect, to ask: Can Jesus' parables be understood unchristologically? Without attempting a definitive answer to the question, we can more modestly rephrase it for our present purposes as follows: Is it possible to apply a literary approach to the parables that will avoid a purely historicist reading like Jeremias', on the one hand, and still not require a confession of belief as in Ricoeur's approach, on the other? In other words, can we read Jesus' parables as narratives, but without attributing to narrative, *qua* literary form, a logocentric, virtually revelatory potency?

THE RABBINIC PARABLE

In response to these questions, I wish to propose the Rabbinic *mashal* as a model for reading the parables as non-revelatory but ideological narratives. While it is clearly impossible within the limits of this essay to offer a full exposition of the Rabbinic *mashal,* a few introductory comments on its rhetorical function and strategies are in order.

1. The vast majority of *meshalim* are preserved in Rabbinic literature within exegetical contexts like midrash where they appear to serve as tools of scriptural exegesis. For the Rabbis themselves, scriptural exegesis was the *mashal*'s primary source of value. "Do not treat the *mashal* lightly," they said (clearly suggesting that some did). "For by means of the *mashal* a person is able to understand the words of Torah . . ." (*Shir Hashirim Rabbah* 1:8).

2. In fact, though, exegesis is not so much the real object of communication of the *mashal* as it is the parable's ostensible occasion—its *raison d'être,* as it were, and divine sanction, the source for its authority.

3. In terms of its actual rhetorical working, the *mashal* can best be defined as an allusive narrative which is told for an ulterior purpose. Like parables and fables in other literatures—the *ainos* in classical Greek literature, for example—the *mashal* draws a parallel between the fictional tale that it relates and a concrete situation at hand, known to the *mashal*'s audience; rather than draw the parallel explicitly, however, the *mashal* tends to leave it to the audience to figure out, upon reflection for itself. This parallel, the *mashal*'s ulterior purpose, constitutes the *mashal*'s rhetorical message, and can generally be categorized in terms of praise or blame, or as a subtype of praise or blame.[50] The particular themes of praise or blame are typically related to the ruling ideas and

beliefs of Rabbinic Judaism. As such, the *mashal* can also be characterized as a form of ideological narrative, that is, a mode of communication
concerned with impressing a certain world-view upon its audience.

4. When a *mashal* is presented orally within a living social context,
one assumes that its audience can grasp its rhetorical message without
additional help. Once the *mashal* is transferred to a literary context,
however, and the recitation of the parable itself becomes a narrative or
part of a larger narrative, it also becomes necessary to provide the new
audience of the *mashal*—its second-hand audience, a reader for
example—with the information he or she will need to grasp the *mashal*'s message. This displacement of the *mashal* from one context to
another is the origin of the *nimshal,* the so-called explanation which
accompanies the *mashal* in its normative form. Yet as this account of its
origins suggests, the *nimshal* is not really an explanation for the *mashal*'s narrative but a medium for providing the *mashal*'s new audience
with the information necessary to grasp its meaning. The actual form of
the *nimshal* can therefore vary considerably from *mashal* to *mashal.*
Sometimes, it explains the narrative's symbolism at great length; at
other times, as in most Rabbinic texts where the *mashal* is usually
presented within a midrashic context, the *nimshal* may consist solely of
the verse which the *mashal* comments upon; while at still other times,
as when the *mashal* appears in a normative context, the *nimshal*'s
information may be provided informally, in the course of the narrative.
In all these cases, though, the rhetorical function of the *mashal*—its
message of praise and blame—remains the determining feature of the
mashal's shape and meaning.[51]

5. While there are some *meshalim* in Rabbinic literature that serve
as illustrations and others that resemble allegories, most Rabbinic parables do not fit at all into these two categories. Neither a simple illustration with a transparent lesson, nor a completely opaque story with a
secret message, the *mashal* is an intrinsically hermeneutical form of
narrative that actively elicits an interpretive act from its audience.

SOME EXAMPLES

It will be easier to grasp the complex workings of the *mashal* and its
rhetoric of praise and blame by looking at an example of the form.
Consider the following *mashal,* which is cited in the Palestinian Talmud,
Berakhot 5c, as part of a eulogy R. Shimeon b. Lakish recited at the
passing of R. Hiyya bar Ada.

It is like (*mashal lemah hadavar domeh le-*) a king who had a son, whom he loved more than anything else. What did the king do? He planted an orchard for his son. When the son obeyed his father, the king would go around the entire world, and whenever he saw a beautiful plant he would plant it in the orchard. And whenever the son angered his father, the king would uproot all the plants.

Likewise (*kakh*): When Israel performs the will of the Holy One, blessed be He, He goes through the entire world, and whenever he finds a righteous gentile, He takes him and joins him to Israel, like Jethro or Rahab. And whenever Israel angers Him, he removes the righteous from them.

Although this *mashal* is presented within a semi-narrative context, it retains the standard bipartite form that eventually becomes part of the regularized form of the Rabbinic *mashal:* first the narrative (with its introductory formula, "it is like," *mashal lemah hadavar domeh,* or a variant), then the *nimshal* (also introduced by the formulaic *kakh,* "likewise"). As one can see from this example, the *nimshal*'s presence in the *mashal* is almost mandatory. Consider the possibility of reading the *mashal* without the *nimshal*. The *mashal*'s audience could probably figure out without too much difficulty the identities of the various stock figures in the narrative: the king is God, the son the people of Israel, and so on. But a reader would have a far more difficult time determining exactly what the motifs of uprooting and adding the plants symbolize except for some kind of general punishment and reward. And if the reader attempted to find an exact correspondent for the symbol of the garden, he or she would be led entirely astray, for as one sees in the *nimshal* (or doesn't), the garden has no precise referent.

Similarly, a common reader would most probably mistake the message of the *mashal,* which is not eulogistic praise of the deceased sage, as one might expect, but rather a rationalization for the sage's death and of God's justice as it is implicated in this untimely death of a righteous sage.[52] Such theodical justification is close to apologetics, and the *mashal*'s rhetorical function can be categorized as apologetic praise which is, however, very different from eulogy, or praise of the dead.

A second example of the Rabbinic *mashal,* the following parable, from the Tannaitic collection Sifre Deuteronomy (312), employs a different rhetorical strategy in commenting upon Deuteronomy 32:9, "For the Lord's portion is His people, Jacob the lot of His inheritance."

It is like (*mashal le-*) a king who owned a field and gave it to tenant-farmers. The tenant-farmers began to plunder the field. So he took it away from them, and gave the field to their children, but soon they were more wicked than their predecessors. So he took the field away from the children, and gave it to their children, but soon they too were more wicked than their predecessors. [Finally] a son was born to the king. He said to the tenant-farmers: Get off my property. I do not want you on it. Give me back my portion that I may acknowledge it (*makiro*).

Likewise (*kakh*): When Abraham came into the world, there issued forth from him inferior progeny (*pesolet,* lit. dregs)—Yishmael and all the children of Keturah. When Isaac came into the world, there issued forth from him inferior progeny (*pesolet*)—Esau and all the chiefs of Edom—and they were more wicked than their predecessors. But when Jacob came, there issued forth from him no inferior progeny, but all his sons were born upright people (*kesheirim*). As the matter is stated: "Jacob was a perfect man, dwelling in tents" (Gen 25:27). Now from what point does God acknowledge His portion? From Jacob, as it is said, "For the Lord's portion is His people [which is] Jacob, the lot of His inheritance" (Deut 32:9).

As in the previous *mashal,* this narrative's overall rhetorical function is praise, though here the *mashal* praises the entire nation of Israel. In this example, however, praise is presented along with blame: of the children of Ishmael and Esau, Rabbinic code-names for the Arab and Roman nations. Since there can be no real praise without some blame, a combination of praise and blame is not entirely unusual; and as in this *mashal,* comparative praise and blame are frequently used in order to make explicitly polemical comparisons. In this example, God's election of Israel as His chosen nation—the nation by which He recognizes His portion—is made at the expense of the Gentile nations whom He rejects on account of their wickedness.

This polemic against the Gentiles may possibly be directed against the claim that true faith—what Paul, for example, calls justification—was already achieved by Abraham, the patriarch and father of many nations, and not solely by Jacob and his descendants, the Israelites who alone received the Law.[53] This suggestion is corroborated by the narrative's startling implication that Jacob alone is God's child; all the others, Abraham, Isaac, and their respective descendants, were merely tenants on the land.

As the reader will notice, however, this last point is at best implied. It is nowhere made explicit in the *mashal* or in the *nimshal;* indeed, the implication itself derives mainly from an inconsistency between the *mashal*'s narrative and the *nimshal.* In the narrative, the king first entrusts the field to the tenant-farmers, then to *their* children, and then to *their* grandchildren—all of whom prove themselves unworthy—until at last the king has a son to whom he gives the field—or so we assume; the narrative never actually carries the story that far. In the nimshal, however, Jacob, or Jacob's children, turn out to be the authentic heirs, but they are in fact Abraham's great-grandchildren, just like the other nations who are rejected as unfit to receive God's inheritance.

This particular discrepancy may underline the radical claim of polemical exclusion that the *mashal* makes, but it also points to a more general stylistic feature of the *mashal.* Besides internal contradictions and similar inconsistencies between the *mashal* and the *nimshal,* the poetics of narrative in the *mashal* builds upon and exploits numerous points of discontinuity—rhetorical silences, unexplained or unmotivated deeds, excessive or exaggerated gestures. All these serve as effective rhetorical gestures and point to the different kinds of hermeneutical space that the *mashal* encloses, both in its narrative as well as in the *nimshal* and its explicit interpretive acts. In addition, there can be any number of undetermined symbols that allow for additional meanings to be read into the *mashal* by different audiences, though always within certain delimited boundaries prescribed by the *mashal*'s own readability.[54]

In this *mashal,* for example, it is not entirely clear precisely what the field in the narrative symbolizes, whether it is the special covenantal relationship that God establishes with the nation of Israel or the actual land of Israel (with a glance toward the contemporary historical reality of Roman imperial possession of the land); the narrative appears to stress the land for its own sake, while the *nimshal* clearly points to the covenantal relationship. Should the implication of the narrative be sacrificed on account of the *nimshal*'s specification? Or should the narrative be privileged over the *nimshal?* It is not clear. The reader is being left with a partially indeterminate reading that he or she must decide upon by filling the gap in meaning.

Yet however he or she reads the symbol, the reader is inevitably led to conclude that the *mashal* goes beyond mere praise of Israel for its worthiness as God's chosen nation. God Himself, as it were, praises Jacob/Israel as the possessors of His inheritance. He rejects the other nations, and acknowledges His portion as His own through the existence

of Israel, as the concluding exegesis of Deuteronomy 32:9 implies. Whatever its more specific nuances, the overall function of this *mashal* can
therefore be characterized as polemical praise.

THE MASHAL AS A KEY TO THE WICKED HUSBANDMEN

The Rabbinic *mashal* serves many other rhetorical functions—
complaint, regret, lamentation, and mockery, to name only a few—but
for our present purposes the two examples we have discussed will suffice. These two *meshalim* also use traditional narrative motifs that appear in the parable of the Wicked Husbandmen. The narrative of that
parable contains the following motifs:

(1) man plants a field (vineyard; orchard; garden)
(2) he leases it to tenants
(3) he goes off to a foreign province
(4) he requests the tenants to send him products/fruit from the field
(5) tenants reject request and effectively rebel against owner (beat servants; kill son to inherit land) [## 4 and 5 are repeated three times]
(6) owner punishes tenants

The *meshalim* from *Sifre Deut.* and from the Palestinian Talmud use
several of these motifs in different combinations and, as we have seen,
for different rhetorical and exegetical purposes. For example, the anonymous author of the *Sifre Deut. mashal* combined the motifs of the man
who plants a vineyard and leases it to tenants (##1 and 2) with the motif
of the wicked tenants who abuse the property (#5), but he used the
motif of the single son who is the rightful heir as the solution to the
owner's dilemma (as in #6). The eulogy parable also uses the motif of
the man who plants a field (specifically an orchard) and combines that
motif directly with the other motif of the single son to whom he gives the
orchard. In that *mashal,* however, the son may be said to play the roles
of both the wicked tenants (that is, when he disobeys his father) *and* the
rightful heir (when he obeys his father); in each case, the king responds
in the appropriate way.

Still other Rabbinic *meshalim* could be cited to show how these
traditional motifs appear in the *mashal;* nearly all the motifs in the
Wicked Husbandmen can be shown to have at least partial parallels in
Rabbinic *meshalim.*[55] Even from the two examples we have looked at,
however, we can observe the range of symbolic values that can be repre-

sented by a single traditional image, motif, or character. For example, in the *Sifre mashal*, the field may represent either Israel's specific status as God's elect nation, or the land of Israel; in the *mashal* from the Palestinian Talmud, the orchard itself does not have a clear symbolic value except, perhaps, as the community of Israel in its entirety.

In both *meshalim*, the image of the son as rightful heir symbolizes the Jewish nation; yet in the *Sifre mashal* the son is deliberately contrasted with the tenants and their children. As both *meshalim* testify, the figure of the son need not necessarily represent God's actual son, and not even a specific individual, as the figure of the son in the parable of the Wicked Husbandmen has typically been interpreted as symbolizing. In regard to this last point, we may also recall a fact recently pointed out—that the adjective modifying the son in both Mark's and Luke's version, *agapetos,* usually translated as "beloved," probably means (on the basis of translation usage in the Septuagint) the "only" or "sole" son, equivalent to the Hebrew *yahid*.[56]

Whom does this "son" represent? To answer this question, let us turn to the rhetorical function of the parable. As in the *Sifre Deut. mashal,* the blame of the wicked husbandmen entails a degree of praise for the son. Still, the Wicked Husbandmen is primarily a *mashal* blaming the wicked husbandmen. Who, then, are the wicked husbandmen? In the various interpretations discussed earlier, they have been understood as representing either the Jewish nation in its entirety (Matthew, Irenaeus, and others); the wealthy landowners (Jeremias); or merely, it would seem, fictional narrative agents, not genuine historical personages, who perpetrate the evil deed necessitated by the parable's process of metaphorical transformation (Ricoeur).

There remains, however, still another possible candidate. Although the Wicked Husbandmen does not have a formal *nimshal* such as might be found in a regularized Rabbinic *mashal,* the information that would be offered in a *nimshal* is in fact supplied by the narrative in the gospeltext that surrounds the parable. As the reader will recall, Jesus is on his way to Jerusalem when he is met by various Jewish leaders—in Mark, the chief priests, the scribes and elders. Mark continues (11:28–33):

> And they said to him: By what authority are you doing these things, or who gave you this authority to do them? Jesus said to them: I will ask you a question. Answer me, and I will tell you by what authority I do these things. Was the baptism of John from heaven or from men? Answer me. And they argued with one another. If we say, From

Heaven, he will say, Then why did you not believe him? But shall we say, From men?—they were afraid of the people, for all held that John was a real prophet. So they answered Jesus: We do not know. And Jesus said to them: Neither will I tell you by what authority I do these things. And he began to speak to them in parables. . . .

Jesus then relates the parable of the Wicked Husbandmen, after which the narrative continues:

And they tried to arrest him, but feared the multitude, for they perceived that he had told the parable against them; so they left him and went away.

This narrative, the literary context of the parable, is generally dismissed as secondary; secondary it is no doubt, because it derives from the literary stage of redaction, but it is not necessarily irrelevant to the parable's meaning. On the basis of its narrative-context, which is common to all three synoptic gospels, the parable's protagonists, the characters of the wicked husbandmen, obviously correspond to the Jewish leaders—in Mark, specifically to the chief priests, scribes, and elders; in Luke, to the scribes and high priests; in Matthew, to the Pharisees and high priests.[57] The parable condemns these leaders for having attempted to usurp the vineyard and for having beaten and/or murdered the owner's messengers and his son. I will return shortly to the symbolism of the vineyard. But if the wicked husbandmen are the Jewish leaders, then the figure of the son most clearly symbolizes John the Baptist. John's death is the crime for which the parable by implication condemns the Jewish leaders.

To be sure, Mark knew that the Jewish leaders were not the ones who killed John. As Mark himself writes earlier in the gospel (6:17–29), it was Herod who ordered John to be executed, in compliance to the request of his daughter, Herodias. Nonetheless, Mark here represents Jesus as condemning the Jewish leaders for murdering John, in much the same way that Matthew, for example, condemns the Jewish leaders for Jesus' crucifixion. Whether Mark believed that Jesus had himself in mind when he condemned the Jews for John's death is unascertainable; however, it would seem irrefutable that the evangelist wished *the reader* to draw a parallel between the fates of the two men. Indeed, to underscore the parallel between John and Jesus, the evangelist tells the reader, immediately following Jesus' narration of the parable, that the Jewish leaders understand the parable's point and that they wish to arrest Jesus—to do to Jesus, in other words, precisely what they have already done to John, or what the evangelist wishes the reader to believe they did. The Jews' fear of the multitude, however, prevents them from carrying out their wish.

FURTHER REFLECTIONS ON JOHN
AS THE PARABLE'S SUBJECT

Malcolm Lowe has recently offered an interpretation of the Wicked Husbandmen that similarly suggests that the son represents John as he was mistreated by the Jewish leaders.[58] Lowe also proposes that the parable of the Wicked Husbandmen, along with the parable of the Two Sons (Mt 21:28–32) and the Parable of the Great Banquet (Mt 22:1–14; Lk 14:15–24), once constituted a "Baptist-sequence." The sequence began with Jesus cleansing the Temple (Mt 12:13; Mk 11:15–17; Lk 19:45–46) and teaching there, and continued by recounting the story of how the Jewish leaders challenged Jesus by asking him for the source of his authority; in response, Jesus asked them his question about John and then told the three parables blaming the Jewish leaders for their treatment of John; the sequence concluded, according to Lowe, with the citation of Psalm 118:22–23, "The very stone (*even*) which the builders (*habonim*) rejected has become the head of the corner; this was the Lord's doings, and it is marvelous in our eyes." In Jesus' presentation, the verse anticipates the eventual punishment of the Jewish leaders, with the stone symbolizing John.

The major thrust of Lowe's argument is to prove the priority of Matthew's version of the sequence, an issue which goes beyond our present concerns. That question aside, Lowe's article demonstrates the connection between the parable and its narrative context in the synoptic versions; at the same time, Lowe also makes a persuasive case for the integrity of Psalm 118:22–23 and its interpretation as part of the passage. For Lowe, the verse and its exegesis compose a kind of peroration to the passage as a whole.

Viewed from the (admittedly later) perspective of the Rabbinic *mashal,* however, the verse might even be part of the parable of the Wicked Husbandmen. In the light of Rabbinic practice, the possibility that Jesus would have used Scripture in the *nimshal,* or that he would have seized upon a verse as the specific occasion or peg for his parable, cannot be ruled out. The interpretation Jesus gives for Psalm 118:22–23 fits perfectly with the reading of the parable as a blame-*mashal* attacking the Jewish leaders for their treatment of John the Baptist. According to this interpretation, the key words in the verse are *rosh pinah*. This phrase, which is usually translated as "the head of the corner" or as a cornerstone, may have been understood by Jesus as it is translated in the LXX, as *kephalē gonias,* that is, the capstone or keystone in an arch.[59] In other words: the stone which the builders initially rejected because it seemed misshapen proved in the end to be the perfect shape for the capstone (which must be irregularly shaped in order to fit its strategic position at the very apex of the archway).

This interpretation resembles other teachings of Jesus that stress the unpredictability of the advent of the kingdom of heaven, like "many that are first will be last, and the last first" (Mt 19:30; 20:16; Mk 10:31; Lk 13:30), to give only one example. The hermeneutical principle used in this exegesis—that operates by applying a verse's description of an essentially ahistorical process (here, reversal) to the career and fate of a historical or Biblical personage—also accords with what we know about the history of the interpretation of the verse in early Jewish exegesis; in contrast, the messianic-christological application becomes common only in early Christian exegesis.[60] In the present exegesis, however, there may also be an additional, more pointed reference to Jesus' Jewish opponents in the word *habonim* in Psalm 118:22, literally "builders" (from the root *bnh*), which Jesus may be interpreting as though it de- rived from the root *bun,* "to understand, or think" and therefore as a reference to "the thinkers" or "the wise," that is, the Jewish scribes and scholars whom Jesus is condemning.[61]

The interpretation of Psalm 118:22 may therefore constitute a pointed indictment of the Jewish leaders, and reflect the same rhetorical message of blame that is directed against the Jews in the *mashal*'s narra- tive. And, as in the narrative, the rhetoric of the exegesis anticipates the eventual vindication of John by God. When Jesus, at the very conclusion of the narrative, asks his inquisitors what the vineyard's owner will do after he returns, and when he answers, "He will come and destroy the tenants and give the vineyard to others," that answer is not a prophecy but an additional confirmation of the wicked tenants' guilt.

The *nimshal*'s exegesis, however, does not stop here; it continues with the next verse: "This was the Lord's doing, and it is marvelous in our eyes." Which is, in effect, interpreted thus: This is the Lord's doing

even though it is marvelous in our eyes—marvelous being taken in the
sense of being beyond human comprehension. This interpretation comes
almost as if it were a response to the following question: If God indeed
planned to vindicate John's authority, why did He send him to be perse-
cuted and eventually killed? The answer is given by the verse's double
assertion: Even though it may baffle our understanding, and while it
certainly exceeded the understanding of the Jewish leaders whom the
parable condemns, John's rejection and his eventual vindication are
both the work of God. The marvel here is precisely the same perplexity
that has been expressed by scholars who have pointed out how illogically
the vineyard owner behaves when he sends his son to the husbandmen
after they have already mistreated all his servants.[62] The man's behavior
may be illogical—or paradoxical in the radical sense of being inconsistent with common belief or experience. But paradox need not make
God's deeds impossible.[63]

According to this interpretation, the parable's message of blame
can therefore be read on a number of levels, as a "double-narrative" (at
the least), whose "real point," as Donald Juel has written elsewhere,
". . . can be found only at a deeper level, at a level of understanding
accessible only to the reader and not to the characters in the story."[64]
Because the implied reader of the parable is expected to understand its
message more deeply than do the characters of the narrative, these
different levels of meaning can be characterized by their irony, which
progressively increases in tenor from level to level. Thus, on the least
ironic level, the parable's blame is directed at the Jewish leaders for their
treatment of John the Baptist. On a slightly more ironic plane, the blame
is attached to the Jews for their past treatment of John and their present
abuse of Jesus. And finally, on the most ironic level of all, blame is
attached to the Jews in the parable for, in addition to everything else,
their future murder of Jesus as Christ and messiah.

Whether or not Jesus himself identified John's death with his own
predicament we will never know for certain. But Mark (and his fellow
evangelists), as I have suggested, clearly intended *their* audiences, the
readers of the gospels, to see the fates of the two men as parallel. In
Matthew, the parallel is made nearly explicit. In Mark, it remains at the
level of irony. In either case, though, while the Jewish leaders understand the parable as condemning them for one crime, the reader is
meant to see that they are being condemned for at least two—the execution of John *and* the far more horrible crime they are about to commit
against the Son of God.[65]

THE LESSON OF THE WICKED HUSBANDMEN

What can the Wicked Husbandmen teach us about the parables of Jesus in general? The first thing to say is that the parable of the Wicked Husbandmen is unlike all other gospel parables in that it explicitly cites and interprets a prooftext from Scripture. The only other parable even to allude to Scripture is the parable of the Sower (Mk 4:3–20; Mt 13:4–23; Lk 8:5–15), and in that parable Isaiah 6:9–10 is cited in the theory of parabolic speech which accompanies the parable rather than in the parable's narrative or its *nimshal*. Interestingly, though, these two parables—the Wicked Husbandmen and the Sower—are the only two narrative parables found in Mark. No verses are cited in the three narrative parables which are preserved in both Matthew and Luke, or in the five parables found in Matthew alone, or in the two preserved solely in Luke.

It therefore is not clear if the Scriptural citations in the two Markan parables reflect a specific convention of the parabolic tradition that Mark inherited (and which Matthew and Luke did not alter though they did not extend it to the other parables they used). It also remains uncertain if that convention is connected to the later Rabbinic use of Scriptural interpretation as a typical occasion for the composition of *meshalim*. Although exegetical activity akin to midrash is certainly evident in the gospels, particularly in Matthew, it is unwarranted to suppose that Jesus was an exegete of the same sort as the later Rabbis. The evangelists themselves never represent his parables as being essentially exegetical, not even in the Wicked Husbandmen or in the Sower. For our present concerns, however, it is not the exegetical dimension *per se* that distinguishes the *mashal* but its use of narrative as a rhetorical instrument of praise and blame.

THE OTHER NEW TESTAMENT PARABLES

We cannot in this essay analyze all eleven parables attributed to Jesus in the three synoptic gospels in the same detail with which we have discussed the parable of the Wicked Husbandmen; but it is worth our while to offer a brief characterization for each parable and its relationship to its literary context.

(1) *The Sower* (Mk 4:3–20; Mt 13:3–23; Lk 8:5–15). The parable itself offers comparative praise/blame of the various types of audiences or bearers who receive and cultivate the message Jesus preaches and

respond to it in different ways. In all three gospels, the parable is presented within the same narrative that describes Jesus preaching to the crowd along with his disciples. In the narrative, after he recites the parable, Jesus is asked why he teaches in parables, and he responds in the famous so-called theory of parabolic speech in the course of which an intepretation is offered for Isaiah 6:9–10. Following the theory, Jesus offers an explicit *nimshal* for the parable. The relationship between the *nimshal,* the parable, and the theory of parables is disputed by scholars.

(2) *Children in the Marketplace* (Mt 11:7–19; Lk 7:24–35). A blame-*mashal* condemning "the masses" for listening neither to the warnings of John the Baptist nor to the teachings of Jesus, the parable is presented within a narrative context that specifies its audience, and has an explicit *nimshal* in the text delivered by Jesus himself.

(3) *The Marriage-Feast or Banquet* (Mt 22:1–14; Lk 14:15–24). The context for the parable is different in the two gospels. In Matthew, this parable is presented immediately after the Wicked Husbandmen; in Luke, Jesus delivers it at a banquet given by a Pharisee. In both cases, though, the message of the parable is clearly blame/condemnation of those guests invited to the feast who refuse to come (=Jewish leaders to whom Jesus preaches), along with the announcement (=praise) of the others whom the host will invite to take their place. In Matthew, the parable has a second part, about a guest who appears at the feast in inappropriate dress; again, this narrative's message is quite clearly blame, but the referent is less clear. There is no explicit *nimshal* for the parable; its information must be adduced from the narrative context.

(4) *The Talents or Pounds* (Mt 25:14–27; Lk 19:12–27). In Matthew, this parable is part of the eschatological discourse, and appears among a series, immediately after the extended simile about the conscientious steward, and right before the parable of the Ten Bridesmaids. The parable communicates comparative praise and blame, with its emphasis falling decidedly upon the latter, condemning the man who fails to take the necessary risks in preparing for the coming redemption. A brief *nimshal* is presented in the form of an epimythium.

In Luke, the parable, which differs in some details from Matthew's version, is delivered in a narrative context, after Jesus is condemned for staying at the house of Zacchaeus the tax collector in Jericho and because the people suppose "that the kingdom of God was to appear immediately."

(5) *The Weeds Sown by the Enemy* (Mt 13:24–30). This parable which is prefaced by the formulaic "the kingdom of heaven is like . . ."

follows immediately upon the Sower, and is accompanied by an explicit *nimshal* (vv. 36–43). The message of the parable is a defense of God's justice in deferring the punishment of the wicked and the reward of the righteous until the end of time. Such justification of God's behavior is a common secondary application of the rhetorical function of praise in many Rabbinic *meshalim* as well; in this parable, the justification also justifies those who wait for the end.

(6) *The Wicked Servant and His Debtor* (Mt 18:23). Also prefaced by the kingdom of heaven formula, this parable is a blame-*mashal* directed against those who do not practice proper charity and forgivance; the punishment such persons will receive at the end of time is used to confirm the message of condemnation. Although the parable has a *nimshal* in the form of an epimythium, it is told in response to Peter's question as to how often he is required to forgive his brother who has sinned against him.

(7) *The Laborers in the Vineyard* (Mt 20:1–16). This parable is an example of apologetic praise in the form of a justification for the behavior of the vineyard owner who pays the last workmen he hires in the day as much as he pays those who have worked for him all day. The parable, however, is accompanied by an epimythium, "the last will be first, and the first, last," which is also Jesus' response to Peter's question as to whether those who have sacrificed much to follow Jesus will enjoy a more privileged position than those who have not. Within this context, then, the apolegetic praise of the owner's paradoxical behavior also contains a grain of blame directed at the workmen who complain about the owner's behavior (=those who have sacrificed much and who might therefore believe they should have a greater reward on that count).

(8) *The Two Sons* (Mt 21:28–32). This parable is recited immediately before the Wicked Husbandmen as part of the same confrontation between Jesus and the Jewish leaders who challenge his authority. The parable presents comparative blame (of the Jewish leaders) and praise (of the tax collectors and harlots who heeded the teachings of John). The parable's *nimshal* is presented in a rhetorical exchange between Jesus and his opponents.

(9) *The Wise and Foolish Maidens* (Mt 25:1–18). Prefaced by the "kingdom of heaven" formula, this parable is presented within the eschatological discourse, immediately before the parable of the Talents, and contains comparative praise (of those who prepare for the arrival of the kingdom) and blame (of those who do not). The parable has a brief epimythium, but its *nimshal* might also be contained in the extended

trope preceding the parable (24:45–51) that compares the wise servant with the wicked one.

(10) *The Rich Man and His Storehouse* (Lk 12:13–21). This parable has an explicit *nimshal* and is also told in response to a request a man makes to Jesus to ask his brother to divide his inheritance with him. The parable condemns the man who wishes to store up material possessions as being covetous, and thus implicitly blames the man for making his request for help to Jesus.

(11) *The Fig Tree Owner and His Steward* (Lk 13:6–9). The parable has no *nimshal* but it is told in the context of a sermon urging repentance. The parable is primarily praise, and appears to urge its audience to repent even after long delay; this positive message is then used secondarily to justify God's waiting for man to repent and his deferring the punishment of the wicked in the hope that they will eventually repent from their wicked ways.

SOME CONCLUSIONS

From this brief survey, we can see that virtually all eleven narrative parables can be categorized in terms of their rhetorical functions, as either praise, blame, or a subcategory of praise or blame. The functions of praise and blame in these parables are essentially directed at four basic topics or themes: Jesus' audience and their reception of his teachings and/or those of John the Baptist (nos. 1, 2, 3, 8); the correct preparation for the kingdom of heaven (nos. 4 and 9); justification of God's behavior in rewarding and punishing those who have hearkened to Jesus' teachings and those who have refused to listen (nos. 5 and 7); the proper religious behavior to be practiced (nos. 6, 10, 11). As we have also seen, and as might be expected, the rhetorical functions of several parables overlap categories: in no. 7, for example, apologetic praise or justification is combined with blame of the beliefs of some members of Jesus' audience.

While this survey shows how the parables can be understood within the literary contexts in the gospels, it does not prove that either the parables or their narrative contexts are in their "original" form. Nor does it indicate that the meaning that the context gives the parable was its "original" message. While it would be tempting to suggest that the ladder of increasingly ironic readings I have constructed for the parable of the Wicked Husbandmen might correspond to strata in the history of the parable's gradual contextualization and accompanying reinterpretation—with the least ironic meaning being the earliest, the more ironic a later supplementation—such a suggestion is mistaken for the reason that all three readings, regardless of their irony, are equally embedded in the narrative's literary and rhetorical exchanges. It has been toward those exchanges and strategies enacted in the gospel texts as we have received them that my approach to the parables in this paper has been directed. As to what Jesus originally spoke or meant, it seems to me difficult to move beyond reasonable guesses based on probability and historical plausibility. Where at least two gospels preserve the same literary context or very similar ones for a single parable, it would appear more likely that context might be related to the one in which the parable originated. But there is obviously no proof for this, only the force of tradition combined with probability.

The same hesitations about original texts and meanings apply to the *mashal* within its various literary contexts in Rabbinic literature. We know even less about the provenance of Rabbinic traditions than we do about the New Testament parables. Many *meshalim* were most likely composed by the anonymous editors and redactors of midrashic collections. Despite their oral-like features, these *meshalim* were literary compositions, written by men who were completely familiar with the conventions of the oral tradition. In these cases, the *meshalim* are literally original to their "secondary" contexts in the midrashic collections.

What our study of the New Testament parables in the light of the Rabbinic *meshalim* has shown is that the parables can be read intelligibly and fruitfully within their literary contexts, and that if read this way, the results are consistent with what we know about the form and function of the *mashal* from Rabbinic literature. This does not mean that, in the end, there is no difference between the New Testament parables and the Rabbinic *meshalim,* just that the real differences between them may not lie in characteristics intrinsic to the compositions but in external factors, specifically in the radically diverging ways in which the parables and meshalim were later preserved and understood in subsequent Christian and Jewish traditions. The differences between the two bodies of texts may therefore reside, we might say, within their *nimshalim* rather than in the *meshalim* themselves, that is, in their subsequent literary and theological contextualizations; and in the values, transcendent or mundane, that their respective religious traditions historically attributed to them.

NOTES

1. The most recent bibliography on scholarship about the parables of Jesus and the Rabbinic *mashal* is to be found in Bradford H. Young, "The Parable as a Literary Genre in Rabbinic Literature and in the Gospels," Ph.D. dissertation, The Hebrew University, Israel: 1986. The most complete bibliography is in Robert Johnston, "Parabolic Interpretations Attributed to Tannaim," Ph.D. dissertation, Ann Arbor, Mich.: 1978, pp. 1–123. See also W.S. Kissinger, *The Parables of Jesus: A History of Interpretation and Bibliography* (Metuchen, N.J.: Scarecrow Press and the American Theological Library Association, 1979); James C. Little, "Parable Research in the Twentieth Century," *Expository Times*, Vols. 87–88 (1976), pp. 356–60, 40–44; 71–75.

2. Adolph Jülicher, *Die Gleichnisreden Jesu* (Freiburg:I.B. Mohr, 1886 (1888, 1899, 1910); repr. Darmstadt: Wissenschaftliche Buchgesellschaft, 1963 (1969, 1976), Vol. 1, pp. 169–172.

3. For one example, see G.V. Jones, *The Art and Truth of the Parables* (London: SPCK, 1964), p. 240:

> There is a qualitative difference between all the Synoptic parables and the versions reproduced by Thomas which emphasizes the superiority of the Synoptic parables over all others and, on another level, illustrates the contrast which Julicher perceived between Jesus' teaching methods and those of his contemporaries—if this term can be extended to cover other practitioners of the rabbinic tradition of much later date. It is the difference between superior and inferior artistry.

Cf. also W.O.E. Oesterley, *The Gospel Parables in the Light of their Jewish Background* (London: SPCK, 1936), pp. 10–11; Maxime Hermaniuk, *La parabole évangelique* (Vol. 38, series II of Universitas Catholica Lovaniensis, Louvain: Bibliotheca Alfonsiana, 1947, p. 194); and Joachim Jeremias, *The Parables of Jesus* (trans. by S.H. Hooke from 6th German ed., 1962; Rev. ed., New York: Scribner's, 1963), p. 12. See also Little's quotes from Jeremias, p. 40.

4. See, for example, I. Abrahams, "The Parables," *Studies in Pharisaism and the Gospels* (1917; New York: Ktav, 1967), pp. 90–107; and A. Feldman, *The Parables and Similes of the Rabbis* (Cambridge: University Press, 1927).

5. In addition to the dissertations of Young and Johnston (note 1), see Jacob Petuchowski, "The Theological Significance of the Parable in Rabbinic Literature and the New Testament," *Christian News from Israel*, Vol. 23–4 (1972–74), pp. 76–86; David Flusser, "Jesus' Parables and the Rabbinic Meshalim" (Hebrew) in *Yahadut Umekorot Hanatsrut* (Tel Aviv: Sifriyat Po'alim, 1979, pp. 150–209; idem, *Die rabbinischen Gleichnisse und der Gleichniserzähler Jesus*, 1. Teil: Das Wesen der Gleichnisse (Bern: Peter Lang, 1981); Clemens Thoma and Simon Lauer, *Die Gleichnisse der Rabbinen*, 1. Teil, Pesiqta deRav Kahana (PesK) (Bern: Peter Lang, 1986).

6. David Stern, "Rhetoric and Midrash: The Case of the Mashal," *Prooftexts,* Vol. 1 (1981), pp. 261–291; "The Function of the Parable in Rabbinic Literature" (Hebrew) in *Jerusclem Studies in Hebrew Literature,* Vol. 7 (1985), trans. into English as "The Rabbinic Parable: From Rhetoric to Poetics," *SBL 1986 Seminar Papers,* Atlanta: 1986, pp. 631–643; and my forthcoming book, *Parables in Midrash* (Cambridge, Mass.: Harvard University Press, 1989).

7. On the dangers of hasty comparative approaches, see Morton Smith, "A Comparison of Early Christian and Early Rabbinic Tradition," *Journal of Biblical Literature,* Vol. 82 (1963), pp. 169–176.

8. Jülicher, pp. 117, 146; translated in Little, p. 357.

9. Jülicher, p. 317; translated in Kissinger, p. 76. See also pp. 52–69 for Jülicher's simile-allegory discussion. The focus of Jülicher's distinction between allegory and parable was that where an allegory has many points of comparison between its *Bildhälfte* (i.e. the vehicle) and *Sachhälfte* (the tenor), a true parable has only a single point of contact between the two sides, that is, the so-called *tertium comparationis.*

10. Cf. Jülicher, p. 24. For the best recent discussion of the treatment of the Markan passage in modern scholarship, see Frank Kermode, *The Genesis of Secrecy* (Cambridge, Mass.: Harvard University Press, 1979), pp. 23–47, 149–152.

11. Jeremias, p. 115.

12. Jeremias, p. 11.

13. See John W. Sider, "Rediscovering the Parables: The Logic of the Jeremias Tradition," *Journal of Biblical Literature,* Vol. 102 (1983), pp. 68ff.

14. Norman Perrin, *Jesus and the Language of the Kingdom* (Philadelphia: Fortress, 1976), p. 106.

15. The best clarification of what is at stake in describing the parables as allegory is in Madeleine Boucher's *The Mysterious Parable* (Washington, D.C.: CBQMS, no. 6, 1977). In addition, see Raymond E. Brown, "Parable and Allegory Reconsidered," *Novum Testamentum,* Vol. 5 (1962), pp. 36–45. M.D. Goulder, "Characteristics of the Parables in the Several Gospels," *Journal of Theological Studies,* N.S. Vol. 19 (1968), pp. 51–69; John Drury, "The Sower, the Vineyard, and the Place of Allegory in the Interpretation of Mark's Parables," *JTS,* Vol. 24 (1973), pp. 367–79; C.F.D. Moule, "Mark 4:1–20 Yet Once More," *Neotestamentica et Semitica: Studies in Honor of Matthew Black,* eds. E.E. Ellis and M. Wilcox (Edinburgh: T. and T. Clark, 1969), pp. 95–113; John Bowker, "Mystery and Parable: Mark 4:1–20," *JTS,* Vol. 25, 1974, pp. 300–17; J.D.M. Derrett, "Allegory and the Wicked Vinedressers," *JTS,* Vol. 25, 1974. Cp. as well John Dominic Crossan's recantation of his earlier views concerning the non-allegorical character of parable, in "Parable, Allegory, and Paradox," in *Semiology and Parables,* ed. Daniel Patte (Pittsburgh: The Pickwick Press, 1976), pp. 247–81.

16. Paul Fiebig, *Altjüdische Gleichnisse und die Gleichnisse Jesu* (Tübingen: J.C.B. Mohr, 1904), pp. 25–73, 93–155. The most complete and sympathetic

review of the many recent attempts to provide a positive non-allegorical definition of the parable from Jeremias and on is to be found in Perrin, *Jesus and the Language of the Kingdom,* pp. 89–205. For several practical demonstrations of these views, see the various contributions in *Semiology and Parables.*

17. C.H. Dodd, *The Parables of the Kingdom* (London: Nisbet, 1935; rev. New York: Scribner's, 1961), p. 5.

18. Dodd, p. 159.

19. Dodd, p. 10.

20. Sallie TeSelle, *Speaking in Parables* (Philadelphia: Fortress, 1975), pp. 78–79. Cf. also Robert W. Funk, *Language, Hermeneutic, and the Word of God* (New York: Harper & Row, 1966); Ernst Fuchs, *Hermeneutik* (Bad Canstatt, 1958); and Eta Linnemann, *Jesus of the Parables,* trans. J. Sturdy (New York: Harper & Row, 1967).

21. See Mary Ann Tolbert, *Perspectives on the Parables* (Philadelphia: Fortress, 1979).

22. See in particular Paul Ricoeur, "Biblical Hermeneutics," in *Semeia* Vol. 4 (1975), p. 75. In the same volume there is a lengthy bibliography of Ricoeur's other writings on metaphor. Cf. David Tracy, "Metaphor and Religion: The Test Case of Christian Texts," *Critical Inquiry,* Vol. 5 (1978), pp. 91–106.

23. Ricoeur, pp. 33–34.

24. Ricoeur, p. 89.

25. Paul Ricoeur, *The Conflict of Interpretation, Essays in Hermeneutics* (Evanston: Northwestern University Press, 1974), pp. 48–49.

26. Paul Ricoeur, "The Bible and the Imagination," in *The Bible as a Document of the University,* ed. H.D. Betz (Chico: Scholars Press, 1981), p. 53.

27. By the term "narrative parable," I mean to distinguish the type of compositions I will discuss in this essay from extended similes or illustrations, on the one hand, and from exempla or anecdotes, on the other. Similes and illustrations, like the Mustard Seed (Mk 4:30–32 and parallels) or the Tree and Its Fruit (Mt 7:16–20), tend to take the form of extended figures, rhetorical questions, and so on, rather than of past-tense narratives, and they describe a way of acting rather than a course of action. In contrast, anecdotes, exempla, or pronouncement stories, like the Prodigal Son (Lk 15:11–32), the Good Samaritan (Lk 10:29–37), or the Dishonest Steward (Lk 16.1–10), usually depend upon a rhetorical claim to historicity—that they happened once upon a time—unlike the *mashal* which acknowledges its fictionality. The distinction between the narrative parable and the two other types has often been made in parable-scholarship although the recent literary approaches tend to blur the differences. As many scholars have noted, the Hebrew term *mashal,* translated in the New Testament as *parabolē,* is used to describe a wide range of literary forms—from parables to allegories, proverbs, and simply famous sayings—and therefore is of no use as a generic marker. For a good survey of the terminology—*mashal* and *parabolē*— see Boucher, pp. 86–89.

28. The major differences between Mark's version of the parable and the versions in Matthew, Luke, and in the Gospel of Thomas are as follows: (1) While Mark and Matthew's opening descriptions of the vineyard virtually quote Isaiah 5:1ff, Luke only alludes to the prophet's passage. (2) Mark and Luke describe the son as *agapētos,* "beloved" or "sole" (see discussion in paper); Matthew and Thomas do not. (3) Matthew has a plural number of servants; Mark and Luke have only a single servant. (4) Mark has the owner initially send three individual messengers, then "many others," who are in turn beaten, wounded, treated shamefully, and killed, and finally, the son, who is killed; Matthew has two groups of servants who are beaten and then the son who is killed; Luke has three individual servants who are beaten, then the son who is killed; Thomas has two servants, who are beaten, and then the son who is killed.

29. Luke cites Psalm 118:22 alone, and then quotes the stone logion as in Matthew.

30. Irenaeus, *Against Heresies,* 36:2, in *The Ante-Nicene Fathers,* eds. A. Roberts and J. Donaldson (Grand Rapids: Eerdmans, 1956), Vol. 1, p. 515. For other medieval interpretations, see Kissinger, passim.

31. Jülicher, pp. 405ff.

32. Jeremias, p. 70.

33. Jeremias, p. 72. Note, however, that in the critical text, Thomas has only two messengers and then the son: *The Nag Hammadi Library,* ed. James M. Robinson (New York: Harper & Row, 1977), pp. 125–26 (Logion 65).

34. Jeremias, p. 73. For a recent reformulation of the undoubted certainty of the identification of the son in the parable with the divine sonship of Jesus, though in specific reference to the narrative in Matthew, see Jack Dean Kingsbury, "The Parable of the Wicked Husbandmen and the Secret of Jesus' Divine Sonship in Matthew: Some Literary-Critical Observations," *JBL* Vol. 105 (1986), pp. 643–55.

35. Jeremias, p. 71.

36. Kermode, p. 44.

37. Ricoeur, "The Bible and the Imagination," p. 56.

38. A.J. Greimas, *Du Sens* (Paris: 1970), p. 188. For helpful exposition, see Susan Rubin Suleiman, *Authoritarian Fictions* (New York: 1983), 150ff. For other applications of Greimas to the New Testament Parables, see Daniel Patte, *What Is Structural Exegesis?* (Philadelphia: 1976).

39. Ricoeur, p. 59.

40. Ricoeur, p. 59.

41. Ricoeur, p. 65.

42. Ricoeur, p. 66.

43. Ricoeur, p. 68.

44. Ricoeur, p. 66.

45. J. Hillis Miller, "Parable and Performative in the Gospels and in Modern

Literature," in *Humanizing America's Iconic Book,* eds. G.M. Tucker and D.A. Knight (Chico: Scholars Press, 1982), p. 59.

46. The classic critical discussion of the Romantic view of the symbol remains Paul de Man's "The Rhetoric of Temporality," in *Interpretation: Theory and Practice,* ed. C.S. Singleton (Baltimore: Johns Hopkins University Press, 1969), pp. 173–209. For an exhaustive critique of Ricoeur from a hermeneutical perspective, see Hans Frei's penetrating analysis, "The 'Literal Reading' of Biblical Narrative in the Christian Tradition: Does It Stretch or Will It Break?" in *The Bible and the Narrative Tradition,* ed. Frank McConnell (Oxford: University Press, 1986), pp. 36–77.

47. Miller, p. 59.

48. Miller, p. 67. Although readers familiar with Hillis Miller's important and original literary criticism may be somewhat astonished at the distinction he posits in this essay between sacred and secular, note should be taken of the contradictory (or, in his words, paradoxical) features that he assigns to sacred parables as well as to secular ones; see in particular pp. 62–65 and 69–71.

49. Walter Benjamin, "Some Reflections on Kafka," in *Illuminations,* trans. H. Zohn (New York: Shocken, 1968), pp. 143–44. See also Jill Robbins, "Kafka's Parables," in *Midrash and Literature,* ed. G. Hartman and S. Budick (New Haven: Yale University Press, 1986), pp. 265–84.

50. See W.J. Verdenius, "AINOS," *Mnemosyne,* Vol. 15 (1962), p. 389; G. Nagy, *The Best of the Achaeans* (Baltimore: Johns Hopkins University Press, 1979), pp. 234–41, 281–86.

51. See the exchange between Daniel Boyarin and myself on the *nimshal* in *Prooftexts,* Vol. 5 (1985), pp. 269–80.

52. See W. Bacher, *Aggadot Amorei Eretz-Yisrael* (Tel Aviv: Dvir, 1926), Vol. I, pt. 2, p. 130n. 4. R. Hiyya b. Ada was the disciple of Shimeon b. Lakish.

53. See, in particular, Romans 4, 10; Galatians 3–4; John G. Gager, *The Origins of Anti-Semitism* (Oxford: University Press, 1985), pp. 217–23, 235–41, 250–52; E.E. Urbach, *The Sages* (trans. from the Hebrew by I. Abrahams, Jerusalem: Magnes, 1975), pp. 529–31; H.W. Basser, *Midrashic Interpretations of the Song of Moses* (Series 7, Vol. 2, American University Studies, New York: Peter Lang, 1984), pp. 132–37.

54. For further discussion of the *mashal*'s narrative poetics, see my discussion in Chapter II of my book, *Parables in Midrash.*

55. A great number of *meshalim* combine in different ways the motifs of a king (or father) who plants a field (vineyard, orchard, etc.) and gives it to his son: for a few examples, see Devarim Rabbah 5:7; Tanhuma (ed. S. Buber), Leviticus, p. 78; Midrash Psalms (ed. S. Buber), p. 51: Yalkut Shimeoni, I. 225. For the motif of the owner/king leasing the field to tenants, see Bereishit Rabbah 61:6; Shemot Rabbah 43:9; and Abot deRabbi Natan A (ed. S. Schechter), p. 64. For examples of the king who goes off to a foreign province, see Eikhah Rabbah 3:21 and Pesikta Rabbati (ed. M. Ish-Shalom), p. 104b. For the king

requesting his subjects to send him produce, see the rough counterpart in Vayikra Rabbah 11:7; for equivalent motifs describing the rebellion of the king's subjects (with no exact counterparts to our parable, however), see Bereishit Rabbah 5:1 (=28:2) and Shemot Rabbah 45:3. For an example of the king punishing the rebellious subjects, see *Mekhilta,* Shirta 10, *ad* Ex. 15:8.

56. See Young, pp. 332–33 and notes.

57. On the Jewish leaders, see Flusser, *Yahadut* . . . , pp. 426–27, where he identifies them with the Temple leadership.

58. Malcolm Lowe, "From the Parable of the Vineyard to a Pre-Synoptic Source," *New Testament Studies,* Vol. 28 (1982), pp. 257–63. Cf. as well J.A. Fitzmeyer, *The Gospel According to Luke (X–XXIV)* (Anchor Bible, Garden City: Doubleday, 1985), p. 1278.

59. See Fitzmeyer, p. 1282; and Grundy, p. 429.

60. In early Jewish interpretation, the verse is most commonly applied to David: see Midrash Psalms, p. 487, for this interpretation too, and Midrash Tannaim (ed. D. Hoffmann), p. 10; Babylonian Talmud Pesahim 118a; Midrash Hagadol on Deut. 1:17 (ed. S. Fisch), p. 32. A pseudo-Davidic psalm reflecting this exegesis has also been published by D. Flusser and S. Safrai in *Sefer Zikaron Livehoshua Grintz* (Tel Aviv: Kibbutz Hameuhad, 1982). For another interpretation, see Midrash Psalms (ed. S. Buber), p. 487 where the verse is applied to Jacob and interpreted along the same lines as those in the mashal in Sifre Deut. 312 discussed earlier. For discussion, see Young, pp. 342–46 and 366 note 40. For early Christian interpretations, see Acts 4:11 and I Peter 2:1–10, and for discussion, James L. Kugel and Rowen A. Greer, *Early Biblical Interpretation* (Philadelphia: Westminster Press, 1986), pp. 132–33.

61. For another example of an analogous pun on *bun-bnh,* see Babylonian Talmud Berakhot 64a for the famous midrash attributed to R. Eleazar in the name of Rabbi Ḥanina on Isaiah 54:17. It is worth noting that this midrash, which is recited in the daily liturgy as a kind of peroration to the hymn *Ein Keloheinu,* is mistranslated and misinterpreted in virtually every English prayer-book. See Ḥanoch Yallon, *Pirkei Lashon* (Jerusalem: Mosad Bialik, 1971), pp. 123–125. For a midrashic interpretation which plays on the pun between *even* (stone) and *boneiha* (her understanders), see B. Ta'anit 4a. Note as well that a punning connection between the *even,* "stone" in the Psalms verse and the word *ben,* "son," has often been cited to prove that the interpretation of the verse is christological; see R.H. Grundy, *Matthew* (Grand Rapids: Eerdmans, 1982), p. 429 and bibliography there; but the pun on son may refer as well to the son in the parable's narrative.

62. For a summary and criticism of this view, see V. Taylor, *The Gospel According to St. Mark* (London: 1966, repr. Grand Rapids: Baker Book House, 1981), p. 472.

63. This paradox may be connected as well to the connection that Mark, for example, makes between the arrest of John and the beginning of Jesus' ministry:

see Mark 1:14, particularly the awkward phrase *meta de to paradothenai,* literally "after the delivering up." Taylor (p. 165) notes that the use of the articular infinitive with no qualifying clause (e.g. "to prison") suggests the fulfillment of God's will, which Jesus understood as a sign to begin preaching.

64. Donald Juell, *Messiah and Temple* (Missoula: 1977), p. 55.

65. It may also be possible to read the parable as a kind of allegory of the character Jesus' confrontation with the Jewish leaders as it is described in the gospel narrative surrounding the parable. Their confrontation begins when the Jewish leaders challenge Jesus' authority, his right to preach and teach disciples. Earlier in the narrative when they first discovered Jesus in the Temple, the Jewish leaders asked Jesus for the source of his authority. To that challenge, Jesus responded by asking the Jewish leaders his own question: What do the Jews believe about John's baptism? Was it authorized from heaven or from men? Jesus tells the Jews that he will answer their question if they will answer his. Of course, he knows (or confidently—and correctly—assumes) that they won't. And as a result, he refuses to reply directly to their question; instead, he tells them parables.

This confrontation between Jesus and the Jewish leaders is over the question of authority: initially, Jesus' authority to teach as he does, and subsequently, John's authority as a prophet. But by using the parable, Jesus effectively extends this controversy to challenge the authority of the Jewish leaders themselves. In terms of the parable's symbolism, ownership of the vineyard might be viewed as the narrative equivalent to the possession of rightful authority. The wicked husbandmen, as it were, mistake possession of the vineyard for ownership, and the parable not only shows the illegitimacy of the wicked husbandmen's (=Jews') claim to authority; it also exposes their attempt to usurp the ownership, first by denying the authority of the rightful owner (by refusing to send back the fruits) and later by murdering his son. The husbandmen's boast that they have become the owners of the vineyard by killing the son has no legal basis (as some have claimed: cf. Jeremias, p. 75, and F.W. Beare, *The Earliest Records of Jesus* [New York: Macmillan, 1962], p. 208; but see Grundy, *Matthew,* p. 425 and his reference to M.I Rostovzeff). Rather, the boast shows only that in addition to being criminals, the husbandmen are stupid, indeed presumptuously stupid. The upshot of the parable's blame of the Jewish leaders intentionally adds insult to condemnation. For a comparable *mashal* that adds insult to injury, see Eikhah Rabbah 1:10.

A Fresh Analysis of the Parable of the Wicked Husbandmen in the Light of Jewish-Catholic Dialogue

Aaron A. Milavec

Every Christian is familiar with the parable of the wicked husbandmen. For hundreds of years this parable has been read in the churches, and the ordained pastors have routinely explained to their congregations that Jesus used this parable to expose the murderous extremes to which the Jews were capable in their resistance to God and in their pursuit of selfish interests. According to the terms of the parable, the Jews had finally gone too far. Murdering "the Son," Jesus Christ, was the last straw. God's patience was strained to the breaking point. As a result, God abandoned Israel—the Jews were to receive no more prophets—and God decided to give his inheritance to the Gentile Church. In such terms, the parable of the wicked husbandmen has carried a long legacy of anti-Judaism within the Christian tradition.

The purpose of this paper is to provide the results of a fresh investigation of the original intent of Mark's version of the wicked husbandmen. In part, this investigation concludes that while Mark did perceive some allegorical elements within the parable of the wicked husbandmen, he did not understand "the son" to represent Jesus nor the "others" to represent the Gentile Church. As such my study calls into question the nearly universal perceptions of both past and present Christian scholars relative to the allegorical content of Mark's parable and presents in its place a disturbing image of what Mark might have originally meant in the ears of his first century listeners.

Before proceeding to a line by line study of the text, I want to position my study by providing a brief historic overview of the interpretation of the wicked husbandmen during the Patristic Era and during the Post-Holocaust Era.

THE INTERPRETATION OF THE WICKED HUSBANDMEN DURING THE PATRISTIC ERA

Anti-Judaism was not always characteristic of Christianity. As long as the congregation of Jerusalem founded by the Twelve Apostles was the Mother Church, Christianity was too manifestly Jewish to have any tinges of anti-Judaism. When selected institutions or practices of Judaism were criticized (e.g. as when Stephen delivers a sharp critique of the Temple in Acts 7), this criticism was motivated by the intramural zeal of a prophetic reform movement to purify Judaism in the wake of the Messianic Age.[1] To have downgraded Judaism *as such* would have been tantamount to downgrading their own religious existence.

This initial situation did not remain. The Roman siege of Jerusalem had the effect of partly destroying and partly dispersing the Mother Church in 68–70 C.E. At the same time, the predominantly Gentile congregations of Rome, Antioch, and Alexandria were pioneering modes of pastorally adapting their Jewish roots to the Hellenized urban settings in which they found themselves. With the Mother Church silenced, these cosmopolitan centers of Christianity, which were searching for an identity within the Empire apart from "the rebellious Jews," took the measures necesary to positively distinguish themselves from the Jews.

The Constantinian era brought the gift of Roman toleration to the Christians in 313 C.E. Within two years, however, the self-chosen clerical advisors of the emperor had persuaded him that the Roman State ought to be less tolerant to the Jewish synagogues of the Diaspora which continued to rival the Christian churches in their appeal to potential Gentile converts. Thus, in 315 C.E., an Imperial Edict forbade Romans from converting to Judaism. In subsequent years, two other potential sources of religious conversions were also checked: Jews were forbidden to intermarry or to possess Gentile slaves.

Emboldened by their preferential status within the empire, the next generations of Christians openly sanctioned the practice of *exalting the things of the Church by downgrading the things of the Synagogue*. By the later decades of the fourth century, this practice had become so fashionable that Archbishop John Chrysostom, the brilliant preacher, saint, and patriarch of Antioch, routinely stigmatized the synagogues as "dens of thieves," "lairs of demons," "congregations of Christ-killers."[2]

When it came time to summarize the Christian complaint against the Jews, John Chrysostom could appeal to the wicked husbandmen as the unique parable from the mouth of Jesus Christ wherein he exposed the whole chain of events by which God abandoned Israel and transferred His blessings and inheritance to the Christian Church. Thus, Chrysostom's homily on the wicked husbandmen begins as follows:

> Many things does he [Jesus, the Lord] intimate by this parable: (a) that God's providence had been exercised towards them [the Jews] from the first; (b) that their disposition was murderous from the beginning; (c) that nothing had been omitted [by God] relative to a heedful care of them; (d) that even when the prophets had been slain, he [YHWH] had not turned away from them, but had sent his very Son; (e) that the God of both the New and of the Old Testament was one and the same; (f) that his death should effect great blessings; (g) that for the crucifixion, their crime, they were to endure extreme punishment: the calling of the Gentiles and the casting out of the Jews.[3]

Since religious texts have a conservative-unitative function (that of evoking and imposing modes of feeling and thinking upon a widely dispersed body of adherents[4]), it is only natural to suppose that John Chrysostom was not a complete innovator in his reading of the wicked husbandmen. His genius consisted in providing a masterful synthesis of the common beliefs which had been slowly growing up around the wicked husbandmen like barnacles on the hull of a ship below the waterline. Chrysostom's sermons and writings were thus prized as intimately combining both intellectual satisfaction and religious identity. Together, this unbeatable combination served to insure a pattern of exegesis surrounding the wicked husbandmen which became both the spontaneously given and the stubborn orthodoxy for future generations of Christians.

Religious prejudice, from the vantage point of the outsider, appears to be irrational since a judgment is made before the facts are in. From the vantage point of the insider, however, prejudice appears as the logically compelling assessment of the known character of things.[5] In the case of Chrysostom and his contemporaries, this intellectual persuasion was also wedded to religion as the *imitatio dei,* the striving to take on the dispositions and judgments of God. Thus, if God loves the poor and is anxious to relieve their distress, as selected texts from the Bible attest, then it is incumbent upon the one attached to God to act likewise.

Similarly, if God hates the Jews and is anxious to punish them for their infidelities, as selected texts from the Bible attest, then it also follows that the one who loves God is committed to the same course of action. From the vantage point of the committed believer, God's prejudice with respect to the poor and God's prejudice with respect to Jews were both intellectually evident and religiously demanding.

THE INTERPRETATION OF THE WICKED HUSBANDMEN DURING THE POST-HOLOCAUST ERA

After the existential shock occasioned by the Holocaust, Christian scholars considered themselves bound to use their modern scientific methods of biblical criticism to rid the New Testament texts of every form of subjectivism and ideological bias. Anti-Judaism was considered to be unsatisfactory on both counts. As a result, overt denigrations and inflammatory name-calling are no longer associated with either the scholarly or the pastoral treatment of the wicked husbandmen. What remains, however, is the nearly universal belief that the parable of the wicked husbandmen describes, in thinly veiled terms, the Jewish killing of Jesus: the fateful event which occasions the Lord's punishment of Israel and the transfer of His inheritance to the Christian Church. Hence, while overt anti-Judaism has been curtailed, the theological framework which engendered this devaluation of Judaism continues to operate under the untouchable rubric of being the objective content of what the wicked husbandmen originally meant for the inspired writers and their contemporaries.

If the tacit content of the parable of the wicked husbandmen is to associate the punishment of Israel with the death of Jesus, then, in and of itself, the parable is anti-Jewish. A minority of scholars, more especially Gregory Baum and Rosemary Ruether, have boldly faced this possibility and admitted that some segments of the New Testament present an unfair negative bias against the Jewish people and their religious heritage.[6] Even the 1985 Vatican "Notes on the Correct Way to Present Jews and Judaism" allows that "it cannot be ruled out that some references hostile or less than favorable to the Jews have their historical context in conflicts between the nascent church and the Jewish community."[7] If such texts are indeed present, it remains for the present discernment of God's ways to challenge and to correct past discernments. Consider, for example, that the Christian reader of the Bible repeatedly encounters texts which indicate a divine sanction upon certain forms of slavery yet, guided by stubborn patterns of discernment informed by the teaching church, never thinks that the Word of God inspires Christians to reestablish or sanction slavery in God's name. In parallel fashion, when Roman Catholics are deeply persuaded that "the Jews should not be presented as repudiated or cursed by God as if such views followed from the Holy Scriptures,"[8] then it would also follow that when a Catholic encounters texts presenting the Jews as so repudiated or cursed, he/she would simply pass over these texts as histori- cally conditioned remnants of a defective earlier understanding which is now no longer operative. Unhappily, the long-standing traditional reli- gious interpretation of texts has not yet been entirely emptied of its anti- Jewish content, and this process will occupy the best efforts of scholars and teachers for many generations to come.

Relative to the parable of the wicked husbandmen, the allegorical identification of "the son" with Jesus has been routinely accepted by almost every Christian scholar during the last forty years.[9] Joachim Jere- mias, the German scholar who has dominated all discussion on the para- bles of Jesus since the mid-50s, accepted the version of the wicked hus- bandmen in the Gospel of Thomas as a more primitive version of the same parable in the Synoptics, precisely because it betrays no intention to allegorize. Jeremias concluded that "neither the sending of the three servants nor that of the son had originally any allegorical significance" and that "the introduction of the figure of the only son is the result, not of theological reflection on the Messiah as Son of God, but of the logic of the story."[10] Nonetheless, when Jeremias treated the Synoptic versions of the wicked husbandmen, he did not display the slightest hesitation in affirm- ing that a program of progressive allegorization was in play which, at all points, served further to identify "the son" with Jesus of Nazareth.[11]

Jeremias' spell upon subsequent scholarship has been so compelling that it was not until the 70s before a few serious scholars ventured to challenge the traditional allegorical interpretation. One such scholar, John Dominic Crossan, found "serious difficulty" with Jeremias' thesis on the grounds that the church could hardly have proceeded to allego- rize the wicked husbandmen "without an allusion to Jesus' resurrec- tional victory built *intrinsically* into the story itself."[12] Crossan's article has been widely read and cited in bibliographies; yet, in point of fact, Jeremias' earlier thesis continued to dominate the scene. For example, Michel Hubaut, in his 1975 doctoral dissertation, included the Crossan article just mentioned in his selected bibliography; yet, in his text, he fails to offer even a single substantive difficulty relative to the son=Jesus identification.[13] Going even further, Hubaut created new arguments in order to reinforce what he perceived as weak links in Jeremias' original thesis. For example, Hubaut argued that the very incredibility of Mark's version of the wicked husbandmen as opposed to the inherent credibility of the shorter version found in the Gospel of Thomas requires that the reader assume the son=Jesus identification:

> On the level of a mundane story . . . this sending of the son by a father able to be persuaded that his son will be better treated is, if not impossible, then at least unbelievable. Only the allegory permits us to understand [and credit the story]: after the failure of the prophetic missions, God sends his Son, Jesus-Christ.[14]

In sum, the critical scholarship of the post-Holocaust era has continued to maintain the son=Jesus identification which formed the basis of Chrysostom's fifth century homily. I myself, consequently, began my own study of the issue with this frame of mind. How my mind was changed will become clear shortly.

While modern critical scholarship has maintained the son=Jesus identification, one does not find the same consensus relative to the allegorical interpretation of the consequences of the son's death. Leopold Sabourin, a Jesuit scholar writing in 1982, offers a fairly representative interpretation in the following terms:

> In the parable of the wicked tenants, then, Matthew expands the ecclesial aspect and reduces the christological, by accentuating the guilt of unbelieving Israel. He maintains the continuity of the economy of salvation in his concept of a reign (or kingdom) of God embracing the old and new covenants. To produce or not to produce fruits is a question of life and death for the people of God. The tenants' hostile attitude manifests the state of mind of the whole people. The definitive punishment is at hand: the transfer of the kingdom to another people, able to produce the fruits. J. Jeremias, who understands the parable as an allegory, identifies "the other nation" with the Gentile church.[15]

Sabourin is well aware that elsewhere in Matthew's Gospel Jesus is presented as upholding the "permanent value" of the Mosaic Torah and that "Judaism has not been rejected by God but is called, together with the Gentiles, to share in God's saving love."[16] Nonetheless, like so many others before him, when he analyzed the wicked husbandmen he quickly forgot all this and fell back into old patterns: (a) "the tenants' hostile attitude manifests the state of mind of the whole people" and (b) the "definitive punishment" for "unbelieving Israel" is identified as "the transfer of the kingdom to another people = Gentile church."

In contrast, it is sobering to find Joseph A. Fitzmyer, also a well-recognized Catholic scholar, making a bold departure from Sabourin's identifications the basis of his investigations in Luke. Fitzmyer concludes that the tenants cannot be safely identified with the Jewish people generally since the Jewish crowds are habitually presented as warmly receiving Jesus. The tenants are to be identified exclusively with "the scribes and the chief priests" (Lk 20:1, 19 & par.) who are repeatedly presented as rejecting Jesus (Lk 4:16–30; 7:31–35; 11:29–32, 49–54; 13:34f; Acts 4:1–3; 7:51–58). The punishment foreseen by the parable is that these uncooperative Jerusalem leaders will be replaced by "Palestinian Jews who accepted him and Gentiles, who will together form the reconstituted Israel."[17] Fitzmyer, claiming to be following Luke's own line of thought, is one of the few scholars who correctly perceives Lukan Christianity as essentially a Jewish enterprise:

> Luke does not describe a Jewish people that, as a whole, has rejected Jesus and his message, but among whom there are some exceptions. "Israel" continues to refer to the Jewish people. . . . It does not refer to a church made up of Jews and Gentiles, but to Jews who have accepted the Christian message and to whom the promises of old have been fulfilled, with whom Gentiles have been associated for a share in those realized promises. It is *not* a *new* Israel, but a reconstituted Israel.[18]

From such a vantage point, the wicked husbandmen quite clearly moves away from being a Jewish-Gentile allegory as the scholarly consensus has supposed and again becomes, even on an allegorical level, a veiled description of a Jewish-Jewish rift.

From this brief survey of modern scholarship, one can perceive that the bulk of Christian scholars have continued to maintain the allegorical intent of the Synoptic writers relative to the identification of "the son" with Jesus and the "others" with the Gentile Church. The comparatively few dissenting voices have been largely drowned out by the sheer multiplicity of voices singing in nearly perfect harmony.

AN ANALYSIS OF THE WICKED HUSBANDMEN
TAKEN VERSE BY VERSE

The parable of the wicked husbandmen is found in Mark 12:1–12, Matthew 21:33–46, Luke 20:9–19, and the Gospel of Thomas, logion 65, where it is followed by the cornerstone saying in logion 66. The three most important versions, uniformly translated following the RSV, are shown in the accompanying chart.[19]

GThom 65–66	Mark 12:1–11	Matt 21:33–43
(65) [1]He said, "There was a good man who owned a vineyard. He leased it to tenant farmers so that they might work it and he might collect the produce from them. He sent his servant so that the tenants might give him the produce of the vineyard. They seized his servant and beat him, all but killing him. The servant went back and told his master. The master said, 'Perhaps ⟨ they⟩ did not recognize ⟨him⟩.' He sent another servant. The tenants beat this one as well. Then the owner sent his son and said, 'Perhaps they will show respect to my son.' Because the tenants knew that it was he who was the heir to the vineyard, they seized him and killed him. [2]Let him who has ears hear."	[1]And he began to speak to them in parables. "A man planted a vineyard, and set a hedge around it, and dug a pit for the wine press, and built a tower, and let it out to tenants, and went into another country. [2]When the time came, he sent a servant to the tenants, to get from them some of the fruit of the vineyard. [3]And they took him and beat him, and sent him away empty-handed. [4]Again he sent to them another servant, and they wounded him in the head, and treated him shamefully. [5]And he sent another, and him they killed; and so with many others, some they beat and some they killed. [6]He had still one other, a beloved son; finally he sent him to them, say-	[33]"Hear another parable. There was a householder who planted a vineyard, and set a hedge around it, and dug a wine press in it, and built a tower, and let it out to tenants, and went into another country. [34]When the season of fruit drew near, he sent his servants to the tenants, to get his fruit; [35]and the tenants took his servants and beat one, killed another, and stoned another. [36]Again he sent other servants more than the first; and they did the same to them. [37]Afterward he sent his son to them, saying 'They will respect my son.' [38]But when the tenants saw the son, they said to themselves, 'This is the heir; come, let us kill him and have his inheritance.' [39]And they took him and cast him out of the

(66) Jesus said, "Show me the stone which the builders have rejected. That one is the cornerstone."

ing, 'They will respect my son.' [7]But those tenants said to one another, 'This is the heir; come, let us kill him, and the inheritance will be ours.' [8]And they took him and killed him, and cast him out of the vineyard. [9]What will the owner of the vineyard do? He will come and destroy the tenants, and give the vineyard to others. [10]Have you not read this scripture:

'The very stone
    which the builders rejected
has become the
    head of the corner;
[11]this was the
    Lord's doing,
and it is marvelous
    in our eyes'?"

vineyard, and killed him. [40]When therefore the owner of the vineyard comes, what will he do to those tenants?" [41]They said to him "He will put those wretches to a miserable death, and let out the vineyard to other tenants who will give him the fruits in their seasons."

[42]Jesus said to them, "Have you never read in the scriptures:

'The very stone
    which the builders rejected
has become the
    head of the corner;
this was the Lord's doing,
and it is marvelous
    in our eyes'?
[43]Therefore I tell you, the kingdom of God will be taken away from you and given to a nation producing the fruits of it."

Among these three versions, there is commonly thought to be a dependency. Some scholars have conjectured that Thomas' version represents the most primitive form of the parable which Mark reworked for inclusion within a specific context in his Gospel.[20] While this hypothesis cannot be established, it does seem safe to say that Thomas retains a simpler version of the wicked husbandmen devoid of any context in the life of Jesus. On the other hand, scholars almost universally agree that Matthew wrote with a copy of Mark's Gospel in hand.[21] Matthew thus provides us with an instance of a contemporary who read Mark, who interpreted his intent, and who editorially reworked his material for use with another audience. Accordingly, the versions of Thomas and Matthew can be used by way of clarifying and contrasting the intent of Mark as we proceed to the verse by verse analysis.

1. Mark's version of the parable begins with the phrase, "A man planted a vineyard. . . ." The version of the wicked husbandmen found in the Gospel of Thomas opens with stark brevity: "There was a *good* man who *owned* a vineyard." Mark, in contrast, has the man going through the actions of personally constructing the vineyard. A chain of five verbs is linked together by the rhythmic repetition of "and . . . and . . . and . . ." The Greek word order looks as follows:

> A vineyard—a man planted
> *and put around [it] a hedge
> and dug a winepress
> *and built a tower
> and leased it to tenants
> and went into another country.

A professional storyteller today might well object that Mark's wordy details serve only to distract his hearers and to stall the build-up of the story. From this vantage point, the economy of language found in Thomas' and Luke's openings is preferable. From the vantage point of most scholars, however, Mark's wordy details are deliberately crafted for the purpose of evoking, in Jewish ears, a resonance with the famous parable of the vineyard found in Isaiah 5:1ff. Isaiah's parable details the personal activity of preparing the vineyard using six verbs linked by the repetition of "and." The word order of the Greek text[22] begins as follows:

> A vineyard—my beloved had on a very fertile hill
> *and a hedge he put around [it]
> and cleared [it of stones]
> and planted choice vines
> *and built a tower in the midst of it
> and hewed out a wine-vat in it
> and he looked for it to yield grapes.

One can now easily see that Mark's version has some parallels but is certainly not identical with Isaiah's. Even in the case of the two phrases (indicated by "*") wherein the parallelism is closest, Mark did invert the word order of one and shortens the other. One could explain this dissimilarity by conjecturing either that Mark was using a Targum of Isaiah which he copied verbatim or that Mark was merely writing a makeshift remembered version of the LXX. However, the fact remains that no Targum has yet been found which more closely parallels Mark's opening, and later copyists did not see fit to correct what they identified as "Mark's faulty memory of Isaiah." Thus, putting these conjectures aside, it seems safest to assume that Mark wished to evoke Isaiah's parable, yet deliberately tried not to imitate it.

Isaiah's parable contrasts sharply with Mark's insofar as it introduces no husbandmen. After detailing the careful preparations made by Isaiah's "friend" the punchline immediately follows: "He expected it to yield [good] grapes, but sour grapes were all that it gave" (Is 5:2 & 4). A few lines later, Isaiah explains this to mean, "He [YHWH] expected justice, but found [unlawful] bloodshed; integrity, but only [found] a cry of distress" (Is 5:7). What follows from this? The prophet registers YHWH's complaint (Is 5:3f) and delivers YHWH's judgment:

> I will take away its hedge for it to be grazed on, and knock down its wall for it to be trampled on. I will lay it waste, unpruned, undug; overgrown by the briar and the thorn. I will command the clouds to rain no rain on it (Is 5:5f).

When one analyzes the mood transitions within Isaiah's extended parable, the following three movements are evident: expectation, disappointment, and future destruction. When the wicked husbandmen begins with a recitation of the deeds of a man building a vineyard, the hearer might thereby be disposed to expect a story in which the same mood transitions flow. As it turns out, the hearer's tacit expectations will not be disappointed.

Special attention should be given to the fact that Mark does not repeat verbatim the Greek opening of Isaiah's parable. If Mark had simply repeated Isaiah's opening words, then he would have set up the misleading expectation that Jesus was about to repeat the familiar *old* parable. By borrowing and noticeably modifying the familiar opening, an artful storyteller evokes the mood and theme of a familiar story at the same time that he signals a *new* version of this old parable is about to be presented. Thus, continuity functions to evoke the familiar mood transitions while discontinuity functions to signal that a novel production is about to unfold.

This artful use of continuity-discontinuity can be seen among the variety of vineyard themes found within the prophetic literature.[23] For example, Jeremiah, a prophet living a full century after Isaiah, is credited with the following:

> I [YHWH] have planted you, a choice vine, a shoot of soundest stock.
> How is it that you have become a degenerate plant, you bastard vine
> [Israel]? (Jer. 2:21).

In this abbreviated parable, the mood transition parallels that of Isaiah: expectation and disappointment. YHWH is presented as having selected the "soundest stock" which ought to have given rise to the choicest fruit. From within its larger context, the fidelity and righteousness of the founding fathers and mothers of Israel is metaphorically presented as the source of expectation which has been bitterly disappointed by the infidelity and wickedness of their children. Contrasts are also apparent. Isaiah does not focus on the planting of "a shoot" and Jeremiah makes no mention of his vines yielding "sour grapes."

Hosea, a contemporary of Isaiah living in the Northern Kingdom, also provided us with an abbreviated vineyard narrative:

> Israel was a luxuriant vine yielding plenty of fruit. The more his fruit
> increased, the more altars [to other gods] he built (Hos 10:1).

Hosea does not focus here upon YHWH as the one who painstakingly builds Israel, but upon Israel who, like a choice vine, bears abundant fruit and prospers. Such prosperity, however, instead of leading Israel to be grateful to the one who planted and nurtured her from the beginning, leads instead to the treacherous step of claiming that her well-being is "the pay my lovers [foreign gods] gave me" (Hos 2:12).

From just these two selections, various tentative conclusions can be drawn which will be shown to have a bearing upon Mark's parable: (a) It can be surmised that the Jewish horizon of understanding was quite rich in playing out intricate variations wherein the changing fortunes of Israel were figuratively portrayed in the language of the vineyard. (b) While every vineyard parable has some metaphorical associations, it cannot be supposed that every element within every parable necessarily has a one-for-one allegorical correspondence.[24] (c) An element in one parable can have a decisive allegorical significance, while this same element, when found within another context, can have either no allegorical significance or a distinguishably different one.

2. Mark continues: "When the time came, he sent a servant to the tenants, to get from them some of the fruit of the vineyard" (Mk 12:2). Jeremias and Dodd take this to be a realistic portrait of events.[25] Galilee, at the time of Jesus, had many absentee landlords who, according to stipulated agreements, were entitled to claim part of the produce as their own during the harvest season. That a servant should have been commissioned to execute this relatively simple task also fits the standard practice of the day. On a deeper level, however, the Jewish horizon of understanding brings to this narrated event interpretative thrusts which enrich the meaning of the parable.

In the first place, it is "the time"—the *kairos*. Such a term could simply mean that it is "the time for the harvest" as suggested in Mark 11:13 when Jesus approaches a fig tree on his way to the temple and fails to find any fruit "for it was not the season (*kairos*) for figs."[26] Yet, such a term could also mean "the eschatological time"—the *kairos* when the Kingdom of God is at hand (Mk 1:15) and/or when the master of the universe will suddenly return and demand an accounting of those servants whom he has put in charge (Mk 13:33f). Furthermore, since the prophetic literature frequently associates the time of harvest with the appointed time of God's judgment (e.g. Is 17:5, 18:4, 27:12), the deliberate ambiguity surrounding this term puts Mark's Jewish listeners on the alert.

"He sent a servant." On one level, this can simply mean that the absentee landlord understandably functions through his intermediary, the servant or slave, who has been commissioned to act in the name of his master. Yet, on another level, since Mark's narrative evokes something of the theme and mood of Isaiah's parable, a Jewish reader is always ready to recognize herein a resonance with YHWH who, in the course of history, functions through His chosen intermediaries. Thus, for example, YHWH again and again calls both Moses (e.g. Num 12:7f; Jos 1:2, 7; Neh 1:7f; Dan 9:11; Mal 4:4) and David (e.g. 2 Sam 7:5, 8; 2 Kgs 19:34, 20:6 Is 37:35; Jer 33:22, 26) "my servant." In the prophetic literature, YHWH, in general, addresses His people under the collective term "Israel/Jacob, my servant" (e.g. Is 43:10; 44:1; 44:21; 48:20; Jer 46:27f). More especially, however, it is the prophets that YHWH calls "my servants" (e.g. Jer 7:25; 25:4; 26:5; 29:19; 35:15; Am 3:7; Zech

1:6). The notion of "sending" further inclines the hearer to preferentially imagine the prophets as "the servants" of the parable:

> From the day your ancestors came out of the land of Egypt until today, day after day I [YHWH] have persistently sent you all my servants the prophets (Jer 7:25 and also 25:4).

In sum, the very unfolding of the narrative evokes the strong suspicion that the narrator is alluding to YHWH's sending prophets to Israel for the purpose of having His people turn their hearts toward God and produce the fruits of repentance. As the parable further unfolds, the hearer will affirm or disconfirm this allegorical intent.

3. "And they took him and beat him and sent him away empty-handed" (Mk 12:3). Up to this point, the narrative had related a string of initiatives defining the character of "the person"[27]—the *anthrōpos*—who personally created the vineyard. Now, for the first time, the husbandmen take the initiative—"seizing," "beating," and "sending away." The contrast between "the man" and "the husbandmen" is slowly unfolding.

Given the undercurrents which have already been suggested as guiding the Jewish listener, it might have been expected that the tenant farmers would not respond to the servant's request. The mood moves rapidly from expectation to disappointment just as in the case of Isaiah's parable which was evoked in the opening lines. Furthermore, the Jewish reader is forced to remember that the prophets sent by YHWH to Israel were not well received. The Jewish tradition amply testifies to this.[28] Hence, the earlier suspicion that Mark wants his hearers to make the association servant-prophet is confirmed.

WHETHER MARK ALLUDES TO PARTICULAR PROPHETS

Given this allegorical identification which most scholars accept as indicating Mark's intent,[29] it is necessary to inquire whether Mark wanted his hearers to identify particular prophets based on the clues that he offered relative to their rejection. The particular treatment afforded each of the servants in Mark is as follows:

1st servant	they beat
2nd servant	they wounded in the head and insulted
3rd servant	they killed
many others	some they beat, some they killed
beloved son	they killed him and cast him out

The word studies of A. Weisner have demonstrated that the Greek vocabulary in this sequence does not represent any specialized afflictions reserved for the prophets within the LXX.[30] It remains to be seen whether Mark offered clues which have a clear association because of internal references in his own Gospel.

Within the New Testament, the verb *derein* (to beat, strike, flay) has twelve occurrences. Mark uses this same verb to describe the storm on the Sea of Galilee where "the waves beat into the boat" (Mk 4:37). This term is too general and too widely used to apply it to any particular prophet.

The second servant is described as "wounded in the head." The Greek term,, *kephalaioein,* could also mean "to decapitate." Immediately, one might think of John the Baptizer; yet Mark himself failed to use this verb to describe the decapitation of John within his own Gospel (Mk 6:27). As such, it seems certain that Mark did not intend to associate the second servant with John.

The third servant is killed. A lot of prophets were beaten and otherwise abused, but only a few were actually put to death.[31] Since Mark does not offer any further precision, it becomes impossible to identify any specific prophet as being evoked by the third servant.

The phrase "many others" provides a general characterization which appears to find a middle course between the narratives of Nehemiah and Chronicles. Nehemiah took the unhistorical position of ascribing a violent death to *all* the prophets during the Israelite monarchy: "They killed the prophets who admonished them" (Neh 9:26). In contrast, in Chronicles this same period is summarized saying, "They ridiculed the messengers of God, they despised his words, they laughed at his prophets" (2 Chr 36:16). Mark, in his own parable, neither embraced the overstatement of Nehemiah nor the understatement of Chronicles but followed a middle course.

At this point in the narrative of the wicked husbandmen, we conclude that the limited allegorical intent of Mark extends to identifying servants-prophets without suggesting that the details offered suffice to identify each prophet by name. Michel Hubaut's extensive study of the modifications found in the Matthean and Lucan parallels concluded that these parallels offer only a general characterization of the abuses suffered by the prophets without encouraging further identification.[32] As for "the beloved son" being identifiable as Jesus or John, this will be taken up momentarily.

After the first servant returns home empty-handed and beaten, Mark immediately focuses on the second sending: "Again he sent to them another servant, and they wounded him in the head and treated him shamefully" (Mk 12:4). The modern reader might well be surprised that Mark does not detail the reaction of the owner as his mistreated servants return. Against the Jewish horizon of understanding, however, it might seem perfectly normal to anticipate rejection as the occupational hazard of the prophets. Nonetheless, even the Jewish listener would note that the tenants have become bolder in their treatment of the servants who show up at their doorstep. They beat the first one and sent him home empty-handed. The second is physically injured in the head and psychologically mistreated as well. With the third sending, the opposition to the owner escalates to murderous proportions: "And he sent another and him they killed" (Mk 12:5).

Any sane individual would, at this point, say, "Enough of this," and begin to take action against the tenant farmers running his vineyard. Not so "the man" in this parable: "And so with many others, some they beat and some they killed" (Mk 12:5). The owner seems to be a slow learner or a glutton for punishment. What can be achieved by repeating again and again the same abortive mission? Here something of the deeper layers of this parable begins to show through: "the man" doesn't surrender to the nasty tradition of violence which his tenant farmers have created for themselves. He refuses to respond to violence by violence. On the contrary, he appears to be a confirmed pacifist who believes that repeated gentle measures will serve to bring his opponents around to taking his rights into account.

The closest, modern image that comes to mind is the wave upon wave of frail, unarmed Indians who unmenacingly walk up to the file of British policemen in the film *Gandhi*. Each new group is mercilessly beaten with long police batons. They only halfheartedly protect themselves and return no blows whatsoever. Each fresh group of Indians comes forward as though they were completely oblivious to the blood and pain of those others who have gone before them. They hold their heads high and say nothing as though their very presence would somehow soften the ideological brutality of the beefy policemen who are systematically bent upon breaking their stupid resistance to British rule. In the heart of an American nourished on the myths of John Wayne and Clint Eastwood, this sort of non-violent resistance is sheer craziness.

This is the beauty of a parable. It can stretch one's mind into imagining that God might just be crazy enough to run his affairs by treating others much better than they deserve. In fact, God just might be the kind who doesn't resist the evildoer and who offers the other cheek when He is smitten on the right cheek (Mt 5:39). Repeated, gentle measures are offered as a fitting response to violent and abusive treatment. How long can this go on?

The parable responds: "He had still one other [servant], a beloved son" (Mk 12:6). The Greek text here is very rough, but the implication appears to be that, having sent all his servants, "the man" has only one left, and this servant is also a "beloved son."[33] Within the Jewish patriarchal household, every minor "son" is, de facto, a "servant" (*pais*), but it is unusual to find a son described as a "slave" (*doulos*) as is the case here.[34] Yet, in the context of religious servitude, the condition of being "son" and "slave" find frequent association. For instance, YHWH claims Israel as his "first-born son" (Ex 4:22f; Jer 31:9) and the people of Israel accordingly constituted YHWH's "slave" (Ez 28:26; 37:25) or "slaves" (Is 54:17; 56:6). In parallel fashion, Mark has Jesus acknowledged by heavenly voices as "beloved son/Son" (Mk 1:11; 9:7); yet, he does not hesitate to be known as "slave" (Mk 10:43–45). Hence, being "son" and "slave" at the same time fits well into a religious context and, in the context of our parable, may well be intended to emphasize both the physical and spiritual bonds that bind this father to this son.

The text continues: "Finally, he sent him to them, saying, 'They will respect my son.' " This is the first indication of the inner logic which has been sustaining the owner during the repeated cycles of anticipation and disappointment. Paradoxically, the use of direct discourse here serves to heighten the new sense of anticipation without making the least reference to past disappointments or to the risk involved in this final sending. The storyteller wants us to regard the owner-father as ready to send his only son as his last-ditch effort to bring his tenant farmers around. Here again, any prudent owner of an estate would have sent a sizable armed guard with his son, but not this one. Following his policy of doggedly repeating gentle measures, he sends his son unaccompanied, all the while hoping that his son can accomplish what his other servants could not.

In contrast, the Gospel of Thomas provides a much more credible story line. In the first place, the owner sends only two servants. Neither of them is killed. In the second place, the owner responds immediately to the report of the returning first servant by saying, "Perhaps they [the husbandmen] did not recognize him." After all, the husbandmen had to be cautious not to hand over the fruit of their labor to just anyone who shows up at their door and pretends to have been sent by the owner. The second servant suffers the same treatment; hence, the owner does not repeat that strategy. He adopts another: "Then the owner sent his son and said, 'Perhaps they will show respect to my son.' " We are not told that this is his "only" son. Nor are we led to believe that the owner is so naively hopeful as in the case of Mark's father. The issue is one of recognition. They were hesitant or unwilling to recognize the first and second servants as *authorized* to act in behalf of the owner. Now that the son is being sent to them, they ought to have no hesitation in recognizing him as someone fully authorized to act in behalf of his father, the owner of the vineyard.

The upshot of Thomas' version is that the strategy does partially succeed: the husbandmen do recognize the third one sent as "son." But then the surprise unfolds—the husbandmen recognize this "son" as "heir to the vineyard" and proceed to seize and kill him. Thus, in the end, by a curious twist, the owner's repeated concern for "recognition" does come to pass at the price of revealing the shocking perversity of the husbandmen. Mark's version, in contrast, has the husbandmen showing their perversity long before the son is sent, and the father naively shuts his eyes to this and says to himself, "They will respect my son." The hearer is asked to believe, therefore, that there is something in the son's presence which is calculated to convert them from their manifest perversity and to bring them around to doing what they ought to have done at the arrival of the first servant. Since the hearer can hardly believe that "the son" can have such a massive impact upon the husbandmen who have already demonstrated their murderous disregard for the owner's rights, Mark's version short-circuits any suspense about whether they will recognize him as authorized to act for the owner.

"But those tenants said to one another, 'This is the heir; come, let us kill him, and the inheritance will be ours.' And they took him and killed him, and cast him out of the vineyard." Alas, the expected scenario comes to pass.

This tragic ending must incline modern listeners to doubt whether any Jew could imagine God being portrayed by this sort of father-owner. Is not God wise? Is not God able to know the future? Would not God take measures to safeguard his innocent son? Within the Jewish horizon of understanding, however, a God who is wise and all-knowing can still send his messengers to a people whom he knows are unwilling to turn from their evil ways. The God of Israel does not stand back and, armed with superior intelligence, wait for just the right moment when just the right intervention in human affairs will result in an unqualified success. History is messy. The God of Abraham, Isaac, and Jacob, the God of

Sarah, Leah, and Rachel, cannot engage His people in history without entering into its messiness. Plans to change or to improve a person or a society are always somewhat ill-timed and somewhat ineffectual just because of the stubborn character of the human condition.

From this it follows that prophetic criticism, no matter how divinely enlightened and how ultimately beneficial for a given society, will always be generally unwelcome and provoke stubborn resistance. Jewish history repeatedly confirms this. This is so much the case that, when prophets are presented within the Jewish chronicles as welcomed by the people, the instinctive response of the inspired writer is not to praise God for the triumph of grace but to suspect that we are here dealing with "false/lying prophets" who have polluted their announcements of God's designs in accord with their private delusions (e.g. Jer 14:14; 23:16, 26f) or princely bribes (e.g. Mi 3:11, Ez 13:19) or idols "enshrined in their hearts" (e.g. Jer 2:8; 5:31; 23:13; Ez 13f). In contrast, the "true/truthful prophets" are routinely presented as delivering a message of YHWH which provokes resistance that culminates in deeds of violence aimed at intimidating and silencing them (e.g. Jer. 11:21). At no time do the Jewish records speak of "the divine hand" rendering the prophet perfectly immune from the cutting edge of the thrown stone or the fired bullet.[35]

If the Jewish horizon of understanding embraces what we have said in the last two paragraphs, it then follows that Mark's version of the wicked husbandmen comes through as the *true Jewish* story—the *true Jewish* account of how God does indeed act in history. The version of Thomas, by contrast, does not go far enough by way of breaking through the parameters of human wisdom and foresight which serve to guide our everyday existence. Here again, the very absurdity of Mark's version illustrates the probative value of parables at their best. They take us into mental places which we are hesitant to frequent. They trick us into capturing the absurd wisdom of God's ways as operative in a world in which God will have the last word.

WHETHER MARK ALLEGORIZES JESUS AS "THE SON"

Now we can raise the question as to whether Mark wanted his listeners to recognize "the son" in his parable as Jesus or John or some other prophet? From what we have concluded already regarding the unspecifiability of the other servants, it would seem consistent to suppose that the final servant would also be unspecifiable. On the other hand, one has to acknowledge that the narrative does offer a much more vivid characterization of the final servant than any of the previous ones. A tally sheet might include the following items:

(a)   only remaining servant
(b)   beloved son
(c)   future heir of the vineyard
(d)   sent as the final mission
(e)   details regarding his death:
        seized and killed in the vineyard
        then cast out of vineyard
        by husbandmen wishing to seize inheritance

Does this tally sheet evoke the image of Jesus for Mark's hearers? Possibly. Mark presents Jesus' contemporaries as regarding him as a prophet (6:15; 8:28). In addition, Jesus refers to himself as a prophet (6:4; 13:32?) and as a servant (10:43–45; 9:35?). Mark has also accustomed his readers to regard Jesus as "Son/son of God" and even as "beloved Son/son" of the Father (Mk 1:1, 11; 3:11; 5:7; 9:7; 13:32; 15:39). Mark has not focused upon Jesus as "heir" unless, of course, the Messiah is tacitly understood "to inherit" the people Israel from the One who created and nurtured him. Jacob Neusner, in his exhaustive study of texts referring to "the Messiah" within formative Judaism, did not find a single instance in which the Messiah is regarded as "heir" or is spoken of as "inheriting."[36] Hence, it is doubtful that Mark's hearers would have associated "the son" with the expected Messiah in the first place.[37] Neither has Mark developed the notion that Jesus is to be counted as "the last" or "final" messenger. Popular Judaism appears to have specified the identity of the final prophet as Elijah (Mk 9:11 & par.; Mal 3:23). Yet, according to Mark, some of the crowds did regard Jesus as Elijah (6:15; 8:28). It would appear unusual that Mark would rely upon the false identification of Jesus as Elijah in order to sustain the son=Jesus identification within his parable.

If Mark had so desired, he could have developed the identity of Jesus to embrace items (a) to (d) in the tally sheet above by simply including in his Gospel the opening lines found in the Letter to the Hebrews:

In many and various ways God spoke of old to our fathers by the prophets; but in these last days he has spoken to us by a Son, whom he appointed as heir of all things . . . (Heb 1:1).

Had Mark himself embraced a theme such as this, which was created some twenty years after his Gospel in a center of Hellenized Judaism, it would be self-evident that "the son" in the parable of the wicked husbandmen was to be identified as Jesus. Given the absence of such a thematic in Mark, however, one has to be prudently inclined to conclude that Mark had no specific referent in mind for any of the servants within his parable, "the son" included.

Even if Mark's hearers were prepared to recognize Jesus as "heir" and as "last sent" because of oral traditions which were not sounded within Mark's written text, the actual details of the killing of "the son" would still be troublesome. According to Mark, the son is killed within the vineyard and then "cast out" (Mk 12:8) without a burial. Jesus, on the contrary, was handed over to others (Romans) who crucified him outside of the city where he was properly buried. If Mark had wanted his hearers to associate "the son" with Jesus at this point in his Gospel, would he not have included details that are already known from Jesus' own predictions of his death (8:31f; 9:30f; 10:33f) or, alternatively, have included details that would await subsequent confirmation within the Passion Narratives to come? Any artful storyteller would have used such a device. Mark does not.

Jeremias and others have discounted the disconfirming specifics relative to the death of "the son" on the basis of their conviction that Matthew read Mark and modified his parable in order to further harmonize the specifics of the parable to favor the son=Jesus identification. John A.T. Robinson, on the contrary, has shown that Matthew takes some steps forward and some backward in this regard. A step forward consists in altering the order of events relative to the son's death: "And they took him and cast him out of the vineyard, and killed him" (Mt 21:39). Jeremias' comment on this is instructive:

> According to the Markan form of the story, the son is killed inside the vineyard, and his body is then thrown out of it. This feature of the story simply emphasizes the full extent of the husbandmen's iniquity: they go on to wreak upon the corpse the final indignity of throwing it over the wall and denying to the slain so much as a grave; nothing here recalls the incidents of the passion of Jesus. Not so Matthew (21:39) and Luke (20:15): on the contrary, they represent the son as being first cast out of the vineyard, and then slain outside it—a reference to the slaying of Jesus outside the city (John 19:17; Heb 13:12f). Thus, in Matthew and Luke, we meet with a christological coloring of the parable. . . .[38]

Jeremias highlights the enormous significance implied by Matthew's altering the order of Mark's verbs in order to place the "casting out" prior to the "killing." Jeremias presumes that Matthew and Luke were motivated by the intent of evoking "the slaying of Jesus outside the city." At this point, Robinson is quite right in critically drawing our attention to the fact that "this point is not emphasized in the two gospels concerned" as one might rightly expect "but only in John 19:17 and Heb 13:12f."[39] To this objection I would add that Jeremias' presumption that the vineyard could suddenly become an allegorical image for the city of Jerusalem is also suspicious. Such an identification, to my knowledge, has no precedent whatsoever within either the Jewish or Christian literature. But beyond this, Robinson also draws attention to the fact that Matthew drops the identification of "the son" from the account of Mark (a) as last sent, (b) as the "only" son, and (c) as the "beloved" son. In Matthew's retelling, the owner sends out two groups of servants, the second containing "more than the first" (Mt 21:36) which are all badly treated. Then, in contrast, Matthew has the owner sending a single individual, saying, "Afterward he sent his son to them" (Mt 21:37). Robinson reflects upon this saying, "Mark here appears to be the *most* allegorical and Matthew the least!"[40]

Springing off Robinson's critique, I would go even further and surmise that Matthew, who is recognized to have finely developed Jewish instincts, must not have perceived that Mark had provided essential clues directed toward an identification of "the son" with Jesus or else *he would not have removed three indicative clues* from his version of the wicked husbandmen. This negative conclusion also means that the inversion of the "casting out" and the "killing" has nothing to do with removing a perceived obstacle to the facts of Jesus' death. Even if one were to allow the unprecedented association of vineyard with the city of Jerusalem, the verb *ekballein* ("to cast out") never appears associated with the trial, handing over, and death of Jesus. Matthew, had he perceived some incompatibility, could easily have said "handed him over to those outside the vineyard who killed him." But he does not! This can only mean that Matthew *did not see* in Mark's parable what Jeremias and others have become habituated to seeing because of their training within the Christian tradition. In effect, what Matthew *did not see* is more trustworthy in reconstituting the original horizon of understanding for interpreting Mark than what such luminaries as Jeremias claim to have seen when they mistakingly categorize Matthew as having "pursued the allegorizing method consistently to the end."[41]

Mark's introduction of "the son" can be entirely accounted for in terms of the internal direction of the story itself. Prior to the appearance of "the son," the repeated sendings have manifested the progressive disrespect and violence of which the husbandmen are capable. The introduction of the last servant as "the son" allows the full measure of the father's reliance upon gentle, repeated measures to be felt. Any other father would cringe from the thought of risking the last and most precious person in his household. But not this father! He would sacrifice even his son if he judged that his son could move the recalcitrant husbandmen to respect and compliance. Furthermore, only the sending of "the son" allows for the forthcoming twist of irony whereby the husbandmen recognize "the heir" and kill him by way of insuring that the inheritance will be theirs (Mk 12:7 & par.).

Jeremias argues that "the arrival of the son allows them to assume that the owner is dead and that the son has come to take up his inheritance."[42] John A.T. Robinson doubts that this assumption is correct. He argues that, if it were, (a) "the son" would more probably be regarded as "the new owner" by the husbandmen rather than "the heir" and (b) the killing of "the new owner" would effect nothing if "the son" had his own children who would then become the legitimate heirs.[43]

In any case, whatever assumptions the husbandmen may have made, it is apparent that the naive hope of the father implied in his words, "They will respect my son," was soundly shattered and that the husbandmen acted in the full recognition of whom they were killing. An examination of the version of the Gospel of Thomas, which is devoid of the deliberate attempts to evoke the vineyard parable of Isaiah, further suggests that the introduction of "the son" can be seen as a natural ingredient in a story which is unfettered by allegorical considerations.

Now, to summarize the results of this study, the following arguments are put forward. (a) The fate of each earlier servant-prophet does not invite a specific identity. (b) The details regarding "the son" manifest little consistency with Mark's details regarding Jesus' death. (c) Matthew altered Mark's version without any perception of any Christological clues. (d) The introduction of "the son" can be accounted for entirely on the grounds of the internal consistency of the narrative story.

To this set, additional minor reasons for refusing to find a son=Jesus identification in Mark's narrative might be the following: (a) No resurrection or vindication or future glory is envisioned for "the son" in the parable.[44] (b) Given the life-of-Jesus setting of the Gospel, the parable would be allegorically presenting a forthcoming death as an already-accomplished death. (c) Mark never presented Jesus as making veiled Christological claims for himself at any other point in his Gospel.

If "the son" is not Jesus, is he perhaps John the Baptist? Those few who have argued for this point to the fact that the parable of the wicked husbandmen follows immediately after Jesus has tacitly vindicated his own authority by making reference to the source of John's authority (Mk 11:29–33). In so doing, John is specifically identified "as a prophet" (11:32). A further positive indicator is the fact that Mark's Gospel associates John's ministry with the eschatological prophet (Mk 1:2f) or with Elijah (Mk 1:6 = 2 Kgs 1:8; Mk 9:12f), the prophet whom, according to Jewish tradition, God had taken up alive into heaven in order to preserve him there in readiness to send him back just prior to the final days (Mal 3:23f). In this perspective, John might well be understood as the last messenger-prophet who is sent just prior to the Lord's coming.

Unfortunately, here is where the positive evidence stops. Neither John nor Elijah is specifically called "son" or "heir" within any of the Jewish or Christian sources. And the actual circumstances of John's death as they are related in both Mark and Matthew do not harmonize with the specifics offered in the parable. Both accounts agree that John was beheaded by a Jewish king (Herod Antipas) who both admired and feared him (Mk 6:20 & par.). The king was tricked by his sister-in-law, Herodias, into having him executed: an order which left him "exceedingly sorry" (Mk 6:26 & par.). John's disciples "came and took his body and laid it in a tomb" (Mk 6:30 & par.). If either Mark or Matthew had it in mind to evoke in his hearers the son–John identification, one would think that he would have deliberately harmonized the clues of the parable to suggest striking features of John's mission and/or John's death. Given the absence of such clues, we conclude that none of the servants, the son included, have any specifiable referent either for Mark or for Mark's readers, Matthew included.

"What will the owner do? He will come and destroy the tenants and give the vineyard to others" (Mk 12:9). Mark now uses a direct question by way of breaking off the parable and focusing attention upon the impact of the parable upon Jesus' listeners. The use of a direct question, at this point, may in part be motivated by the fact that Isaiah makes use of direct questions to develop the full intent of his parable (Is 5:4ff). If so, Mark has artfully framed his parable by evoking Isaiah's parable at both the beginning and the end.

The direct question identifies "the man" of the parable as *kyrios* (lord, owner, person-in-charge) for the first time. The direct question also breaks with the habitual use of the aorist tense and shifts into the future: "What will the lord of the vineyard do?" The word *kyrios* is frequently used in the LXX and the NT to refer to "YHWH." For example, the Masoretic text of Isaiah writes, "Prepare a way . . . for YHWH," which the LXX renders as "Prepare the way for the *kyrios*" (Is 40:3). Mark opens his Gospel citing the LXX, and his readers understand that *kyrios* is the appropriate designation for "YHWH" in this place. Hence, this linguistic habit allows the word *kyrios* in the direct question to refer (a) to "the man" who constructed the vineyard and (b) to the Lord who will come in the final days and render judgment. The fact that Mark uses *anthrōpos*, a term which could not be used for "YHWH" by any stretch of the imagination, as the initial designation for "the man" in the parable and then, suddenly, refers to "the man" as *kyrios* prepares his listeners to discover yet another feature of the one who has been gradually revealed as (a) constructing the vineyard, (b) sending servants, and (c) finally sending his last servant, his beloved son.

This *anthrōpos* is not weak and timid, as some might surmise on the basis of his repeated and futile sending of all his servants. He is also clearly the *kyrios* who "will come and destroy." Here again, the transition of moods already evoked by the opening lines of the familiar parable of Isaiah comes to completion: anticipation, disappointment, and destruction. In the case of Isaiah, the entire vineyard, which has produced only sour grapes, is destroyed. In the case of Mark who introduces the husbandmen as the tenant farmers working the vineyard, only the husbandmen are to be destroyed. This is the critical twist wherein Mark turns aside from the thrust of Isaiah's parable. *Israel is not to be destroyed.* The vineyard is quite capable of producing a good and abundant harvest of fruit just as the Lord prepared it to do. The problem, however, is that the husbandmen who have been placed in charge of the vineyard have refused to accept the long line of prophets which have been sent by the Lord and, consequently, have to be destroyed and replaced "by others."

WHAT MARK INTENDS BY "THE HUSBANDMEN" AND THE "OTHERS"

Who are "the husbandmen," and who are "others" who are their future replacements in Mark 12:9? To respond to the first question, recall that Mark wishes to evoke for his hearers Isaiah's parable wherein the vineyard planted by the Lord is representative of Israel, God's chosen people. Even though Isaiah's parable makes no mention of tenants, one could presume that those who manage the vineyard in someone else's absence would be precisely those who manage Israel in the absence of the Lord. If there is any doubt in the mind of the listener on this matter, one has only to wait for the response of Mark 12:12 to be certain that "the chief priests, the scribes, and the elders" recognize themselves as being presented as "the husbandmen." On this identification, I have not yet found a single scholar who would disagree. In a larger context, however, when Mark's parable is construed as depicting the whole of Jewish history wherein God repeatedly sends prophets, "the husbandmen" would include not only the existing Jerusalem leaders but all those leaders within Israel in the past epochs who have resisted the prophets as well.

It is noteworthy that Matthew modifies Mark to imply that "the Pharisees" are to be included with the "chief priests" as applying this parable to themselves (Mt 21:45). In this context, Matthew betrays his tendency to enlarge upon the opposition of the Pharisees and marginally to implicate the Pharisees in the treacherous plot to eliminate Jesus violently. Even though the Pharisees are not known to have resisted any known prophet, Matthew's Gospel goes so far as to accuse both "scribes and Pharisees" equally of being "the sons of those who murdered the prophets" (Mt 23:31) and are, consequently, turning out to be just like them. Mark, to repeat once again, does not give any indication that he would include the Pharisees among those referred to by "the husbandmen."

Who, then, are "the others"? Various responses have been forthcoming: (a) the Gentile Church, (b) the Jesus Movement, or (c) the apostles. The majority of scholars identify "the others" as the Gentile Church. They come to this conclusion because they are persuaded that allegorical identification rules all dimensions of the parable and that, since Jesus is "the son" killed by "the Jews," it follows that "the Gentile Church" does take over the vineyard. Allegorically this is very awkward for the Gentile Church did not at any point even aspire to replace the Jewish authorities and to take over the direction of Israel.

This awkward identification is partially removed when one understands that the Jesus Movement is essentially a Jewish renewal movement bent upon the eschatological renewal of Israel. Earlier in this essay I cited Joseph A. Fitzmyer to this effect. Within this framework, Gentiles are the wild branches grafted onto the roots of Israel's spiritual heritage. As such, therefore, the Christian Church is not an alternative to Judaism but an alternative within Judaism. This specification of "the others" has the advantage of harmonizing with (a) the notion that Israel is not destroyed and (b) the historical fact that Jesus and his disciples understood their calling to be as Jews for Jews. Nonetheless, even if the Jesus Movement is perceived as transforming Judaism from within and thereby giving a fresh direction to Israel in the future, it does not seem consistent to suppose that absolutely everyone within the Jesus Movement should end up as leaders within the reconstituted Israel. Rather, it would seem more fitting to suppose that some well-defined group within the Jesus Movement should replace the well-defined Jerusalem administrators to whom God formerly entrusted the direction of the vineyard.

Thus, among the three choices offered above, the best prospect might appear to be identifying "the others" as "the Twelve." This harmonizes well with Matthew's tradition wherein Jesus promises his disciples that "in the new world, when the Son of Man shall sit on his glorious throne, you who have followed me will also sit on twelve thrones, judging the twelve tribes of Israel" (Mt 19:28; Lk 22:30). Since Matthew presents "the scribes and Pharisees" as currently occupying "Moses' seat" (Mt 23:1), it appears that, in the age to come, when the twelve tribes of Israel are again restored, the Twelve will occupy "Moses' seat." Yet, here again, it is quite difficult to transpose this meaning into Mark's text since he has nothing in his Gospel which parallels Matthew 19:28. Quite to the contrary, following the widely received thesis of Theodore Weeden, Mark consistently presents the Twelve as defective in understanding and working at cross purposes with Jesus.[45] Following this distinctive Markan portrait of the Twelve, one could hardly expect that Mark's hearers would perceive such as these as worthy candidates for taking charge of the vineyard. It would appear, therefore, that Mark's Gospel does not offer any readily identifiable association with the "others." But, there is more to come.

If the *kyrios* "will come and destroy" at the end of time, then it would also follow that the transfer of the direction of the vineyard will take place *after* the final judgment. This means that neither at the time of Jesus nor at the time of Mark's writing of his Gospel has the transfer yet been effected. Hence, even if Mark perceives "his church" as having the promise of producing fruit for the Lord at the harvest, the actual transfer of power is still something the Lord will do! This future expectation accords well with the sense of the scriptural citation which Mark inserts in his text relative to the rejected stone becoming the future head of the corner.

"Have you not read this scripture: 'The very stone which the builders rejected has become the head of the corner; this was the Lord's doing, and it is marvelous in our eyes.' " Note that the Gospel of Thomas lists the parable of the wicked husbandmen and a saying about "the stone which the builders have rejected" one right after the other without implying that they were used together on any specific occasion. Mark, and the other two Synoptics who take over his basic text, all agree upon integrating these two into a single setting in the life of Jesus. In addition, the stone saying in the Synoptics is modified and identified as being a text of Scripture (Ps 118:22f).

In my judgment, J. Duncan M. Derrett has gone to the heart of Mark's use of this text when he has shown that, within the Jewish horizon of understanding, the Davidic Messiah would be immediately perceived as "the stone which the builders rejected" in Psalm 118:

> The psalm is about David, and therefore inferentially about the Messiah. It is a passover psalm and therefore relates to the redemption theme. David is the pattern of the redeemer. . . . David, though a younger brother and lacking in prestige, was chosen to effect that ancient redemption [from the Philistine menace]. The specialists, even Samuel, David's own family, Goliath, then Saul and others rejected and overlooked him. Yet he was chosen, evidently by God. David was the *real* builder of Solomon's Temple, and in a real sense the completer of the Jewish state. . . . The psalmist emphasizes that the junior and the unlikely can (as frequently in Jewish history) be the means of God's purpose. "It is wonderful in our eyes."[46]

In effect, therefore, Psalm 118 recaptures the Davidic Messiah as a type of Cinderella story wherein rejection by the builders of society does not get in the way of God's plan to exalt the poor and the humble. In a world in which the followers of Jesus are keenly aware that he has been rejected by the divinely ordained builders of Israel, it must have seemed natural to recall how David too had unpromising beginnings and suffered repeated rejections. Mark's community, which believes that this Jesus of Nazareth is God's choice for the Messiah, would, as a consequence, be keen to perceive Psalm 118 as sustaining their own future vision of things.[47]

Mark's overall plan, therefore, is to present Jesus as boldly standing up to the chief priests when they question him and having him present the counter-question about the source of John's authority. They rejected John, whom the people recognized as a true prophet, and, by implication, they are destined to reject Jesus as well. The position of the parable of the wicked husbandmen drives home this point. The opening images of the parable serve to evoke the changing moods of Isaiah's parable. There immediately follows the incredible image of YHWH patiently sending vulnerable messengers to those whom he has set in charge of Israel. His determination reaches a climax when, with only his son left, he decides to send him as well. When this last hope is exhausted, YHWH abandons his gentle measures and prepares to come personally to avenge the crimes of the husbandmen and to appoint "others" to manage his vineyard. Who are these "others"? They are deliberately left undetermined. Not even Jesus felt that it was up to him to assign places in the Kingdom of God (Mk 10:40). However, by examining the case of David ("the very stone which the builders rejected"), one can surmise that many of those now officially despised will be among the "others" whom the Lord will choose.[48]

The effect of Psalm 118, therefore, is that it acts as an explosive postscript to the parable. According to the terms of the parable, the Lord placed the husbandmen in charge of his vineyard. Hence, the judgments of the chief priests and their associates are being tacitly recognized as divinely authorized. Yet, immediately following, there is a revolutionary appeal to the future return of the Lord as the moment for true and final justice, checking the wickedness of the husbandmen and making some surprising reversals. The invoking of this future superior court has the powerful effect of exposing the provisional nature of the authority and judgments of those whom the Lord has placed in charge. Those who came to judge the worth of Jesus and to challenge his authority are now themselves being judged.[49] Those who came to challenge his authority are now themselves exposed to an affront on their authority. The tables have been turned. No wonder "they tried to arrest him" (Mk 12:12).

CONCLUSION

If this study with its conclusions is substantially correct, then the legacy of anti-Judaism attached to the parable of the wicked husbandmen from the patristic period down to our present day cannot be judged as part of the original inspiration guiding Mark in the creation of his Gospel. Positively speaking, however, the foregoing attempt to recreate the original horizon of understanding provides a fresh interpretation of the parable which is decidedly favorable to Judaism in the following ways:

1. Mark's parable implies that Israel will continue to exist as God's favored until the end of time. In this regard, Mark evokes and modifies Isaiah's parable of the vineyard. The mood transitions (expectation, disappointment, and future destruction) are retained, but, by introducing the husbandmen within Isaiah's general motif, Mark shifts YHWH's wrath from Israel as a whole to the Jerusalem leadership. In so doing, Mark implies that Israel is quite capable of producing fruit for its Lord in due season when the vineyard is under capable management by "others" who, at this time, are themselves officially despised by the present management which despises their Lord as well.

2. The replacement theme in Mark consistently implies a Jewish struggle stemming out of Jewish origins. Mark makes no racial distinctions within his parable. By implication, Jewish servants are sent to collect the produce from Jewish husbandmen. They, out of their disregard for the owner and not out of their Jewishness, progressively shame and injure those sent. The "others" who will inherit the vineyard are also Jews. Psalm 118 caps this off by offering a Jewish case study illustrating how a Jew despised by the official establishment rose to the top as part of the Lord's doing. Gentiles and Gentile interests simply have no role within the horizon of this narrative.

3. Finally, Mark's parable fails to make any triumphalistic claims for Jesus or for the Jesus Movement. Rather, it consistently follows the mind and heart of Jesus' training: "Whoever would be great among you must be your servant, and whoever would be first among you must be slave to all" (Mk 10:43f). In the end, by not exactly specifying the "others" but by allowing the Lord God to be the one who makes the critical choices, Mark allows each one to be preoccupied with conforming one's life to God's standards. In so doing, Mark may be acting against a false reliance that some within his own community may have because they know who the Messiah is or have been trained under his direction.

By extension, even today, Mark's parable stands much more to caution and to judge the Church than to assure her of her superiority over the Jews. Whenever the Church's divine mission leads her to either an institutional triumphalism or to a mistreatment of her own prophets, Mark's parable judges her as unfit to be the "other." The same, of course, can be said of those synagogues which, while claiming to be the inheritors of the prophets, nonetheless disgrace and injure them by their deeds.

In the end, consequently, critical inquiry carefully scrapes away the

anti-Jewish image that had been carefully painted over the basic outline
of the parable of the wicked husbandmen. Another image, older and
fresher, appears.[50] This image is not that of Christian superiority and
Jewish guilt for the death of Jesus, which has for so long been displayed
in the Church. Rather, this new image has the potential for unsettling
the onlooker by tearing away those religious assurances which shield
one from the terrible judgment of the living God. It remains to be seen
whether this image will ever be displayed within those churches that call
themselves Christian.

NOTES

1. For our purposes here, it suffices to remember that vehement criticism
and threats of destruction of the Temple have a large role within the Jewish
prophetic tradition (e.g. Is 1:11–20; Jer 7:1–15) and cannot, in themselves, be
construed as anti-Jewish. According to Acts, the primitive church continued
Jesus' practice of going to the Temple in order to pray and teach (e.g. Lk 24:53;
Acts 3:1; 5:42), but this did not prevent Stephen from preaching that "Jesus of
Nazareth will destroy this place" (Acts 6:14). This ambiguity regarding the
Temple has been studied by Joseph B. Tyson in *The Death of Jesus in Luke-Acts*
(Columbia, SC: University Press, 1986), pp. 90–110. The role of the Temple in
Mark has been studied by Donald Joel, *Messiah and Temple* (Missoula: Scholars
Press, 1977).

2. John Chrysostom, *Patrologia Graeca* 48.845, 849f, 851f, 854, 861, 881.

3. John Chrysostom, *Homilies on the Gospel of Matthew*, 68.1.

4. Aaron Milavec, *To Empower as Jesus Did* (N.Y.: The Edwin Mellen
Press, 1982), pp. 249–51; David Tracy, *The Analogical Imagination* (N.Y: Crossroad, 1981), pp. 105, 322f.

5. Gadamer explored the function of prejudice by showing that everyone
comes to some understanding of "x" only by virtue of a set of predispositions
which tacitly guide the process of recognizing and judging "x." These tacit
predispositions can be regarded as "legitimate prejudices" when they lead to
truth or as "illegitimate" when they lead to a distorted recognition/judgment of
"x." Cf. Hans-Georg Gadamer, *Truth and Method* (N.Y.: Seabury, 1975), pp.
235–253.

6. Gregory Baum, in his early book *Is the New Testament Anti-Semitic?*
(Glen Rock, N.J.: Paulist, 1965), endeavored to maintain that the New Testament texts are not by themselves tainted by anti-Judaism but that the later
interpretations of the Church gave them this coloring. With the appearance of
Rosemary Ruether's study, *Faith and Fratricide: The Theological Roots of Anti-
Semitism* (N.Y.: Seabury, 1974), Baum wrote in the preface that Ruether had
changed his mind by demonstrating that the canonical texts themselves are

already colored by an antagonism toward the religion of Israel. John M. Oesterreicher, in his *Anatomy of Contempt* (South Orange, N.J.: Seton Hall University, n.d.), strongly reproved Ruether for her "lopsided exegesis" and endeavored systematically to sustain Baum's earlier position. Douglas R.A. Hare advanced these exchanges by distinguishing various forms of anti-Judaism in his study, "The Rejection of the Jews in the Synoptic Gospels and Acts," *AntiSemitism and the Foundations of Christianity,* ed. by Alan T. Davies (N.Y.: Paulist, 1979), pp. 27–47. Jewish contributions to this discussion include Samuel Sandmel, *Anti-Semitism in the New Testament?* (Philadelphia: Fortress, 1978) and numerous excellent works by Michael J. Cook: (a) *Mark's Treatment of the Jewish Leaders* (Leiden: Brill, 1978); (b) "Anti-Judaism in the New Testament," *Union Seminary Quarterly Review* 38/2 (1983) 125–137; (c) "Interpreting 'Pro-Jewish' Passages in Matthew," *Hebrew Union College Annual* 54 (1983) 135–146; (d) "The Bible and Catholic-Jewish Relations," *Twenty Years of Jewish-Catholic Relations,* ed. by Eugene J. Fisher (N.Y.: Paulist, 1986), 109–124.

7. Vatican Commission for Religious Relations with the Jews, "Notes on the Correct Way to Present Jews and Judaism in Preaching and Catechesis in the Roman Catholic Church," 3.21. Eng. tr. from *Origins* 15/7 (4 July 1985) 102–107.

8. *Ibid.,* 4.22 citing from *Nostra Aetate,* 4.

9. Of thirty studies devoted to the Synoptics which I randomly selected, every one of them unqualifyingly associated "the son" with Jesus. These include works by Francis Wright Beare, Gunther Bornkamm, Rudolph Bultmann, John Dominic Crossan, C.H. Dodd, James D.G. Dunn, Joseph A. Fitzmyer, Joachim Jeremias, Xavier Leon-Dufour, John P. Meier, John L. McKenzie, John A.T. Robinson, Rosemary Radford Ruether, Leopold Sabourin, Donald Senior, Edward Schweizer, Carroll Stuhlmueller, Vincent Taylor, and Herman C. Waetjen. In the periodic literature referenced in *Religious Index One: Periodicals* over the past twenty years, only one study opposes this association. Jane E. and Raymond R. Newell, in "The Parable of the Wicked Tenants," *Novum Testamentum* 14 (1972) 226–237, argue that Jesus used this parable to challenge those sympathetic to the zealot movement. The husbandmen, in this perspective, are the Jewish freedom fighters who are resisting the unjust claims of the foreign landowner who was Rome. The French school of semiotics has sometimes avoided traditional allegorical associations in its quest to specify the inherent transformations within the story. Cf., e.g., J. Almeida, "Les vignerons meurtriers," *Sémiotique & Bible* 11 (1978) 18–47 and Louis Martin, *The Semiotics of the Passion Narrative,* tr. by A.M. Johnson of 1971 French ed. (Pittsburgh: Pickwick Press, 1980).

10. Joachim Jeremias, *The Parables of Jesus* (N.Y.: Charles Scribner's Sons, 1954), p. 74.

11. *Ibid.,* pp. 76f.

12. John Dominic Crossan, "The Parable of the Wicked Husbandmen," *Journal of Biblical Literature* 90 (1971) 455.

13. Michel Hubaut, "La parabole des vignerons homicides," *Cahiers de la Revue Biblique* 16 (Paris: J. Gabalda, 1976).

14. *Ibid.*, p. 41, my tr.

15. Leopold Sabourin, *The Gospel According to St. Matthew* (Bombay: St. Paul, 1982), vol. 1, p. 65. While Jeremias initially identifies the "other people" as the Gentile Church, in the end, Jeremias identifies "the meek" as being the implied future inheritors. Cf. Jeremias, *op. cit.*, pp. 68 & 76.

16. *Ibid.*, p. 69.

17. Joseph A. Fitzmyer, *The Gospel According to Luke: The Anchor Bible* 28 & 29 (Garden City: Doubleday & Co., 1981 & 1985), p. 1281.

18. *Ibid.*, p. 191.

19. John Dominic Crossan, *Sayings Parallels* (Philadelphia: Fortress, 1986), p. 151.

20. E.g. John Dominic Crossan, *Four Other Gospels* (N.Y.: Winston Press, 1985), pp. 59–62. J.M. Robinson and H. Koester, in *Trajectories through Early Christianity* (Philadelphia: Fortress, 1971), pp. 130–32 & 166–187, argue that the parabolic material in the Gospel of Thomas rests upon a tradition independent of the Synoptics.

21. John A.T. Robinson, in "The Parable of the Wicked Husbandmen: A Test of Synoptic Relationships," *New Testament Studies* 21 (1974–75) 443–461, concludes that the parable of the wicked husbandmen offers substantial evidence for Matthew's dependence on Mark but that nothing definitive can be said relative to either Luke's availability to or dependence upon any other Gospel writer.

22. Jeremias, *op. cit.*, p. 71, n. 80, explains that it is evident Mark used the Greek LXX rather than the Hebrew text from the fact that the Hebrew text reads "he dug it up" while the LXX incorrectly renders this as "he put around it a hedge."

23. Is 5:1–7; 27:2–5; Jer 2:21; 5:10; 6:9; 13:13; 12:10; Ez 15:1–8; 17:5–10; 19:10–14; Hos 2:14–17; 10:1. Also see Ps 80:7–15; Cant 1:6; 2:15; 8:11f; 2 Baruch 57:2; 4 Ezra 5:23. For rabbinic parallels, see the article of David Stern, "Jesus' Parables From the Perspective of Rabbinic Literature," in this volume, esp. n. 49. For early Christian usage of vineyard motifs, see Jean Daniélou, *Les symboles chrétiens primitifs* (Paris: Editions du Seuil, 1961), pp. 42–47.

24. When a parable with limited allegorical intent is reflected upon within a tradition, there is a tendency to suspect that it has further hidden meanings which can be deciphered by dint of further decoding the unallegorical elements therein. Paul Ricoeur, in *Interpretation Theory* (Fort Worth: Texas Christian University Press, 1976), pp. 25–37 & 55–57, rightly specifies that any discourse which is made available through writing to persons no longer restricted by the original context will be found to exhibit a "surplus of meaning/signification" for these new inquirers. In point of fact, rabbinic reflection upon Isaiah's parable gradually developed the edifying habit of identifying the "hedge-enclosure" which YHWH built around the vineyard as "the Torah" or "the rules of ritual

purity" which protected Israel from harmful contacts with outsiders. This inspired and inspiring extension of Isaiah's intent, however, does not embrace an
image employed among the prophets and should not be identified as the *original
intent* of the author. In a parallel fashion, one finds Mark himself endorsing a
tendency exhaustively to allegorize the Parable of the Sower (Mk 4:3–20). Modern scholars have correctly cautioned us that Mark, in so doing, has shifted the
meaning of the parable away from Jesus' original intent. Cf., e.g., Eduard
Schweizer, *The Good News According to Mark* (Richmond: John Knox Press,
1970), pp. 95–98, and Jeremias, *op. cit.,* pp. 149–151.

25. C.H. Dodd, *The Parables of the Kingdom* (N.Y.: Charles Scribner's Sons,
1961), p. 97, & Jeremias, *op. cit.,* p. 75.

26. Even in this context Mark uses the expectation-disappointment mood
surrounding the fig tree as a framing device for signaling the expectation-
disappointment of Jesus as he enters the Temple, finds that its operations have
failed in their purpose, and prophetically halts the priestly sacrifices in favor of
making the Temple "a house of prayer for the nations" (Mk 11:17, evoking the
critique of Jer 7:1–15).

27. The New Testament is generally careful in using the word *anthrōpos* when
a human being is referred to without any distinction between male and female.
Thus, according to Genesis, "God created *anthrōpos* in the image of him/
herself . . . male and female . . ." (Gen 1:27). In effect, the Genesis tradition
imaged God as male and female. Thus, the actual use of the word *anthrōpos* in
the opening lines of the parable of the wicked husbandmen more capably signals
a possible reference to God than would the use of the word *anēr* which could
only signal "a man" as contrasted with a woman. Traditional English usage
obscures the Greek intent by rendering *anthrōpos* as "man." On the other hand,
traditional Anglo-American culture has habituated us to regard "the man" as
being the more appropriate metaphor for God than "the person."

28. Jeremiah, for instance, describes the harassment evoked by his role as
God's messenger to Israel. He receives death threats (Jer 11:21), his friends
abandon him (20:10), the priest Pashhur has him beaten and put in stocks (20:2),
and the royal officials have him beaten and put under house arrest (37:15) and
later abandoned in a muddy well to die (38:9). Added to this open hostility,
Jeremiah faces the inner suffering of associating himself with the plight of his
people (4:19–22; 8:18–23; 13:17–19) and feeling that his whole life has been a
waste (20:18).

29. Only those few scholars who read the parable of the wicked husbandmen
entirely outside of the context of Isaiah's parable deny such an association. Cf.
Newell, *op. cit.,* pp. 235f. Crossan, in *Four Other Gospels,* pp. 53f & 60, concludes that Thomas, as it stands, either offers "a warning against the evil consequences of material greed" or presents a "grasp your chance" approach to the
Kingdom of God. Mark's use of Isaiah 5, and his situating the parable in the life
of Jesus as he does, immediately negates such potential meanings.

30. Alfons Weiser, *Die Knechtsgleichnisse der synoptischen Evangelien, Studien zum Alten and Neuen Testament* 29 (München: Kösel-Verlag, 1971), p. 53f.

31. Edward Schillebeeckx, *Jesus* (N.Y.: Seabury, 1979), pp. 275f, and J. Lindblom, *Prophecy in Ancient Israel* (Philadelphia: Fortress Press, 1962), pp. 203f & 296f.

32. Hubaut, *op. cit.,* pp. 36–41.

33. The order of the Greek words reads thus: "Still one (*hena*) he-had a-son beloved." The verb appearing where it does separates off the first part, "still one," from the second, "a beloved son." Accordingly *hena* has the force of a pronoun replacing the word "servant" and not of an adjective modifying "son." Hubaut, *op. cit.,* pp. 43f, indicates that certain ancient copyists, uneasy with the association servant-son, altered the word-order to read, "Still one son he-had beloved." The Vulgate translation substituted the participle, *habens,* for the verb "he-had" without changing the word order: "*adhuc ergo unum habens filium carissimum.*" This has the effect of reducing *unum* to an adjective that can only be translated to say, "and therefore having one beloved son."

34. The Greek language distinguishes between the words *pais* and *doulos,* while English translations render both of these terms as "servant." The word *pais* appears to direct attention to the insignificance or smallness of the one being referred to and can be applied to slaves as well as to children. The word *doulos,* in contrast, most often refers to involuntary servitude. In the religious context, this term aptly captured both the inequality and the attachment of the one devoted to God's service. Thus, the righteous person, is often specified as *doulos* (e.g. Ps 18:12, 14; 26:9; 30:17). In the Greek literature of late Judaism, *doulos* entirely dominated over *pais* as the term to express "servants/slaves of God" (e.g. 2 Mac 7:33; Jub 23:30; Josephus, *Antiquities* 11.4.4). Following this usage, Paul frequently specified his identity as being that of a "slave of Jesus Christ" (Rom 1:1; Phil 1:1; Gal 1:10). For further information, see ThDNT 2:267f & 5:675–686. The word *hyios,* in addition to designating physical sonship, also referred to spiritual sonship in both the Hebrew and Christian Scriptures. See ThDNT 8:334f, 354f, 359f, & 364f.

35. In the Elijah and Elisha traditions, YHWH periodically intervenes to protect his prophet(s), e.g., as when two bears came out of the woods and mangled the forty-two boys who had been calling Elisha a "baldhead" (2 Kgs 2:23f). Cf. Lindblom, *op. cit.,* pp. 62–64.

36. Jacob Neusner, *Messiah in Context: Israel's History and Destiny in Formative Judaism* (Philadelphia: Fortress, 1984).

37. Jeremias, *op. cit.,* p. 73, even acknowledges this point.

38. *Ibid.*

39. Robinson, *op. cit.,* in n. 21, p. 449.

40. *Ibid.*

41. Jeremias, *op. cit.,* p. 72.

42. *Ibid.*, pp. 75f.

43. Robinson, *op. cit.* in n. 21, p. 448.

44. Crossan, "The Parable of the Wicked Husbandmen," p. 455. Jeremias, *op. cit.*, p. 74, also noted the absence of any reference to the resurrection in the parable and postulated that Psalm 118 was appended to the parable precisely because it is "the primitive Church's favorite proof-texts for the resurrection and exaltation of the rejected Christ" (cf. Acts 4:11; 1 Pet 2:7).

45. Theodore J. Weeden, Sr., *Mark—Traditions in Conflict* (Philadelphia: Fortress, 1971), pp. 23–51.

46. J. Duncan M. Derrett, *Studies in the New Testament*, Vol. 2 (Leiden: Brill, 1978), p. 62. David Stern, in his article published in this volume, also notes that rabbinic midrash has Psalm 118:22f referring to David's lowly origins.

47. Luke 4:11 uses this same segment from Psalm 118 as part of Peter's defense before the high priest and his associates. In this context, Psalm 118 illustrates how the one that the Temple establishment had crucified was, in fact, God's choice as Messiah. For other references to Jesus as "the stone," one can consult ThDNT 4:272–77.

48. It is not necessary to decide if Jesus actually did use Psalm 118 in this or in any other context. It suffices to acknowledge that the parable and Psalm 118 could have been used by Jesus in the situation in which Mark placed it. In point of fact, many commentators (e.g. A. Jülicher, R. Bultmann, W.G. Kümmel) regard the entire complex of Mark 12:1–12 to be the creation of the early church. Among those who accept that some form of the parable of the wicked husbandmen was uttered by Jesus himself (e.g. C.H. Dodd, J. Jeremias, V. Taylor), no one has supposed that Jesus made use of Psalm 118 on the same occasion. In part their hesitancy is based upon the conviction that "the stone" could not yet be understood as referring to Jesus. What Derrett (n. 46) has shown is that the immediate reference is to David and, consequently, need not refer to Jesus as such but to the Lord's pattern of confounding "the builders" by choosing the most unlikely candidate for the most exalted offices in Israel. In this understanding, Psalm 118 serves to hint at what sort of "others" the Lord may place in charge of Israel on the last day without necessarily deciding for any given person.

49. The appeal to a higher judgment in this context prepares the reader for Jesus' similar appeal when he is being questioned by the high priest. In this latter context, Jesus affirms that he is the Messiah (a proposition which the high priest is not willing to accept) and then immediately appeals to the future and final judgment ("You will see the Son of Man sitting on the right hand of Power" [14:62]). It is this latter appeal which tacitly challenges the high priest's authority to definitively judge Jesus. As such, it might well be that Mark wants us to understand Jesus' juridical challenge to constitute the "blasphemy" (14:64) upon which he is condemned. Matthew 26:64 and Luke 22:67f seem to favor this

interpretation by retaining the charge of blasphemy even when Jesus declines to answer the direct question of the high priest.

50. Frank Kermode, in *The Genesis of Secrecy* (Cambridge: Harvard University Press, 1979), correctly cautions those interpreters who "sometimes think of earlier interpretations, transmitted by institutions, as having attached themselves to the original, and as having tended to close it off, lowering its potential rather as mineral deposits clog a pipe and reduce its flow" (p. 40). A few lines later, however, Kermode acknowledges that "what it meant and what it means are both actualizations of its hermeneutic potential, which, though never fully available, is inexhaustible." Applying this to the parable of the wicked husbandmen, I would say that the late Fathers of the Church discovered within the parable of Jesus a passionate resonance with their own historically conditioned antagonism toward Jews. The contemporary Church, having abandoned its teaching of contempt, is now once again in a favorable situation for rediscovering some lost meanings and even for pioneering new understandings which harmonize with the recently recovered sense that there exists a common heritage which unites Christians and Jews.

II.
LITERARY-CRITICAL
REFLECTIONS
ON PARABLE AND STORY

New Ways with Bible Stories

Frank Kermode

Any historical account of the rise of modern literary studies in the
Bible would probably begin with Erich Auerbach's *Mimesis,* now over
forty years old. But the unquestioned brilliance and originality of that
work, and of the essay "Figura" which supplements it, do not quite
explain the forms taken by more recent studies of biblical narrative; they
haven't been directly indebted to Auerbach. The methods used, which
are various, hardly resemble his, although it would probably be true to
say that his bold formulation of a realism, drastically modified, that
embraces the biblical narratives and the modern novel, left less conscious traces. He offered a new explanation of the importance for later
literature of the Passion narratives; and what he wrote in his first chapter
about the differences between the narrative style of Homer and that of
the Jewish Bible must also have left a deep impression. Yet most recent
studies of biblical narrative seem to come at the subject from rather
different angles.

One may here offer some over-simple explanations of the motivation of this kind of scholarship. First, there is a development that is
primarily Jewish. Roughly speaking, it ceased to seem necessary for
Jewish critics to make an arbitrary separation between the interests and
assumptions of the secular academy and the ancient tradition of Bible
study in which many of them had been trained—sometimes just on the
other side of the street, though conventionally a world away from the
classrooms where they studied a more modern and less sacred literature.
As we shall see, the new secular interest in "the poetics of prose" or
narratology now seemed applicable to the Bible texts. And, conversely,
the peculiar imaginative boldness of rabbinic commentary, the tradition,
I may call it for short, of midrash, might—for some, though not for the

most devout—appear to have a relationship with other forms of interpretation, at a time when philosophies and methods of interpretation had begun to grow more interesting.

There were comparable changes in attitudes toward the Christian Bible. The Gospel narratives were restored to attention *as* narratives. In his important book *The Eclipse of Biblical Narrative,* published in 1974, Hans Frei showed how in the eighteenth century interest in the factuality of the narratives came to supplant consideration of them as stories. Facts, not writing, were the object of scholarly consideration, and the difficult relation between history and the history-like, or, to express the point in a formula of Jean Starobinski's, between what is written and what it is written about, was forgotten. Even before Frei's book *story* was beginning to attract interest, as if, by conscious effort, one could restore the undifferentiated view of fact and story that had prevailed before "scientific" scholarship began to treat narrative as a mere veil over historical occurrence.

THE MYSTERY OF NARRATIVE

This change could probably not have occurred without a prior development, the new interest in the way narratives work—one might say, in the mystery of narrative. People began to ask such questions as: In what sense do stories have structure? Since its primary function seems to be explanatory and persuasive, how does narrative also generate secrecy—call for so much explanation from the reader to whom it ostensibly offers explanations? Such questions may be asked of all narrative, but seem particularly appropriate to texts that have suffered many centuries of explanation. (One consequence of the wish to ask such questions was the renewal of attention to parable, and to the sort of rabbinical commentary which assumes inexhaustible stocks of secrets requiring interpretation.)

We easily assume that narrative has a natural drive toward plainness and clarity. We fall into its pattern naturally when recounting the events of a day at the office, or a quarrel or an encounter of any kind; it is the obvious way of explaining not only what occurred but the significance of what occurred. Of course we may also use it for concealment, or to forestall unfavorable interpretation. It was an ancient complaint against the Gnostics that by altering the narrative sequence of the Gospels they distorted the *logia;* and the idea that the Scriptures plainly offered all the explanations necessary to salvation and conduct continued to seem intuitively right. Yet such notions coexisted with the contrary assumption, common to Jew and Christian in their different ways, that there were *secrets* in the text, and that they could be brought to light only by devoted research. In this respect the Rabbis and the Fathers anticipated ambitious modern secular commentary, which really became possible only when certain texts were granted a pseudo-canonical status. And one might almost say that it was a rediscovery to the apparently infinite possibilities of interpretation, and a new understanding of the necessary obsolescence of commentary (partly dependent on the grant of a quasi-sacred status to secular texts) that impelled the secular scholars to look again at the originally sacred texts. For their part, the traditional guardians of those sacred texts, their confidence in simple historical foundations impaired by two centuries of scientific scholarship, were ready to consider the new approaches to narrative that were coming from the secular critics. Bible scholars and secular critics were now able to greet one another on the same common ground.

On the whole they have not concerned themselves with deconstructive analysis; they use more traditional methods, though with a new intensity. But they are a varied company, and generalization is difficult. For example, it is true of some but by no means of the majority that they have simply bracketed the question of historical reference; some, perhaps most of them, regard it as inescapable. But by and large they agree that whatever else the Bible may be it is certainly, in the first place, a form of literature; and they go on from there in their different ways. Some are indebted to the Formalist revival of the Sixties, French and Soviet, some to various kinds of "reader-response" theory, some to the severe style of narratological analysis developed in Israel. Some are eclectic. On one other matter they tend to agree. Though not disrespectful of traditional scholarship, they choose to treat narratives in the forms in which they have come down to us, ignoring speculative earlier versions (truer, perhaps, to fact) which may lie behind them.

For example, when James S. Ackerman analyzes the story of Joseph's brothers in Egypt he must, if he is to discuss the text as the Bible actually offers it, account for a good deal of repetition in speech and action. In traditional scholarship this is regarded as the result of a redactor's clumsiness in conflating his sources. Ackerman doesn't offer to refute that view; his concern is with the *effect* of this doubling on our reading of the story. It may give emphasis, it may retard the progress of the plot in rhetorically important ways, for instance by delaying the recognition scene between Joseph and his brothers. This is so whether the doubling is the result of mere clumsiness, or whether it was done by a redactor of much greater skill than scientific criticism supposed—a writer so far from clumsy that he carefully organized the narrative to this end. Ackerman would probably agree with Robert Alter that it is usually more sensible to assume skill than inspired incompetence; but that choice makes no difference to the effect of the passage.[1]

In this respect there is not much difference between attitudes to Old and New Testaments. For instance, it is sometimes argued that the scene in which Mary confronts Jesus before the raising of Lazarus must be an interpolation because it (partly) doubles the meeting of Jesus with Martha. This view seems to me unlikely, indeed incredible; but in any case it would not bother our modern analysts, who would simply consider the literary effect of the repetition, and probably conclude that it enhanced the value of the narrative. I shall return to that example later.

Obviously critics who look at the Bible stories in this light have had to rid themselves of an unconscious equation between antiquity and simplicity; they believe such narrative may be extremely complex in its structure and effects, yet in ways very different from modern narrative. That is why most of them refuse to ignore history; they must situate the ancient texts in the past and be mindful of the difficulties entailed by the fact that they themselves, the interpreters, exist in an historical context which is in obvious respects remote from that of the texts they are studying, though not completely cut off from it.

Tzvetan Todorov has remarked that the tacit application to ancient texts of recent criteria of value—such as stylistic unity, non-contradiction, non-digression, non-repetition—can only result in a deceptive or patronizing reading. Robert Alter adds that if we applied these criteria to such books as *Ulysses, The Sound and the Fury, Tristram Shandy* and *La Jalousie,* we should adjudge them also to be "shoddily 'redacted' literary scraps."[2] I might add a favorite example of my own: Theodore Dreiser condemned Ford's *The Good Soldier* on the ground that Ford had found a good story but ruined it by clumsy execution—he should have begun at the beginning and gone straight on to the end.[3] Presumably we should all agree that what is inept here is the comment, not the novel. And when talking about ancient narrative it is clearly right not to be blinkered by any modern prejudice, however natural it seems. Good narratives take a great many forms at different times, and even at one time. It is in this sense that the analyst, with his attention on the text before him, is nevertheless an historian.

DAVID, BATHSHEBA AND URIAH

What I propose to do now is to give some simple instances of the modern interpretation of narratives from both the Jewish and the Christian Bibles, and then ask briefly what we are to conclude from them. I shall have to leave aside the matter of parable, though it is obviously interesting as providing the sort of narrative which is formally incomplete *without* interpretation; perhaps it is so only more obviously than other narrative, but the point, which is on some approaches central to the whole question, I have at present no time to expound. Instead I shall ask you to think first about the familiar story of David, Bathsheba and Uriah.

I choose this episode because it was the subject of a famous article by Menakhem Perry and Meir Sternberg, first published in Hebrew in 1968. In a revised form it forms the core of Sternberg's book *The Poetics of Biblical Narrative* (Bloomington, 1985). In the intervening years it attracted much comment and is the ancestor of many roughly similar studies.

The theme of the narrative, which runs from 2 Samuel 11:1 to 12:31, is murder and adultery, though until the last part of the sequence there is no open condemnation of David as adulterer and murderer. And although the story contains a variety of incidents—a military campaign, a seduction, the death of Bathsheba's husband Uriah and of her child by David, and so on—it is tersely, even reticently told, even at points which seem to us to cry out for expansion and explanation. Sternberg believes that reticence is an essential aspect of the technique of such narratives; they contain significant "gaps." Of course all stories have gaps—total explanation would be intolerable—and it is not a new discovery that they can be subtly used. For example, Henry James and E.M. Forster both discuss the exploitation in novels of what is not expressly stated, and after their day Robbe-Grillet developed a whole theory and practice of the gap (and indeed of repetition and internal contradiction). Sternberg distinguishes between gaps and blanks, the latter being, roughly, the kind of thing we are not told about even in Leopold Bloom's day, simply because to tell absolutely everything would be pathologically tedious. Gaps are different because they have a positive part in the plot. I think myself that Sternberg is a little too confident that he can invariably tell a blank from a gap, but that there is a difference is undoubted.

In this story of David and Bathsheba he finds many rich gaps. The biblical text is omniscient—the narrator knows what is going on in people's heads, and even what God thinks about it all—but omniscience doesn't entail omni-communicativeness. The omniscient author leaves gaps in which the reader must work for his own meanings. He must work equally on repetitions and what may look like redundant explanations, which also contribute to the effect of the whole. I should add one more point: Sternberg is far from being a libertarian. He believes there are strong constraints on interpretation, and that there is a standard of competence by which interpreters must be measured. Like others before him, he labors to define this "competence."

The Rabbis knew gaps when they saw them. For example, there is a dissonance, or a gap, between David, king of Israel and author of the Psalms, and David, the scheming opportunist, the lecher and murderer of the Bathsheba story. To fill this gap they rather uneasily suggested that it was the custom for Israelite soldiers to divorce their wives before going into battle so that the women, if widowed, could escape levirate marriage; if not, they could remarry their husbands after the war. If it can be assumed that Uriah had done this, David can at least be acquitted of adultery. This may not strike us as competent interpretation; the excuse does rather little for David, and it jars with the whole context. But you see the point: something is required from the reader. Sternberg's modern gap-filling is not moral but technical.

The gaps arise from the habitual reticence of the narrator, and impose on us the need to ask and answer questions: for example, does Uriah know, or suspect, that his wife has been unfaithful? Does he deduce from David's bringing him back from the front, making much of him, and urging him to go home to his own house, that the king badly wants him to sleep with Bathsheba, so that the paternity of the child conceived in his absence can plausibly be attributed to Uriah? If, as seems likely, Bathsheba's bath was a post-menstrual purification, the child couldn't be thought to be her husband's unless he slept with her on this occasion. Or perhaps the bath is mentioned not solely to explain the arousal of David's desire at seeing Bathsheba naked, but also to indicate that he was at least not guilty of ritual impurity? This seems unlikely, but such are the questions raised by gaps. And there is an inexplicitness about the entire tale; for example, we are told very little about the early stages of the love affair, and very little about Uriah.

There is another difficulty. What is David doing in Jerusalem watching Bathsheba when he should be with his troops? The campaign is said to be occurring "at the time when kings go forth to battle," and David is king precisely because he is supposed to be good at leading from the front. Moreover, we are soon to learn that although he avoided the fighting he did not deny himself the glory or the plunder of conquest. Joab, having subdued the enemy city, stood back and waited for David to occupy it formally. Are we to infer that he cheated his subordinate of the spoils, as he had cheated Uriah first of his wife and then of his life? These are possible inferences; yet little is done actively to solicit our disapproval of the king; and when God decrees the death of his child by Bathsheba we are made to feel sorry for David in his wretchedness, and surprised—even impressed?—by his extraordinary recovery when the infant actually dies.

These are samples of the Sternbergian gaps, where competent readers must go to work, each making sense of them in his own way. Normally we do so without reflecting on our procedures; Sternberg is trying to formalize our unexamined operations, performed because we need to do something about what we are expected to know without being told. Why did David send for Uriah? To ask forgiveness? To offer a bribe? To get him to bed with his wife? Why did Uriah stay away from her? For the reason he himself gave, namely that he shouldn't enjoy home comforts while his comrades were still in the tented field? Or because he saw through David's trickery, and wanted him to be stuck with the paternity of the child?

It's not part of the argument that one can always fill the gaps positively. When David and Uriah are together you can ask yourself what David thinks Uriah is thinking: did he know or think that Uriah knew about him and Bathsheba? Did he think or know Uriah didn't know? Was he undecided between these possibilities? And so on. We may have to content ourselves with coexistent possibilities. Sternberg's examination of these matters is always exhilarating, and it seems obvious that once you get hold of the idea that this sort of narrative works as much by what it doesn't as by what it does say, you are on the way to a richer understanding of biblical narrative.

One of the critics who was impressed by the Perry-Sternberg article was Robert Alter. He tells us he had long pondered another strange moment in 2 Samuel, chapter 3. Abner is sent away by David "in peace" (*vayeleikh beshalom*), and this expression is thrice repeated; when Joab arrives he is angry about Abner's safe departure, and asks the king "Why did you send him away, going off?" ("and he is quite gone," King James Version). Here the Hebrew is *vayeleikh halokh,* a partial repetition of the formula of dismissal; and yet this time it recalls a euphemism for dying. Reading the Perry-Sternberg article, Alter came to understand that such near-repetitions make openings into the minds of the characters and the subtle movements of plot. Joab at once follows up his modification of the dismissal formula by assassinating Abner.[4]

Working on his own, Alter added much of value to this kind of narrative analysis. He reminds us how *dialogue* is used to highlight parts of the David story, with the effect that although so much else is going on, the murder of Uriah is made its central theme. Between David and Bathsheba there is a total absence of dialogue; thus adultery is relegated to the position of a contributory cause.[5] Another commentator, Adele Berlin, adds some remarks on the passivity of Bathsheba—she merely interests David by taking a conspicuous bath. We don't know whether she welcomed the king's advances or simply submitted to the royal will. She finds herself in what most women would think a difficult situation— she is an adulteress, pregnant by her lover; then a widow; then a be- reaved mother. But nothing is made of all this; she is not shown as feeling guilt or even grief, though David suffers both. In short, as Berlin puts it, she is "a complete non-person, simply part of the plot." And she doesn't acquire character until, as the wife of David and the mother of Solomon, she is involved in a succession crisis and replaced by Abishag in the old king's bed. Only then is she allowed to take part in the dialogue; no longer simply an agent, she is at last something like a person.[6]

So insights accumulate. Joel Rosenberg considers David's reply to Nathan's parable: the rich man, he says, should pay the value of the poor man's ewe four times over (2 Sam 12:1ff). This is not merely involuntary self-condemnation but unconscious prophecy; for David will pay four times over for the theft of Uriah's wife. Amnon will rape Tamar and be murdered by Absalom; Absalom will be killed by Joab, who had earlier despatched Uriah; and Adonijah will die as a direct consequence of Bathsheba's intercession with her son Solomon on his behalf.[7]

These modern commentators don't presume that they are the first to notice the characteristics they discuss; they are only trying to give more formal accounts of them. One could accumulate evidence to show that earlier commentators had dealt with the reticences of the story— and with the moral difficulties they create—in ways that seemed equally suitable to *them*. The Christian tradition used allegory as a solvent or gap-filler: Bathsheba's bath was an allegory of baptism, David's polyg- amy a figure for the union of many diverse peoples in the faith. But allegory of this kind can solve anything; and for some early commenta- tors the questions to be answered were more human and more commonplace. What was Bathsheba doing on the roof? Was she being immodest? Was the king perhaps seduced by her? Bathsheba, after all, makes an appearance among the ancestors of Jesus in Matthew's genealogy, where she is expressly described as the former wife of Uriah. She is one of the four women, all in various ways ambiguous and surprising presences, who are named in that document. That there was a mystery, a secret, no one could doubt. That the mystery has at any rate for the most part to do with the techniques of story-telling rather than with some allegorical message is the modern view I have been describing.

Perhaps this will suffice to show the modern emphasis on the creative character of reading, and on internal relations rather than on historical reference. It has been argued that in the David stories we witness a transition from myth into "historicized fiction," and there seems no doubt that skills long acquired from the reading of novels can be applied to freshen or even transform our reading of the Bible stories. Such acts of interpretation may be thought of as a modern equivalent of midrash, which, as Rosenberg remarks, knows of no single "correct" reading, but works to make us suspicious of every detail in the text.

NEW TESTAMENT NARRATIVE

The case is not very different in modern readings of New Testament narrative. They have ancestors—not only Auerbach but Austin Farrer and Amos Wilder. The structure of Mark was long thought to be amenable only to form-critical study; any structure it had was imposed as it were from without, in whatever material came into the Evangelist's hands. Farrer sought more or less occult indications of interior structuration (Wilder's approach was different). Now books exploring the literary qualities of Mark and the other gospels abound, some on structuralist principles, some using other modern methods or eclectic assemblages of several such, some dealing with isolated passages and some with whole texts. Once again the tendency is to accept the text as we have it rather than to look for a lost text or texts behind it. Narrow notions of intention are eschewed; what matters is that the patterns, analogues, relations, significant silences and significant repetitions are there to be perceived and developed.

This reaction from the "scientific" scholarly tradition meets, of course, with opposition, some of it very forceful; the new criticism is called a reversion to "pre-critical" methods. Its practitioners not surprisingly prefer to call their methods "post-critical." Yet it is true that they have some affinities with pre-critical interpretative practices. They require fidelity to the literal but deny that this is a bar to interpretative freedom. So the Tannaim claimed that their *derash* was the true sense of Scripture, and therefore identical with *peshat,* the literal sense; and so medieval Christians held that the literal sense of the Jewish Bible was the sense revealed in the New Testament. Of course the great difference between the old and the new is the difference implied by the term "historicized fiction." It took a considerable cultural upheaval to bring on a state of affairs in which it seemed possible, even perhaps necessary, to read the New Testament stories not in order to study their historical reference but to consider them as one might consider other instances of the art of fiction, and to do so in the conviction that this was the way to defend their religious value.

Here are some examples of such readings of Christian narrative. John alone introduces the character of Nicodemus. At his first appearance in Chapter 3, Nicodemus seems to be a type-figure, a specimen upper-class Jew, and Jews in John's Gospel have as their principal function the misunderstanding of Jesus. Nicodemus, "a ruler of the Jews," well-placed, serious, recognizes that Jesus is "a teacher come from God." But we are to infer that this recognition is imperfect because dependent on the miracles ("signs") he has observed—which is the case with most Jewish acknowledgments of Jesus. So his salutation is received not with a courteous word but with a dark saying: "Except a man be born again, he cannot see the kingdom of God." Nicodemus is baffled; Jesus, having prefaced his saying with the "Amen, amen" that vouches for its absolute veracity, has spoken figuratively, and Nicodemus doesn't understand the figure, blindly supposing that Jesus is talking about carnal generation. His rejoinder produces more gnomic sentences, though by verse 9 he should understand that what is being described is a spiritual rebirth "from above." "How can these things be?" he asks.

As so often, Jesus answers the question with another question: "Art thou a master of Israel, and knowest not these things?" It is as if this intelligent man was missing something obvious. And further explanation, which contains an obscure prophecy of redemption, seems not to help Nicodemus. He doesn't go out into the night from which he came; he simply fades away, and the dialogue becomes a monologue. We *could* say, following the critical tradition, that a discourse of Jesus has got attached to a tradition about Nicodemus, or we could hypothesize a careless redactor, who simply forgot to move Nicodemus offstage. Or we could speculate as to what became of him. He had come in out of the darkness to visit the Light, but he may then have retreated into an even blacker darkness, meriting therefore the condemnation of v.19: "And this is the condemnation, that light is come into the world, and men loved darkness rather than light, because their deeds were evil." On the other hand Nicodemus *had* sought the light, and was therefore not one of those who failed to do so lest their deeds should be reproved (v. 20). Some work is here asked of the reader; there is certainly some sort of gap.

It has often been noticed that John likes to make each of his episodes mirror in little the whole narrative, as this one does by prophecy and by implication: the Jews were shown the light but remained dark to the end. But its links with the whole story are too strong to be described as mere reflections or analogues. From the Prologue we know about the cardinal antithesis of darkness and light. We know that in many ways, for example by declaring himself the antitype of Moses lifting up the brazen serpent—"even so must the Son of man be lifted up," v. 14— Jesus affirms a relation of fulfillment to the Old Testament, and the repeated failure of the Jews to understand such typologies is a recurrent theme. So there certainly are reflections. Yet there is something simpler and more striking about the narrative treatment of Nicodemus. He has not in fact disappeared for good. He returns briefly at 7:50. There we learn that some people think of Jesus as "the Prophet" or "the Christ," but the Pharisees obstinately declare that people who support him are ignorant of the Law and accursed. They also say that no prophet can come from Galilee.

It is at this moment that Nicodemus inquires whether the Law allows a man to be condemned without a hearing, a remark which draws upon him the accusation of being a supporter of Jesus. Nicodemus says only one thing, and it sounds like liberal good sense; but the Pharisees read it as pro-Christian, and they may, by an irony, be right. The implication may be either that proper observance of the Law is in fact Christian, or that Nicodemus is of the Christian party without knowing or openly declaring it. And is he still the puzzled, rational fellow of Chapter 3, or does this brief reappearance hint at a development of his capacities?

Another possibility is that John was preparing for the third appearance of Nicodemus at the climax of the story, and, wanting us to keep him in mind, inserted him in the middle as well as at both ends. Yet the final appearance offers no simple and satisfying explanation of his role. It happens at 19:39, when Nicodemus turns up with Joseph of Arimathea, described as a disciple of Jesus; they are bearing ointments to prepare the body for burial. And that is the end of him. We are not told that he had become, or was to become, a disciple. He may simply have wished to honor in death the man he had long since recognized as a great teacher. He may have joined Joseph in order to dissociate himself from the acts and opinions of the Pharisees. If we want to argue that he is no longer among the condemned—or even if we want to argue that he is—we shall have to make up a plot connecting his three appearances, in none of which is he given an unambiguous part to play. John, then, is reticent; he withholds explanations. Narrative certainly serves both to aid memory and to explain; those are its primary functions. But it also deals in oblivion and secrecy.

THE RAISING OF LAZARUS

John is in some ways the most subtle story-teller of the Evangelists. The raising of Lazarus in Chapter 11 is only in his Gospel, and it is unlike the raisings from the dead in the others, not least because of its extended treatment and the ambiguities of its presentation. There can be no doubt of its structural significance, occurring as it does at the great hinge of John's narrative, just before the start of the Passion story. Indeed it is more than anything else what makes his account of the last days of Jesus different from all the others. In John, Lazarus is one target of the chief priests' enmity—they rather absurdly want to kill him for having been resurrected and making converts in the process. Some will say that John put the tale together from disparate parts of the other gospels; but however he came by the material he clearly resolved to treat it differently, for example in the matter of length—forty-five verses from the announcement of Lazarus' sickness to his emergence from the tomb.

Jesus announces that the sickness is not unto death; and for reasons we can only guess at, he delays for two days his journey to Bethany. At v. 14 he announces plainly that Lazarus is dead, with an implication that he, Jesus, had required this to be the case ("I am glad for your sakes that I was not there, to the intent ye may believe"). Six verses later Martha comes out to meet him, with what sounds like a quiet reproach: "If thou hadst been here, my brother had not died." He assures her that her brother will rise from the dead. Martha takes this to mean that he will rise "at the last day," and Jesus tells her, "I am the resurrection and the life." After twelve more verses Mary, the other sister, encounters Jesus, repeating Martha's complaint almost word for word: "If thou hadst been here my brother had not died." We may now have some expectation that

Jesus will repeat his words to Martha; instead, he weeps. He shows signs of great distress, "groaning in himself" (v. 38); and in the account of the dead man's emergence from the tomb it is almost as if Jesus himself were suffering birthpangs, crying out "with a loud voice, 'Lazarus, come forth' " (v. 43). And Lazarus does come forth, still bound in his grave clothes.

Why is the conversation with Martha partly, but only partly, repeated with Mary? It is sometimes suggested, in the "critical" manner, that the author or redactor is clumsily putting together two traditions. That view takes no account of the narrative depth and richness of the passage. The progress of Jesus to the tomb is uncannily slow as v. 30 emphasizes; it is as if, in the midst of all the interruptions, some ritual were being performed. We expect the meeting with Mary to replicate exactly that with Martha, as it might in a folktale (or a rite); perhaps a third encounter will follow, as, with enormous effect, it does, when Lazarus also comes out to meet him. But the meeting with Mary is not a duplicate; there is no repetition of the divine pronouncement ("I am the resurrection and the life"—the *ego eimi,* the "I am," of John is always an affirmation of divinity). Instead there is a man, weeping, capable of human love and grief. He asks where Lazarus has been laid, and says nothing more until the prayer and the command to come forth, which is uttered in a loud voice—the Greek words being exactly the same as those used by Matthew of Jesus uttering his last cry on the cross, also dying to bring about rebirth.

There is here a blend of reticence and express statement. Martha is played off against Mary, the humanity of Jesus against his divinity; this most spectacular miracle is finally a figure for the spiritual sense of resurrection and its human cost. It has many functions, including a part in the political plot. It remembers the plot of miracle or sign misunderstood. One could go on. But the point is its reticence, and its imaginative resource, not inferior to those of the great Old Testament stories.

THE ANOINTING OF JESUS

One final example—this time a story told by all four Evangelists, so that here we have an advantage denied us in the other instances cited, namely that we can see what four different hands made of the same material. The story is of the anointing of Jesus at the house of Lazarus, Martha and Mary in Bethany. At any rate, that is John's story. In Mark and Matthew the anointing is done by a "woman," not otherwise described or named, at the house of Simon the leper (Mk 14:3; Mt 26:6). In both these versions the woman pours the ointment on the head of Jesus; in Mark some, and in Matthew all, of the disciples protest about the waste, and are reproved by Jesus, who says the woman has done a beautiful thing and prepared his body for burial (vv. 3–9, 6–13). Luke places the story earlier in the ministry and says that it happened in the house of Simon the *Pharisee;* he describes the woman as a "sinner" (7:35–50). This woman washes the feet of Jesus and wipes them with her hair before anointing his head. The Pharisee says to himself that a genuine prophet would have known the woman was a sinner; and Jesus, reading his thoughts, replies with a parable-like saying that the woman's love is greater than the Pharisee's, and that her sins, though many, will be forgiven.

Obviously Luke's point would have been lost had Simon himself been a leper and so unclean, for he wanted the contrast between the Pharisee and his loveless virtue and the woman sinner with her faith and devotion. Mark had something else in mind, namely Jesus' choice of table companions, and his wish to act as physician to the sick. John deviates even more widely from the Marcan account than Luke does. With his usual economy he identifies the woman with Mary, the sister of Lazarus. She anoints his feet, not his head—and that is an extraordinary thing to have done; she then wipes his feet with her hair, which is even more extraordinary, more appropriate to Luke's sinner than to a virtuous woman. The protest against waste, which is omitted by Luke and in Mark and Matthew made by several disciples or all of them, is made in John's version by Judas alone. John alone characterized Judas as the thieving pursebearer, now ripe for an act much more wicked than petty theft. His complaint is preceded by a clear indication of its place in his developing career as a criminal: "Then saith one of the disciples, Judas Iscariot, Simon's son, which should betray him . . ." (12:4).

John's version exhibits a concern for causal connection and economy of characterization that is found everywhere in his narrative. Some might prefer Luke's version, which is adorned by a parable and contains a well-wrought contrast between the reserve of the Pharisee and the tenderness of the woman. But John has found a stronger place for the tale; he relates it not only to the coming betrayal but to the earlier scene with Mary before the raising of Lazarus. It is interesting that this tradition of interpretation by narrative (clearly originating in the "midrashic habit") should have been continued in later Christian thought; for the woman not otherwise specified by Mark and Matthew, and the woman who was in Luke a sinner, and Mary, the sister of Lazarus in John, were combined with Mary Magdalene not only in the popular imagination, but also in the ecclesiastic tradition, for the identification is perpetuated in the Roman Catholic liturgical calendar.

When one speaks of connexity in New Testament narratives one should not neglect the deepest connection of all, the connection with the Jewish Bible. I cannot now enlarge on that theme—the creation of fictive history or historicized fiction by the development of ancient narrative germs. It is a dominant characteristic of New Testament narrative. To rewrite the old in terms of a later state of affairs is an ancient Jewish practice. One of the points I've tried to make is that in their manner of writing stories there was much in common between the authors of the two Bibles. A revaluation of their techniques and methods in the light of our own knowledge of what it is to follow—to cooperate with—a story should serve to refresh our perceptions. And it may not be too much to hope that the efforts now being devoted to this end may solve some of the difficulties that have for so long beset modern readers of ancient writings.

NOTES

1. James S. Ackerman, "Joseph, Judah and Jacob," in Kenneth R.R. Gros Louis and J.S. Ackerman, eds., *More Literary Interpretations of Biblical Narratives* (Abingdon, 1982).

2. Tzvetan Todorov, *The Poetics of Prose,* trans. Richard Howard (Ithaca, N.Y., 1977), pp. 53–65; Robert Alter, *The Art of Biblical Narrative* (New York, 1981), p. 21.

3. Frank MacShane, ed., *Ford Maddox Ford: The Critical Heritage* (London, 1972), pp. 47–51.

4. "The Challenge of the Texts," Commencement Address at the Los Angeles School, Hebrew Union College, 1985.

5. Robert Alter, *The Art of Biblical Narrative* (New York, 1981), p. 182.

6. Adele Berlin, *Poetics and Interpretation of Biblical Narrative* (Sheffield, 1983), pp. 26–27.

7. Joel Rosenberg, "Meanings, Morals and Mysteries: Literary Approaches to Torah," *Response,* 26 (1975), 67ff.

Figurative Speech: Function, Form, Exegesis—A Linguistic Approach

Paul Michel

Once upon a time, a wicked government ordered that the Israelites were not to study the Torah. At that time Papos ben Yehuda came and encountered Rabbi Aqiva, who held open meetings and studied the Torah. He said to him: "Aqiva, are you not afraid of the wicked government?" Aqiva replied: "I want to recount a parable to which this can be compared:

A fox was going along the bank of a river and as he saw the fish gathering from place to place, he said to them: "From what are you fleeing?" The fish answered: "From the nets which people cast for us!" Then the fox said to them: "Why don't you come on land so that we, you and I, can live together just like my ancestors and your ancestors once lived together?" The fish replied: "Is it you of whom they say that he is the cleverest of all animals? You are not clever at all, you are stupid. If we are already afraid in the water how much more must we be afraid on land where we are sure to die!"

"And so it is with us", Rabbi Aqiva continued, "if we are already in such a situation as we sit and study the Torah, of which is said 'for it is life for you and length of days' (Deut. 30:20), how much worse if we would go and turn away from the Torah." (*Babylonian Talmud, Berakhot 61b*)

The attitude of Rabbi Aqiva seems questionable to Papos ben Yehuda because he operates out of the following hierarchy of values: saving one's life in face of the Roman occupation is more important than studying the Torah. Rabbi Aqiva's hierarchy of values is just the opposite, and he knows that it is very difficult to change someone's preconceived notions. As a result, Aqiva tells a story in which a hierarchy of values is presented which the questioner accepts as well and which can analogously be transferred to Aqiva's situation. To act in a manner to which you have been destined (fish naturally belong in water) is less dangerous than to act in a manner to which you have not been destined (fish on land). In relation to this hierarchy, all possible dangers in the destined mode of life are of secondary importance (the nets do not catch every fish, but on land every fish is sure to die). Aqiva makes a connection with the introductory question by means of the biblical citation. The Torah is the life principle for the Jew, which, if given up, brings certainty of death. In the face of this, the persecutions of the Romans (like the nets of the fish) are to be ignored. Through the selection of the figure in the story (fox), the questioner, Papos ben Yehuda, is characterized as one who considers himself clever, but whose cleverness is exposed as stupidity.

The anecdote is typical for the culture from which it originates. The pedagogy of the rabbi consists of letting the questioner find the truth himself by telling him a parable. Rabbi Aqiva convinces Papos by means of figurative speech. A parable stands in the service of persuasion.

While in the Graeco-Roman culture we know of only about a dozen parables in which the situational setting has also been handed down,[1] we find approximately 500 to 1,400 parables[2] in the rabbinic tradition which have made their way to us together with their situational contexts (whereby it is of no importance whether that setting is original or was added later). This presents an ideal source of material for investigations like the following.

1. FORMULATION OF THE PROBLEM. TOOLS OF ANALYSIS

The following simple semiotic concept, taken from Ferdinand de Saussure, is our starting point: The text consists of a "signifiant" and a "signifié" ("medium" and "message" respectively). In common texts (ordinary language) (e.g. minutes of a meeting, radio news report), the "signifiant" imparts the "signifié" in an immediate and transparent fashion. In a lyrical poem, the "signifiant" is the primary focus of interest; independent of whatever meaning it intends to convey, the reader/hearer can find a message in the rhythm, rhyme, and intonation: "the medium *is* the message."[3] Parables are more or less hybrids. On the one hand, they have been composed as aesthetical works of art, like lyrical poems. On the other, they are dedicated to their message in the same way as common texts. (More will be presented about the dual nature of the aesthetics of the parables at the end of this essay.) Depending on which aspect is emphasized, the interest of the parable researcher is directed either more to the formal, aesthetical dimension or to that of the contents.

In my book *Alieniloquium*[4] I have focused predominantly on the second dimension by means of an investigation of the dialectical function of the parables. I understand the term "dialectic" in the same sense in which it was used in ancient rhetoric, as that system of speech which serves to convince someone who at first is of a different opinion, but who can be brought to accept the opinion of the speaker on the grounds of a commonly recognized basis of argumentation. Dialectic raises the question of how it is possible to win a hearing, or even outwit the hearer, through mere speech. Which mechanisms are at work, what are the rules of the game? Ancient rhetoric has experienced a renaissance in modern linguistics, especially through John L. Austin's book with the programmatic title "How To Do Things with Words" (published in 1962).

Anyone who ever compared the definitions of "simile," "parable," "example," "allegory," etc. in the various reference books will have noted that all these terms are related to one another.[5] "Related" is meant here in the sense of Ludwig Wittgenstein's theory of "family resemblances." Although each genre mentioned above is unique, any one of them may well share one or another constitutive element with another. Therefore, instead of attempting to define each of these genres as such in relation to the others, it is more helpful to isolate the various elements which form them and then describe them. My aim is to enable as exact a description of these elements as possible by means of a set of very few units. Such a descriptive grid, however, should not only serve the purpose of classification, but rather, beyond that, also demonstrate how dialectic speech functions in parables in general, as well as in individual cases. The goal, then, is to identify the constitutive elements from which each individual case can be systematically constructed.

The following theoretical concepts have proved to be helpful tools for my purpose:

Model

Models are employed where a topic is not well known. We call such a poorly understood topic an *explanandum*. The system which serves as a model, on the other hand, is well known. It is taken from a world of categories completely different from that of the original topic. Corresponding features between the explanandum and the model are highlighted, while irrelevant ones are relegated to the shadows. Models can serve different functions. In the case of parables, the following two are the most significant:

> The function of didactical illustration;

> The heuristic function, in which the model serves to explore certain features of the explanandum hitherto unknown.—This second function has to do with those metaphors in classical rhetoric which are employed because of *inopia verborum*.[6]

The concept of a model has been used in a very fruitful way by Max Black in his metaphor theory and by I.T. Ramsey in the field of theology.[7] Every kind of figurative speech uses models in order to address the issues in question.

Speech Act

A central concept in my own approach is the term speech act, which was introduced into linguistics by John L. Austin and John R. Searle.[8] (See the explanation of the various functions below.)

Formal Logic

To the extent that figurative speech is very often used to posit certain conclusions which are only vaguely implied, one must consult the system of syllogisms as derived from formal logic, and particularly the system of *enthymema*. An enthymeme is an argument in which not all of the premises are explicitly stated, but one of the premises is implicitly understood.[9] Furthermore, logic explains how to analyze analogous and generalizing arguments, which are important for the exegesis of models.

Theory of Argumentation

Classical logic must be expanded, however, when dealing with recommending, dissuading, and evaluating actions. That is particularly true in relation to the theory of argumentation as it has been developed by Stephan Toulmin.[10]

2. THE CONSTITUTIVE ELEMENTS OF FIGURATIVE SPEECH

The constitutive elements of figurative speech can be assigned to the following three categories:

2.1 The *function* of figurative speech. In terms of dialectic, either that which the speaker wishes to substantiate, or the answer to a question from the audience, e.g. "What should I do?" "What is the case?" "Why is something that way and not another?"

2.2 The *formal structure* of figurative speech. This does not refer to literary forms, e.g. the typifying of persons involved, *parallelismus membrorum,* construction according to incremental elements, or expansion to useless minutiae, but rather formal-logical structures such as: "When someone in situation S carries out action A he commits an injustice," or "For all persons P of class C, it is true that they have the quality Q."

2.3 Some *interpretative operations* (types of exegesis) through which the function (2.1) can be obtained from the formal structure (2.2).

The elements of the three categories (2.1–2.3) are interconnected in a systematic-conclusive fashion. Not every formal structure can fulfill each function.

2.1 THE FUNCTION OF FIGURATIVE SPEECH

We begin with a more precise definition of the notion "speech act." The smallest communicative unit, in which a relationship is established among the speaker, the audience, the subject matter and an action, is called a speech act.

This can be illustrated by means of an example. A person with a dog says to a child who wants to pet the animal, "The dog bites." The following aspects of that message (i.e. the communicative point of purpose) can be distinguished:

The *propositional content* (the subject in question): that the dog will bite when a stranger touches it.

The *illocutionary force* (taken from Austin): that the person with the dog has given a "warning" in what he said. (To warn someone is a communicative action.)

There is an infinite number of possible propositional contents, but a finite repertoire of illocutionary forces, e.g. "to warn someone," "to convince someone of something," "to rebuke someone for something," etc. Speech act theory has set for itself the goal of discovering the underlying conditions of an utterance which make it possible for the intended illocutionary force to be successfully communicated (per Searle: "happiness conditions"). Parables are the appropriate size for a speech act (i.e. they are on a larger scale than a single word, yet smaller than complex texts). For this reason, the analysis of parables with the help of speech act theory is very promising.

In ordinary utterances other functions are superimposed upon the illocutionary force. The position within a dialogue or a particular context in which a speech act is expressed is important and can determine whether an opponent "starts an argument," or a proponent "defends his thesis." One could speak here of a *conversational function*.

There are other functions in addition to this. For example, we might speak of *interactional functions* (i.e. by means of an utterance I can try to "gain prestige," or "save face," etc.). Utterances also have *psychological* and *aesthetic* functions.

Finally, each speech act is dedicated to an *action* which aims at a concrete change in the given situation, e.g. "increasing a company's sales," "preventing the neighbor from doing something foolish," etc.

Each type of function makes a specific contribution to the analysis. For the time being I will leave these superimposed functions which I have described out of the picture (taking them up again in section four) and concentrate here on the illocutionary force.

There are basically two main groups of illocutive forces which can be identified in figurative speech. First, the model demonstrates or clarifies *what* an unknown word means or *how* an unknown thing functions, as in the case of the question "What is sin?" The explanandum grammatically has the dimension of a word.

Secondly, the model helps to demonstrate *that* a particular issue in question is actually true: e.g. "Is it true that sins can be removed?" The explanandum grammatically has the dimension of a statement. (It does not matter whether it concerns the proof of a thesis, support for demanding an action, a reason for giving comfort, etc.)

That these two basic functions cannot be identified from the form of the text alone is important (see the parables of the fig rennin below).

Let us take a look at two rabbinic *meshalim* (parables) with prominent illocutionary forces of the second type. The context of the first example explicitly exhibits the function "consoling."

> When Rabban Yohanan ben Zakkai's son died, his disciples came to comfort him. The first disciple made reference to Adam, who had allowed himself to be consoled with the death of Abel. R. Yohanan then said: "Is it not enough that I carry my own grief? Must you remind me of the grief of Adam as well?"

> The second disciple referred to Job, who allowed himself to be consoled after the loss of all his sons and daughters. R. Yohanan once again reacted crossly.

> The third disciple brought Aaron as an example, and the fourth disciple the example of David. Each time no consolation was accepted.

> At last Rabbi Eleazar ben 'Arak told a parable: *A king deposited a certain object with a man so that the man would keep it for him. Each day the man would weep and cry out, saying: "When will this responsibility be lifted from me, so I can live in peace?"* "The same is the case with you, Rabbi. You had a son (. . .) and he departed from the world without sin. And you should be consoled that you could return intact that which had been entrusted to you."

> In this Rabban Yohanan found consolation.[11]

The following parable, which is taken from a Midrash, deals with the question of why God imposed the dietary laws (Leviticus 11) on the Israelites alone, and not on the other peoples of the world as well. The illocutionary force here is "to provide an aetiological substantiation."

> Rabbi Tanhum ben Hanilai said (. . .) "To what may this be compared? *To a physician who went to see two sick people, one whose life was not in danger and the other who was near death. The physician said to the one whose life was not threatened: "You should not eat such and such things!" And in the case of the other man near death, he said to the people: "Give him whatever he wants to eat!"*

> So it is with the people of the world who are not chosen for life in the world to come: "Every creature that lives and moves shall be food for you . . ." (Gen. 9:3). But to the Israelites, who are there to live in Gan Eden: "These are the living things which you may eat among all the beasts that are on earth" (Lev. 11:2).[12]

There are parables which "postulate a norm," those which "suggest a way of acting," others which "clarify a paradox," "make an action-result connection plausible" or "characterize a complex of circumstances," among many others.

2.2 THE FORMAL STRUCTURE OF FIGURATIVE SPEECH

Formal structure is not a very fruitful starting point for the analysis of figurative speech for two reasons. The first is that parables of a certain structure can have completely different functions. One cannot in any way determine which function (or illocutionary force) is at hand based solely upon the structure. Moreover, one must know the question which the speaker intends to answer with the parable. This can be illustrated with the following pair of short parables:

Homer uses the following parable to illustrate how Ares was healed by a wink from Zeus' eyes: *Just as fig rennin quickly solidifies white milk, the liquid milk curdling rapidly while being stirred, the raging Ares was just as quickly healed.*[13] We are dealing here with a parable that illustrates the qualities of an occurrence. It answers the question: "How did the healing of Ares occur?"

Apparently, Empedocles uses the same parable. *Just as fig rennin thickens white milk and binds it.*[14] He uses it, however, with a completely different function. Empedocles had solved the problem of the coexistence of constant change and eternal stability in the cosmos by means of his theory of the elements, which form the world as they alternately divide and combine among themselves. He now applies the parable of the (sour) rennin and the (sweet) milk in order to make plausible his cosmological assertion that something fixed and enduring can be made out of opposing primary elements. In this case, the parable answers the question: "Is it possible that . . . ?" Its function is to support an assertion (thesis).

In order to present the second reason that formal structure makes analysis so difficult, I need to explain something in greater detail. To make sure that a speech act can achieve its goal, several conditions, which Searle has identified, must be fulfilled. Among other things, the proposition must have a certain logical structure. For instance, in order for the question "What time is it?" to fulfill its purpose, the utterance must contain a gap. For me to be able to recommend something to

someone, the recommendation, which has been formulated in the proposition, must be an act which is seen by the addressee as authentic and
desired, and so on. There are only a few logical structures that are suited
to what we have referred to as propositional content, as was indicated
above.

Before the hearer, using Aristotle's logic, can draw conclusions
from a piece of conversation by means of syllogism, it should first be
possible to reduce it to a certain logical structure.

> Examples: The sequential ordering of the characteristics of an individ-
> ual (The following applies to X: it has the qualities a, b, c, d, e,
> whereby—per analogiam—a, c, e can be transferred to X); the struc-
> ture of implication (Whenever the subject x, then the subject y, x
> applies; consequently y applies); the structure of a universal predicate
> (Of all X within the set T, the following applies: X has the quality Q:
> Y belongs to the set T also, therefore Y has the quality Q as well); or
> the structure of a hierarchy of values (In the situation S, X is more
> valuable than Y), etc.

To use a concept from modern structuralism, the *surface structure*
does not reflect the *deep structure*. They are incongruent, and therefore
the necessary logical structures are not self-evident in the text.[15] This can
be seen in the following example.

The sense of the proverb "The cat likes to eat fish, but does not like
to go in the water" is obvious. If I want to be able to apply it to a
concrete situation in life, I cannot take its apparent surface structure (C
wants a, but not b) as a starting point. Rather I have to expose its logical
core: "Unless you put up with adversities, you cannot reach your goal."
This deep structure enables me to draw a conclusion.

A narrator of parables does not necessarily carry an analogy
through in all its details on the narrative surface level. In his narrative he
can focus on the first eye-catching detail and then simply allow the rest
to follow. Moreover, some narrators prefer to cloak a particular precept
or principle (e.g. scientific, social or psychological areas) in a story
rather than in some abstract discursive statement. Both of these stylistic
categories are present in Jesus' parable of the pearl (Mt 13:45). He does
not say, "In a same way that you would give up everything for a precious
pearl, so also, you should also give up everything for the sake of the
kingdom of heaven" (which is what would logically lie at the heart of his

parable), but rather, "The kingdom of heaven is like a merchant in search of fine pearls . . ."

The distinction between surface structure and deep structure can also be seen in the parable of the old garment (Mk 2:21–22 and parallels). The sentence "No one sews a piece of unshrunk cloth on an old garment" does not in itself make any meaningful contribution to the discussion. It is necessary to discover the reason why no one does such a thing, namely, when it becomes wet, the new cloth shrinks severely and, as a result, puts such a strain on the weakened, older cloth that the garment is completely destroyed. The following norm is here in question: "When the new comes, the old proves to be fragile."

In summary, the surface structure is influenced by literary modes and often serves to supply the rhetorical point, or purpose (e.g. the parable may lead up to a question or cause the listener to reflect). It is predisposed to aesthetic formulation. As people who either create and understand metaphors and parables in our ordinary speech or interpret them in a more scientific fashion, we are well versed in a number of strategies which help us to penetrate the surface of the text and, using that text as a source of information, reach the logical deep structure. We delete merely illuminative features, decipher abbreviations, move from a specific case to the general rule involved, and reconstruct the underlying operating principle in order to penetrate to the core of the message.

This core, as reconstructed by the interpreter, is the propositional content of the parable. It is sufficiently abstract and constructed in a form which is logically applicable enough that, on the one hand it represents a paraphrase of the contents of the parable, and on the other supplies a "springboard" for a speech act which sucessfully achieves its goal. I call this virtual entity the *pivot* of the parable,[16] which, being concretized in the real world and supplied with the required illocutive force, yields the communicative point of the parable. In the Phaedrus fables such abstract sentences which build a bridge from the world of illustration (model) to the real world (explanandum) are formulated as "promythion" or "epimythion."

Naturally, the surface structure cannot simply be ignored. Its contribution to the communicative process deserves particular esteem. That can only be appreciated, however, when the difference between it and the logical deep structure has been identified. This subject will be dealt with in greater detail below.

2.3 FOUR INTERPRETATIVE OPERATIONS (TYPES OF EXEGESIS)

A more precise definition of "exegesis" is necessary here. Above all, a pseudo-psychological misunderstanding must be dismissed. Exegesis should not be thought of as an insight into mental processes. It also does not imply that those who are seeking to understand recite to themselves exegetical rules when they are at the point of reaching that understanding. On the contrary, in order to describe exegesis one must establish a scientific construct which, by means of a limited number of defined elements and rules, makes plausible how a statement can supply the answer to a given question, how a statement can form a warning within a certain context, etc.

First, the question arises as to whether a statement is to be understood as "direct" or as a parable. That can only be determined on the basis of how it is embedded in a certain context or a situation. The sentence "The cat likes to eat fish, but does not like to go in the water" is understood differently in the case of two animal lovers who observe a cat lurking at the edge of a goldfish pond, than when we cite it in gossiping with each other about the youth who has an attractive, rich girlfriend, but does not want to marry her. In the second case, the statement in its literal sense does not correspond directly with the situation at hand. The listener has to know certain exegetical rules in order to grasp the point of the statement. He must understand it as figurative speech.

The fact that such *incongruencies* form an impulse for the exegesis of a text was already recognized by the Rabbis. The commentary *Midrash Rabba* comments on Ecclesiastes 9:8 "Let your garments be always white; let not oil be lacking on your head":

> "If the verse were speaking about white garments, how many white garments the peoples of the world have! And if the verse were speaking about good oils, how many good oils the people of the world have! Behold, therefore the verse is speaking of the commandments and the good works and the Law."[17]

It is established here with penetrating hermeneutical insight that the injunction of the preacher Solomon would be meaningless if it were simply to be understood literally. By observing it, the Jews would not distinguish themselves from the Gentiles, which is an essential point of the command. The commentator of the Bible is then forced to understand the verse in Ecclesiastes as an abridged parable, which he more fully relates in the following way:

> *(It is like) a king who invited his servants to a meal, but did not set a time (for the beginning of the meal). The prudent ones among them dressed themselves festively and sat down at the door of the king's house. They said, "The king's house is still lacking something." The foolish ones among them went about their work. All of a sudden the king sent for his servants. The prudent ones among them went in before the king, festively dressed as they were. The foolish ones, however, went in before the king as dirty as they were. And the king was pleased with the prudent ones, but was angry with the foolish ones.*

Midrash understands "to be dressed up every day in white clothes" figuratively as "to be prepared every day for repentance."

If a text is suspected of being written as figurative speech, the next question arises as to how the hearer accesses the communicative point which is actually intended. He not only has the given text as a fixed point for this task, but also the expectation that the question which he posed is answered (in the earlier examples it is the question of how the behavior of the reluctant suitor is to be appraised or which commandments the Jews should observe). In addition, there is the general knowledge of stereotypical mental concepts in world affairs (e.g. that cats are afraid of water; that Gentiles anoint themselves), as well as the ability to submit the given text to certain logical procedures. We turn now to these procedures themselves.

There are different paths which lead from a parable text to the disclosure of its point. In the following, I have designated these "paths" with the letters A, B, C, and D. Each of the them will be presented through the use of an example.

Type A Exegesis

The world of the parable (model) and that of the real world (explanandum) are linked together by a series of *analogies*. The structure of the subject in both worlds is the same. Some elements (central) are corresponding, others (marginal) are not. For example the Israelites venerate the golden calf and God is full of anger. But Moses attempts to placate Him, "O Lord, why does thy wrath burn hot against thy people, whom Thou hast brought forth out of the land of Egypt with great power and with a mighty hand?" (Ex 32:11). *Midrash Rabba* seeks to explain the logic of Moses' argument by means of parables, among which is the following:

> Rabbi 'Avin said in the name of Rabbi Simeon ben Yehotsadaq: *To what may this be compared? To a king who had a desolate field. He said to a gardener: "Go and cultivate it and make it into a vineyard for me!" The gardener did what he was told, cultivated the field and planted vines. They grew and produced wine, but it was sour. When the king saw this, he said to the gardener: "Go and cut down (the vineyard). What good is a vineyard to me that produces vinegar?" The gardener replied: "My lord king! You have spent so much for this vineyard, and now you want to cut it down? Why? Only because its wine is sour. That is only because the fruit is still young and, because of that, it does not produce a good wine yet, but rather a sour one."*

> And when the Israelites had committed that deed, God also wanted to destroy them. But Moses said: "Lord of the world! Did you not lead them out of Egypt (. . .)? The Israelites are still young (. . .). Have a little patience with them, and they will accomplish good deeds before You."[18]

In this parable, two series of statements run parallel to one another. The world of the vineyard and the world of Israel stand in a relationship of similarity. The transition from statements on the one side to statements on the other is permitted when all the predicates contained in the statement are in some way similar to one another. We elaborate this in greater detail:

- Establishing a vineyard is a large investment for the king in the parable, just as leading the Israelites out of Egypt is for God.

- That the cultivated vines only bring forth wild grapes is like an insubordination to the king (see Is 5:1–7), just as the Israelites do not show God any reverence.

- The king is angry about poor wines, just as God is about Israel.

- Young vines do not bring forth good wine in the same way that (a young people does not yet bring forth deeds which please God).

In connection with the last sentence, the statement actually only appears in the model. Its counterpart in the explanandum (written in parentheses) is an empty space, a "gap." That which is to be supplied in the gap as the appropriate counterpart should present itself as a matter of course once the analogy in the previous parallels has proved to be sound. This statement expresses that which the Midrash intended to address, i.e. the motivating force of Moses' argumentation with God.

To the extent that in type A exegesis two worlds are linked together by a series of corresponding elements, such parables tend to become allegories. When confronted with the finished text, we cannot determine whether it is the result of the composition of a series of parallels among the individual elements of a complex whole (e.g. a narrative) or the growing together of individual metaphors to form that complex whole or narrative. According to the old definition of an allegory, "*allegoria fit continuatis translationibus.*"

Type A Exegesis

Type B Exegesis

The only mediator between the model and the explanandum is a *pivot* (see above). There are no one-to-one correlations between the elements of the two spheres.[19]

The twin parable of the tower and the war (Lk 14:28–32) serves as an example. It has to do with how to become a disciple of Jesus.

For which of you, desiring to build a tower, does not first sit down and count the cost, whether he has enough to complete it? Otherwise, when he has laid a foundation, and is not able to finish, all who see it, begin to mock him saying: "This man began to build and was not able to finish!"

Or what king going to encounter another king in war, will not sit down first and take counsel whether he is able with ten thousand to meet him who comes against him with twenty thousand? And if not, while the other is yet a great way off, he sends an embassy and asks terms of peace.

As the smallest common denominator of both parables a general sentence (pivot) such as "great undertakings require great investments" or "great risks require careful consideration" can easily be formulated. The explanandum is "discipleship poses an enormous existential decision." Each hearer of the sermon must himself supply this general challenge concerning careful consideration and great investments with his own specific responses.

Type B Exegesis

Type C Exegesis

In addition to an abstract pivot, *individual elements* of the model can be set *parallel* to their counterparts in the explanandum. But contrary to type A, these correspondences are not features which are necessary for an understanding of the text. Often they either simply appear or aid in understanding.[20]

The parallel construction is an aid when the subject (the narrative) to be clarified or demonstrated by means of the model is very complex (as in the following example) or when the relationship among the elements is not clearly identifiable. Often, however, the excessive formulation of parallel constructions originates simply from the interest of the narrator to spin an illustrative tale. The fable of Stesichoros serves as an example.[21] The people of Himera had called Phalaris (who was a native of Agrigent) to help them against their neighbors and had chosen him as their absolute military leader. When they were at the point of granting him a bodyguard, Stesichoros opposed it by telling the following fable:

> *Like a horse which had a pasture all to itself. But when a stag came and destroyed the pasture, the horse wanted revenge and asked a human if he was prepared to punish the stag with him. The human agreed under the condition that the horse would allow a bridle to be put on and that he himself mount the horse with a javelin in his hand. Ever since it agreed and was mounted, the horse itself has served humans instead of getting revenge.*

"So be careful" Stesichoros said, "that you do not suffer the same fate as the horse through your intention to take revenge on your enemies. For you already have the bridle by having chosen him as your tyrant. But if you now grant him a bodyguard and permit him to mount you, you will serve Phalaris as slaves ever after."

The analysis of the fable is shown here in the form of a table.

Aim of the action	
of the horse	of the people of Himera
is revenge against invaders	
i.e. the stag.	i.e. neighboring people.
The situation *hic et nunc:*	
the horse is	the Himerians are
too weak.	
Alternative:	
Call for outside help	
i.e. of the human.	of military leader Phalaris from Agrigent.
The negative consequences of this action:	
The horse has bridle put on, the human mounts.	(Extrapolated by Stesichoros: the Himerians lose their freedom).

Comparative evaluation
between the original aim and the outcome:
It is better not to revenge injury
than to come under foreign domination.

The last sentence is in the sense of the epimythion of Phaedrus (IV, 4): "*Impune potius laedi, quam dedi alteri.*" This pivot can be easily applied to the above parable. In the form of such an enlightening abstract statement, the Himerians can apply it to their own situation. As a result of the parallel construction of the elements of the model and the explanandum throughout, which is not necessarily essential, the model acquires greater credibility. The extrapolated consequence (written in parentheses) of the loss of independence emerges even more forcefully.

Type C Exegesis

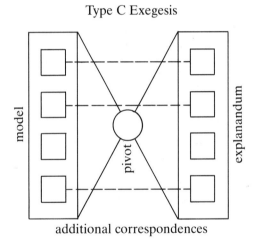

additional correspondences

Type D Exegesis

Every interpretation of parables is confronted with the difficulty that that which is said about the state of affairs of a certain sphere of life (i.e. the world of the model, e.g. agriculture, elementary techniques, economic systems, etc.) has to be transferred into a categorically different world (e.g. the relationship between political powers and their subjects, between God and humanity, etc.). The bridging of this gap by a one-to-one analogy or by an abstract statement (pivot) does not cover all the possibilities. There are parables in which neither an analogy nor a pivot can be found. *Metaphors* are useful in mediating between the world of the model and the world of the explanandum. Metaphors are words that are simultaneously at home in two worlds. Consider the following example: "My soul is eaten away by rust (of sin)." The word "rust" belongs to the world of metallurgy (where the word is employed in common usage) as well as to the world of ethics, as in this particular case. Let us have a look at the following example:

> Rabban Yohanan ben Zakkai used to say: "Why did the Israelites go into exile in Babel and not in other countries? Because the house (the family) of Abraham came from there. Let us make a parable. To what can this be compared? *To a woman who committed an offense against her husband. Where does he send her? He sends her to the house of her father.*"[22]

The model which R. Yohanan offers in answer to the question formulates a rule of the social world: "When a woman commits an offense against her husband, he sends her to the place from which she came." This sentence serves as a *praemissa major* in a syllogism. Furthermore, the rabbi assumes the information that "Israel commits adultery against God" as something that is already well known. This traditional metaphor is based upon many scripture passages in which the bridal relation-

Type D Exegesis

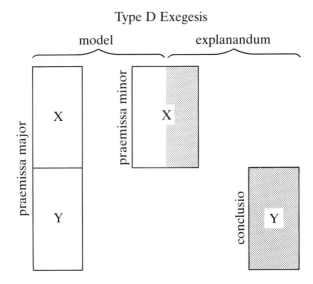

ship between God and Israel is described (Is 54:4–6; Jer 2:2; 3:8–13; 9:1; Ez 16:7–14; Hos 1–3). The *praemissa minor* is expressed in the metaphorical statement: "Israel committed an offense against its spouse." As a result, the conclusion can be drawn by means of syllogism: "God sends Israel to the place from which it came," namely, to the land of Abraham.

3. THE ATOMIZING OF LITERARY GENRES

With the above, we have pointed out that figurative speech can be precisely analyzed by applying the following three categories in each case:

What is the *function* of the parable in the dialectic dispute with respect to the distinction between illocutionary force and superimposed functions as discussed above (see section 2.1)?

Which *formal structure* does the text have with respect to surface structure and deep structure (see section 2.2)?

Which *exegetical operations* lead from the parable text to the communicative point or purpose (the four types of exegesis in section 2.3)?

These three categories are systematically interwoven with one another. We have separated them here in order to analyze them more easily.

I would, therefore, advocate an "atomizing of literary genres." I believe it is more reasonable to describe individual parables, as it were, in a "generative" manner by means of such elements, than to proceed from a set of ready-made genres.[23] In any event, such genres cannot be clearly distinguished because they stand in a close family resemblance to one another. As a result, in determining to which genre a concrete text belongs, more "borderline cases" arise than unambiguous identifications. (In a similar way, chemists can identify every existing substance as a configuration of some of the 103 elements, and they can predicate the non-existence of a certain substance such as "carbon trioxide.") Those, however, who are of the conviction that literary genres are some kind of platonic ideas which are merely reflected in the material world would not proceed in this fashion.

4. ADDITIONAL CAPABILITIES OF FIGURATIVE SPEECH

Up to this point we have acted as if the text of the parable could be translated into an answer to the question in discussion. That must now be corrected. The French saying *traduire c'est trahir* also applies here. Even when we have drawn out the communicative point (propositional content and illocutive force), there is still remaining material which that process has not translated. Between the parable text which has actually been presented, and the point or purpose as reconstructed by the interpreter, i.e. the statement as it might read in discursive, non-figurative speech, there remains a discrepancy. This discrepancy, nevertheless, can only be discerned as a result of this reconstruction. Or, the other way around, this procedure brings to light that the figurative speech which is actually before us has a greater value in comparison to the non-figurative variant. This *surplus value* consists of the dialectical, psychological, aesthetical function (explained above with the introduction of the term "function"). There are several additional characteristics which are applicable to all parables, which I now will briefly explain.

In principle, figurative speech always indicates the application of a model. Models are instruments which further understanding because of their effectiveness in simplification.

When I speak figuratively, I do not refer directly to the problem in question, but consider a distinctly different world. It is precisely this turning away from the problem which is itself one of the best means for solving the problem.

The hearer or reader of the parable must uncover the point himself. That which we discover for ourselves is planted much more deeply in the memory.

When the hearer is challenged to express his own evaluation of a case involving a model, the parable can work as a trap, as with the parable of Nathan (2 Sam 12:1–15): "You yourself are the man!"

As a starting point for communicating by means of parables, the narrator can choose the sphere of the actual world which best serves his purpose. He can skillfully avoid his audience's aversions to certain matters and, instead, tie into areas of experience which are familiar and carry emotionally positive connotations for them. This is illustrated by the following example:

Rabbi Aqiva is asked by the wicked military leader, Rufus: "What is it that distinguishes the Sabbath from all the other days?" *Aqiva replied:*

"What is it that distinguishes you from all other people?" Rufus replied: "It is the will of my king!" "With regard to the Sabbath, it is also the will of the Lord." (Babylonian Talmud, *Sanhedrin* 65b)

Rabbi Aqiva directs the discussion with great skill across the terrain familiar to this military leader. He knows all about the various stages of military promotion, and he uses this knowledge to lay a foundation upon which his dialectical opponent builds.

I want to make one more comment concerning aesthetical surplus. A dialectical intention demands a beauty, which on the one hand is alluring, yet, on the other, does not cause the hearer to merely remain in amazement (which is often the effect of a lyrical poem). The literary pleasure is only meant to serve the purpose at hand. Lucretius justified the literary structure of his work in his way: "Like physicians who spread honey on the rim of a cup when they have to give children bitter vermouth, he would serve the sour teaching (of atomism) within a sweet song."[24] The rabbis captured the tension between the literary fascination and the disposable character of the aesthetic cloak itself with a parable:

> The parable should not be seen as a minor thing in your eyes, for by means of parables everyone can gain access to the words of the Torah. A parable: *Like a king who lost a precious pearl from his treasure. Is he not able to find it with the help of a taper worth an 'Isar?*[25]

NOTES

1. For example, the fable of Menenius Agrippa about the stomach and the limbs, quoted from Livius II, xxxii, 9–11, or the fable of the flute-player and the fish in Herodot I, 141. Concerning the fable of Stesichoros, quoted from Aristotle, see note 21 below.

2. This is the estimation of Clemens Thoma / Simon Lauer, *Die Gleichnisse der Rabbinen*, 1.Teil (PesK) (Bern/Frankfurt/New York: P. Lang, 1986), p. 12.

3. The Czechoslovakian scholar Jan Mukařovský had already in 1948 drawn attention to this principle of poetic speech ("foregrounding"). Excerpts of his important book *Kapitoly z české poetiky* are translated in Paul L. Garvin (editor), *A Prague School Reader on Esthetics, Literary, Structure, and Style* (Georgetown University, Washington D.C., 1955).

4. Paul Michel, ALIENILOQUIUM. *Elemente einer Grammatik der Bildrede* (Bern/Frankfurt/New York: P. Lang, 1987).

5. "Figurative speech" can be utilized as a collective term for the technical concepts "simile," "parable," "example," and "allegory." To simplify matters, I

restrict myself to using the term "parable" in a general way for all of the above concepts.

6. The term *"inopia verborum"* is found in Cicero, *de oratore* III,155. Quintilian (VII, vi, 6) uses *"quia necesse est."*

7. Max Black, *Models and Metaphors* (Ithaca, N.Y., 1962), pp. 22–47. Max Black, "More about Metaphor," *Dialectica* 31 (1977), pp. 431–457. I.T. Ramsey, *Religious Language* (New York: The Macmillan Company, 1957).

8. John L. Austin, *How To Do Things with Words* (Oxford University Press, 1962). John R. Searle, *Speech Acts* (Cambridge University Press, 1969).

9. According to Aristotle (*Rhetoric* I, ii, 13 = 1357a) *enthýmēma* is defined as truncated syllogism in which some premises are understood but not stated.

10. Stephen Toulmin, *The Uses of Argument* (Cambridge University Press, 1958).

11. *Avot de R. Natan* XIV (ed. Schechter 29b/30a); compare *The Fathers According to Rabbi Nathan,* trans. Judah Goldin (New Haven: Yale Univ., 1955), pp. 76–77. This parable demonstrates the advantage of a form of figurative speech which applies a model from a completely different sphere over one which takes its material from the same sphere, since the latter reminds the addressee of other sad events, which directly interferes with the intention of consoling.

12. *Midrash Wayiqra Rabba* 13 (114b).

13. Homer, *Iliad,* E 902–904.

14. Empedocles, fragment 33 (Hermann Diels / Walter Kranz, eds., *Die Fragmente der Vorsokratiker,* Dublin/Zurich, [13]1968).

15. Paul Fiebig has particularly emphasized this point (compare note 20 below). He referred to the "Inkonzinnität" (disharmony) between model and explanandum.

16. I have borrowed the notion "pivot" from Schiller's dramaturgy (from the sketch of the never completed drama *Die Malteser*). Schiller understands "pivot" as the central idea of the drama before it has been formed into words.—The notion "pivot" is *not* applied to parables that have merely an illustrative function (as the above example from Homer), *nor* to parables of type A exegesis (see section 2.3).

17. *Midrash Qohelet Rabba* 9 (ed. Wilna 1887: 23b).

18. *Midrash Shemot Rabba* 43,9 (145a); similar in *Pesiqta deRav Kahana* 16,9 (Thoma/Lauer, above note 3), No. 50 = pp. 237–241.

19. Adolf Jülicher has absolutized this mode of exegesis in his fundamental book *Die Gleichnisreden Jesu* (t. I, Tübingen, 1886; II, 1898). Jülicher accepts only this type of exegesis and, where he does not see a way to interpret a NT parable in this sense, he presupposes that the original words of Jesus have been modified by the editors. This view has been strongly criticized by Paul Fiebig (see note 20).

20. Paul Fiebig drew attention to this transitional form which lies between

parable (type A) and allegory. *Die Gleichnisreden Jesu im Lichte der rabbinischen Gleichnisse des neutestamentlichen Zeitalters* (Tübingen, 1912).

21. Stesichoros (640–555 BCE), poet at Himera in Sicily, quoted from Aristotle, *Rhetoric* II, xx, 5.

22. *Tosefta Baba Qamma* 7, 3 (ed. Zuckermandel, pp. 357f).

23. I understand the term "generative" in the specific sense in which Noam Chomsky used it when speaking of "generative grammar" (*Syntactic Structures*, The Hague/Paris: Mouton, 1957): "The grammar of a language L will be a device that generates all of the grammatical sequences of L and none of the ungrammatical ones" (p. 13).

24. T. Lucretius Carus, *De Rerum Natura*, IV, 11–25 (English translation by C. Bailey, Oxford, 1947).

25. *Midrash Shir HaShirim* 1,7 (3b). '*Isar* is a coin of small value.

Understanding the *Mashal* and Its Value for the Jewish-Christian Dialogue in a Narrative Theology

Lawrence Boadt, C.S.P.

I. INTRODUCTION

The foundation for significant Jewish-Christian religious dialogue lies in the claims of both faiths to the Hebrew Scriptures as normative and canonical. Since Christians have joined the New Testament with the earlier Scriptures, and both faiths have developed divergent and independent traditions of interpretation over many centuries, there are essential disagreements on the authority of the Hebrew Bible, its meaning for the nature of the faith community, and even on what constitute its absolute demands on those who believe in it. But there are also many agreements, not the least of which is the identity and nature of the God who inspires and reveals through that Scripture. Both communities look to its story of Israel's relationship with that God as normative in some way for its own identity and development. And both share about half the legal materials and ninety percent of the prophetic demands as binding on themselves.

To speak of the Bible as a canon often implies the message and purpose of the text beyond the limits and shape of the narratives it contains. It implies the normative meaning for the community rule of action and the formulations of basis truths taught by each religion. But Jewish tradition, like the Christian, lives on the power of its story, retold year after year in liturgy and catechesis, and always applied to our situation today. Recent interest in story theology and the literary potential of narrative to communicate truth shows some promise to unlock more fully the power of the normative stories for contemporary believers. Narratives, and especially those involving metaphor or symbol, work on many levels for the hearer. These levels need to be recovered as part of the ongoing dialogue with the text about how to create a hermeneutic possibility of appropriation for each generation.

Especially in the meshalim, or parable literature, the role of metaphor is central and has a unique power to disclose truth on several levels at once—not just as doctrinal formulation, but as appeal to experience, and as a call to commitment and decision about how I should respond. The biblical stories and parables provide a common entry point for Christians and Jews to discover the revealed message of God and participate in it through the text that transcends the often closed and rigid differences set by the legal forms and doctrinal statements that have separated us. Modern parable theory will not explain all aspects of a text in a common understanding, nor will it replace and do away with the need for doctrinal and regulative norms that identify and distinguish the Jewish and Christian religions. But it will help to rediscover that revelation comes in more forms than legal formulation and creeds.

It will be worth looking first at some of the modern theories about the nature of New Testament parables because here the theology of parable and story has been developed the furthest. This research can next be compared briefly to current explorations of the rabbinic parables of the first to fifth centuries C.E., and then to recent study of the parables of the Old Testament. For all three levels, the technical word in Hebrew is *mashal* (plural: *meshalim*).[1] But its meaning does not remain constant through the ages, nor does it always have a narrow and highly focused meaning in every case. Finally, something can be said about Christian interest in the development of a narrative theology that will integrate the task of taking literary metaphor seriously with the theological task of offering critical reflection on the relation of sacred text to doctrinal belief. Can this provide some positive openings for continued dialogue between Christians and Jews?

II. THE PARABLE IN THE NEW TESTAMENT

The Parable Genre in Recent Study

John Dominic Crossan opens his book, *In Parables: The Challenge of the Historical Jesus,* by quoting the poet W. H. Auden, "You cannot tell people what to do, you can only tell them parables; and this is what art

really is, particular stories of particular people and experiences. . . ."[2]
This is a provocative comment because it highlights an important area of
confusion in modern understanding of the New Testament, namely that
the language of moral persuasion and commandment is far different from
the actual language of Jesus' parables. Parables lean much more heavily
on the language of experience shared by all who have reflected on life
situations and identified their own particular experience with that of other
people whom they have studied or learned about through the years. Art
imitates nature, so the common wisdom goes, and in the case of the
parable, the nature it imitates is that of the questioning human being who
sorts out lessons and models to be followed through a dialogue between
the exploring self and the world in which that self lives.

The New Testament is proclamatory and persuasive literature in
general, a literature that lays a claim on the reader to make an urgent
decision for (or against) its message. Within that broad definition of its
literary function, the New Testament contains many diverse literary
genres, such as gospel, letter, apocalyptic vision, and chronicle; and
within these, still more subgenres, such as wisdom sayings, legal command, catechetical instruction, quotation, dialogue, disputation, infancy
narrative and parable.

The parable is distinguished in turn by several special characteristics: it is always narrative in some fashion, it appeals to experience, and
it proposes some form of lesson for the hearer. We could add that it is
also always artfully crafted in the language of simile or metaphor.

Certain conclusions can readily be drawn from this short list of
parable characteristics. If it is *narrative* in form, the parable naturally fits
the Gospel genre itself, which implies storytelling and action on the part
of Jesus and his disciples. The parable's realism about life and the power
of its message for those who would follow Jesus come from the hearer's
recognition of a close unity between Jesus' own beliefs and actions and
the action in the narrative vignettes he tells. The parables closely reflect
the concerns and questions about Jesus' own identity and his mission by
centering on the nature of the kingdom as the imminent inbreaking of
God, and on the prophetic stance taken by Jesus.[3] At the same time, the
parables are mirror images of life, and offer stories of how concrete
individuals act when confronted by difficult life situations. Parables always center on the moral dimensions of the world we live in, but not on
the answers offered by formal ethical systems or philosophical reasoning.[4] They are also lessons, as Auden so wisely implied, but lessons that
are discovered only by identifying each person's own experience with
that of others, so that one is constantly challenged to look anew at the

common experiences described in the parable and ask about our individual understandings and attitudes in the light of its story. In this way, the parable has an inclusive dimension that forces us to look at our viewpoints from the larger perspective of the community.

Thus the parable is action-oriented, experiential, and didactic, yes, but also artistic. Much of our greatest gain in recent parable research has focused on the narrative art of the parable, especially in its nature as metaphor or simile. Parable research from Jülicher to Jeremias had done an excellent job identifying the historical referents within the parables of Jesus and describing the life situations of first-century Palestine.[5] But these scholars consistently viewed parables as either illustrations or explanations of the sermons of Jesus. They were perhaps influenced strongly by their search for rabbinic parables in the Talmud and elsewhere which would parallel those of Jesus. As we shall note below in the next section, rabbinic parables often served precisely the function of illustrating and explicating halakhic points under discussion. But this does not mean that the parables of Jesus were used in the same way. In fact, as already noted above, they function quite differently in Jesus' own ministry. In the last twenty years, this difference has been explored by a series of writers who view the parables of Jesus primarily as metaphor and all which that implies.

The Parable as Metaphor

C. H. Dodd argued that the nature of the metaphor or simile was to open doubts in the hearer as to its exact application and so force the mind to puzzle over its meaning.[6] Amos Wilder, in a chapter on the parable in his *Early Christian Rhetoric,* goes on to distinguish between merely illustrative parables and those closer to symbol in which the metaphor carries the reality to which it refers.[7] The hearer "not only learns about that reality, he participates in it."[8] Wilder, however, did not go on to draw out some of the more important implications of this remark.

Robert Funk did. He understood the parable as a "language event." The hearer is drawn into the parable because it is metaphorical and puts together two fundamentally unlike referents that force the imagination to draw connections.[9] The impact of the two when joined together produces a personal vision which cannot be adequately described by discursive speech alone. The hearer becomes a participant in creating the meaning of the metaphor by being active in its application. A judgment is called forth on the situation described in the parable based on the effect the metaphorical elements have on the listener. For Funk, a metaphor is creative of meaning, whereas a simile only illustrates a meaning. Thus in the parables of the kingdom, when Jesus says the kingdom of God is *like* a mustard seed, the point is an illustration of how it grows from small beginnings, but if Jesus talks about the kingdom by simply telling the story of the prodigal son or the good Samaritan, then the listener must become involved in the story as metaphor and as a narrative of action, and make a personal judgment on its application. In this metaphorical narrative, the kingdom has confronted the hearer as a bearer of a realistic life situation, as a stimulus to the imagination, and as a demand for decision. At the same time, Funk acknowledges the power of the parable as metaphor to elicit new meanings about reality. The listener is invited to participate in the meaning that the parable unfolds and to choose between the conventional world and the particular world proposed in the parable and to then order his or her own life accordingly.[10]

Dan O. Via

Dan O. Via is also concerned with the parable and theological language.[11] He disagrees with the prevailing view of the parable, originally proposed by Jülicher, which allows only one major point to be taken from its story. He contrasts the parable to the allegory where each referent indeed is intended to have a single meaning. The allegory begins with a conceptual meaning for a connected group of referents and searches for the proper image in which to express this meaning. A true parable, on the other hand, begins with an image and draws out *suggested* meanings. The parable has a richness brought about by the use of metaphorical language, and as a result has multiple points of contact with the one or more referents outside the story or image. As does Funk, Via distinguishes different types of "parable," of which only one has these full metaphoric characteristics. There is (1) the similitude, or likeness, which normally draws a one to one comparison. There is also (2) the example story, which lacks the indirect use of symbol and makes a clear point of illustration in reference to the lesson to be learned from the real world. And, finally, there is (3) the true parable, which is an invented story of a personal action, rather than a stereotypical mode of behavior. Its meaning is not always clear, and in some ways resembles the *ḥidah,* or riddle, which teases the hearer to puzzle out new dimensions in familiar images and actions. In fact, as noted in the section below on the *mashal* in the Old Testament, *ḥidah* and *mashal* are often linked as poetically paired words (Pss 49:4; 78:2; Ez 17:2; Prov 1:6).

Via adds one other significant point to the discussion on parable by insisting that the parable can incorporate many elements drawn from the creator's own imagination and elaboration of the scene, but all these elements point *within* the story itself and not to specific referents outside that will correspond point by point. All aesthetic work is non-referential in this way.[12] Via, too, is critical of the limits of the historical critical approach of Jeremias and others. Not only do we not know enough about the actual history or events of Jesus' life to connect to them the situations described in each parable, but this approach tends to tie the individual parables down to only one possible meaning referent and ignores the broad appeal to common human experience valid for all generations, and the consequent openness to later readers who will hear the parables in their contemporary situations.

Via acknowledges the importance of doing historical critical analysis, but wishes to extend the investigation of parable meaning on into a literary and finally a theological level of understanding. He calls these next two stages the "Literary-existential analysis" and the "Existential-theological interpretation." The word "existential" is included in both levels because, for Via, both a literary participation in the metaphor or symbol, and the resulting response to the theological claims of the text, involve making life decisions—at least on the plane of accepting the vision of life that is introduced, and then relating it to the presence of the divine in that vision.

The strength of Via's presentation overall is that he perceives that the parables of Jesus are at heart metaphors; that these are embodied in narrative which implies action and decision; and that the hearer or reader is drawn into active participation in the creation of the meaning of the metaphor for his or her own life decision.

John Dominic Crossan

John Dominic Crossan has also contributed to the discussion of parable as metaphor.[13] He, too, begins with a critique of (1) the single viewpoint of parables in contrast to that of allegories and (2) an overly historical-critical approach to the parable. Instead he explores the power of symbol and metaphor, as they are understood in poetry, to express something that can be expressed in no other way. "Metaphor can articulate a referent so new and so alien to consciousness that it can only be grasped within the metaphor itself."[14] In a more pointed fashion, Crossan goes on to suggest that the parables are a fundamental expression of Jesus' experience of God, so that they are not just paradigms for us, nor illustrations of his message, but constitutive of the historical reality of Jesus himself. They express and contain Jesus' own response to his experience of the kingdom of God, and of his relationship to his father.

Crossan goes much further than does Via to develop how these parables affect the hearer. There are three key elements that form a sequence: Crossan calls them "advent," "reversal," and "action."[15] The hearer of a parable is confronted by a new understanding and new possibilities of familiar situations, is led to reverse earlier convictions, and is moved to take on a new world with new action to pursue. Parables such as the Pearl of Great Price (Mt 13:44–45) and the Treasure Hidden in a Field (Mt 13:45) are primary examples of this movement. But all parables have some aspect of these elements, and each stresses one or more of the key elements in a special way. Thus, for example, the parable of the Good Samaritan (Lk 10:30–37) is a parable of reversal, while the parable of the Talents in Matthew 25:14–30 is largely a parable of action. Crossan goes on to suggest how this paradigm is particularly appropriate for Jesus' teaching of the kingdom of God, and gives attention to the issues of eschatology and Jesus' linear concept of time. But these are beyond the scope of the present investigation. It suffices to remark that his attention to these further dimensions of the parable in 1973 most probably stemmed from his familiarity with the approach of Norman Perrin to the language about the Kingdom,[16] and to his knowledge of the work by the structural analysts.[17]

In a still later article on "Parable, Allegory and Paradox,"[18] Crossan develops the structural approach and now understands paradox to be at the heart of the metaphoric scene in the parable. In the process, he reverses himself on the role of allegory as a non-metaphorical literary genre, and now sees it, like the parable, as capable of multiple levels of meaning, but also paradoxical and playful with the possibilities of plot. At the same time, he compares the role of parable and allegory with that of myth in the structural analyses of Claude Lévi-Strauss,[19] Pierre Maranda[20] and Roman Jakobson.[21] He concludes that parable serves the opposite role from that of myth. Just as myth reconciles the binary oppositions in human thinking and mediates contradictions in human experiences, so its binary opposite, the parable, creates contradiction out of the certainties of life.[22]

In this article, he has taken the central insight of the reversal theme present in Jesus' parables and made it foundational to all parables as a literary form. Parables are narrative paradox, i.e., paradox formed into story. This is a strong position, and one may legitimately question whether everything considered to be parable in the New Testament really fits under this rubric. Indeed, the very question has been raised by John R. Donahue in his response to Crossan.[23] Should not this insightfulness pursued by Funk, Via and Crossan be regarded as limited to some parables? After all, other so-called parables have been restricted to such categories as the example-story (Via). On the other hand, perhaps there is a still broader definition of parable that should include within it the involving-metaphor, the simple illustration and the example story.

The *mashal* in the Old Testament and in later Rabbinic examples shows just such wider usage, and deserves a brief examination.

III. THE RABBINIC *MASHAL*

Disparaging Rabbinic Parables

From Jülicher onward, modern Christian interpreters of the parables of Jesus have largely distinguished them from the abundant number of *meshalim* or parables that occur throughout early rabbinic literature. Günther Bornkamm's comment is typical:

> The rabbis also relate parables in abundance, to clarify a point in their teaching and explain the sense of a written passage, but always as an aid to the teaching and an instrument in the exegesis of an authoritatively prescribed text. But that is just what they are not in the mouth of Jesus, although they often come very close to those of the Jewish teachers in their content, and though Jesus makes free use of traditional and familiar topics. Here the parables are the preaching itself and are not merely serving the purpose of a lesson which is quite independent of them.[24]

Crossan also insists on this point. Rabbinic parables are almost always didactic stories linked to a life problem or to a given biblical or rabbinic text in a very precise and specific fashion. They are figures that are expendable, and only of value for pedagogical purposes. They are examples to illustrate a dogmatic proposition.[25]

Why should the parables of Jesus be viewed in a different fashion from those of the (other) rabbis? Two factors can usually be cited. The first is dating. Although the general form of the *mashal* is traditional, its precise use and function may change with time, and as far as we know, Jesus' parables substantially predate the use of rabbinic parables as they are now constructed in the Talmudim, Midrashim and related rabbinic works. Thus the setting of the learned academy established after 70 C.E. may have changed the purpose and function of the *mashal* even if the content and general type as comparison remained. Secondly, rabbinic *meshalim* certainly show a much more standardized form than do the parables of Jesus, a form that accents their purpose as primarily that of illustration in the setting of the present rabbinic material.

Recent Study of Rabbinic Parables

Clemens Thoma and Simon Lauer have begun an intensive study of the rabbinic parables.[26] Analyzing the 133 parables of the *Pesiqta de Rav Kahana,* a midrashic work of the 5th–6th century C.E., they have put together a schema of the five major elements found in nearly all rabbinic examples. This includes the *motivation,* or situation which initiates the need for a *mashal* in order to clarify or answer a problem; and the *ḥiddush,* or primary point of disclosure, a specific hinge phrase or aspect on which the main point of the comparison will turn. Both of these elements are introductory to the parable itself and set the context as one of enlightening the meaning of the Torah or making it relevant to a new situation for the contemporary audience.

The actual parable has two clear parts: the *mashal* proper and the *nimshal.* The *mashal* part has a plot with action, and thus is narrative in form, and is not merely a simple comparison. Thoma and Lauer, along with other analysts, such as Louis Isaac Rabinowitz,[27] understand it to be monoepisodic, and generally confined to one point. The *nimshal* is the explanation of the comparison, and can take various forms such as quoting either a passage of Scripture or the opinions of other rabbis; or it can make a direct point-for-point application of the story in the *mashal.* However, the *nimshal* does not always confine itself to the direct explanation of the comparison in the *mashal,* but can sometimes jump back to address the actual problem posed by the original setting (i.e. the motivation) for the *mashal.* Sometimes, too, the *nimshal* is a pre-existing midrash found in other well-known passages and in other contexts as well.[28]

The fifth element is the *addressee,* which is always the community and its life, not in the past situation of the original legal formulation or biblical text, but as lived in the present and directed to succeeding generations.

It is worth highlighting some aspects of what Thoma and Lauer consider important to the rabbinic parable as it is now found in the literature, and not as it may have developed. First, it is always found within a halakhic or haggadic discussion, so that the *nimshal* intends a normative teaching, and this basically serves the decisive disclosure the author desires (the *hiddush*). Up to this point, the analysis of the rabbinic use of parables would tend to support the claims of those critics who see them closer to what New Testament scholars define as allegories and example-stories and illustrations than they do to true metaphorical narratives.

However, Thoma goes beyond the concept of the rabbinic parable as a teaching tool, fashioned in such a way that *nimshal* actually comes first and the *mashal* is created to fit it. He points out that often the story or narrative is larger than the points addressed by the *nimshal,* and he notes that the power of the stories rhetorically and metaphorically often eclipses the legal point or teaching of the *nimshal*. Note the two examples he cites in the article in this volume: the parable of the two luminaries, and the triple parable of the rewarded wait.[29] There is a clear literary dimension in these that transcends the function of the *nimshal* to teach a lesson. Moreover, he goes on to indicate his own personal insight that the parables carry an eschatological viewpoint and salvational history viewpoint that involves the hearer or reader in a larger identity and perspective than the immediate decision signaled by the *nimshal*.[30]

The Approach of David Stern

Thoma himself credits David Stern and David Flusser for helping him to see this literary-theological dimension of the parable.[31] Stern's article in this volume on the parable of the wicked husbandmen in Mark's Gospel is a masterpiece of insight.[32] It is not his first exploration of the metaphorical dimension of the rabbinic parable,[33] but it suffices to bring out important dimensions missed by earlier commentators. He readily acknowledges the connection in rabbinic and medieval Jewish literary tradition between narrative and explanation of the law, or direct exegesis of a scriptural passage. At the same time, he goes on to develop how every parable is more than exegesis; it is allusive as narrative and leaves the task of figuring out exactly what the message is to the reader audience. He is in agreement with many of the Christian students of the parable whose work we have examined. He criticizes the historical reconstruction of parables by Jülicher and Jeremias that sought to discover the one point in each, and that disparaged any allegorical elements in parables as a later didacticism. With Via and Crossan, Stern perceives the rediscovery of the "original words" of Jesus' parables to be largely the product of the dogmatic or ideological positions of the scholar who does the reconstruction.

Stern, however, goes beyond the New Testament scholars to critique the polysemy approach that postulates open-ended possibilities for meaning, or multiple levels of meaning, in the nature of the metaphoric language of the parable. His analysis of the thought of Paul Ricoeur on the subject of parabolic metaphor and "intertextuality" is persuasive indeed; the ultimate meaning Ricoeur postulates seems not to be generated by the dynamic of the parable's literary form but by the theological system already in place for the interpreter (i.e. for Ricoeur himself). But, of course, one does not have to accept Ricoeur in order to see metaphor as a "language event" that transcends ordinary simile comparisons or illustrative lessons.

Stern on the Wicked Husbandmen

Stern proceeds to examine the parable of the wicked husbandmen with a great deal of acuity. He points out the traditional motifs and language that permeate the story, and looks to parallels with the rabbinic parables that will bring into the foreground the common tradition of dealing with the motifs and central symbols of the parable. He also identifies an original *nimshal* in this parable of Jesus and argues that probably all of the New Testament parables had such a formal *nimshal*, a point generally denied by transmission history exegetes of the New Testament. He then analyzes the motivation, or context, into which the parable of the wicked husbandmen is set in Mark's gospel. There is a clear referential purpose to the story in regard to the wicked behavior of the Pharisees in persecuting John the Baptist. It is a blame-*mashal*, as are many of Jesus' parables, a genre also known from rabbinic sources. Its meaning does not come from an allegorical interpretation of the story itself, but from the interplay of the scriptural exegesis of Psalm 118:23 about the cornerstone that was rejected, and the context of the discourse in Mark 11:28–33 about John the Baptist. Thus Stern relocates the discussion on the parables of Jesus back into the wider discussion of

known parables, especially those of the rabbinic tradition, and sees no
particular essential difference between the two groups.

This may be going too far. Certainly, the form and context of the
parable of the wicked husbandmen in Mark 12:1–12, Matthew 21:33–
46, and Luke 20:9–19 all retain a common setting in the polemic of Jesus
with the Pharisees over the role of John the Baptist. But to assert that
the original referent of the parable was blame for the killing of John laid
on the Pharisees is far different from a further claim that the quotation
of Psalm 118:23 serves as a *nimshal* that in fact serves to establish the
source of Jesus' authority to teach. I would concede that the parable may
have originally alluded to the servants as the prophets of old, and that
the son was intended to be John and not Jesus, but the application of the
Psalm's image of the cornerstone to John hardly makes sense—unless
the new structure is actually founded on John redivivus, i.e. Jesus con-
tinuing John's mission, a point that Stern hints at. But then the authority
to which Jesus appeals is not John continued, but the divine sending of a
son, and no one, not even a Jew reading the parable, could miss the
resonance of Jesus' own title as that son, and as the leader of a movement that is new, and the positioning of this story in all three gospels to
be late in Jesus' career where it was clear that he in no way was a
continuation of the mission of John as John conceived it.

Even the use of Psalm 118 is allusive and not clarifying when the
parable is intended to resonate on more than one level. Indeed, "it is
wonderful in our eyes" suggests far more than that the role of John is at
stake in this parable. The role of the story works on at least two consciously historical levels, John and Jesus as similar but distinct missions,
and on at least two (or more) levels about the divine intention that is
both recognized and yet new, and to be heard differently by foe or
friend. The Pharisees see it as a parable of blame, fair enough, but the
original disciple and later believer both know it makes a claim for the
new that a non-believer cannot recognize at all. This is precisely the
point made by Via and Crossan. Stern's work is superb, but it under-
plays the role of paradox, reversal, and newness that operate in Jesus'
parables.

Milavec on the Wicked Husbandmen

We can contrast Stern's approach to the parable of the wicked
husbandmen by comparing it to the study of the same parable by Aaron
Milavec also in this volume.[34] Milavec concentrates on the elements in

the language of the parable that reveal evocative possibilities. E.g. he notes how Mark's version only alludes to the earlier biblical uses of the image of a vineyard, so that the parable will not be identified simply as an allegory built around Isaiah 5:1–5, but touches also the power of texts in Hosea and Jeremiah that open up several other directions for the hearer to follow.[35] In general, Milavec highlights the open-ended and ambiguous quality of the parable narrative in Mark which touches, however, the historical experience of faith known to his Jewish audience from their Scriptures. Although Milavec doesn't orient his observations around the language of metaphor to describe this, he clearly resonates with this approach, and at least knows and appreciates Crossan's work.[36]

But at the same time, his approach to the parable seems to be governed by an outside concern, namely to explain away any anti-Jewish elements in its current forms in the canonical gospels and the Gospel of Thomas. He adopts a basic "reader-response" methodology which highlights the literary qualities needed to touch an audience, but appears to envision the audience itself as those who actually heard Jesus' words and not the audience of Mark's own church many years after. To recover the original parable of Jesus in its pure form addressed to a Galilean audience raises the same difficulties of historical reconstruction for which Jeremias has been criticized.[37]

As the parable stands now, it is contexted in all cases as a paradoxical reversal, and the Christian reader will certainly draw a further conclusion that the son is Jesus, who grants authority to the apostles as the "others" who will inherit the vineyard and till it. They will not be a new community, or a Gentile church, but a continuation of Israel itself with a responsive community leadership that recognizes Jesus as messiah and would not turn away this "son" if he were to come again.

Milavec makes an excellent contribution to understanding much of the literary power and allusiveness of this parable, but does not want to go so far as to say that even a part of the multi-level dimensions are allusions to the Christian community's developed beliefs in Jesus.

Observations

In general, these scholars exhibit definite insight into the metaphorical nature of the parables of Jesus, but tend to view them through the lens of a Jewish tradition different from that of the Gospel communities themselves. Milavec tries to see an earlier Jesus level, and is at least partially successful; but Stern, despite the quality of his insight, is not convincing when he argues that there is some equivalent to the rigorous rabbinic *nimshal* in New Testament parables. Here, the wide variations in the contexts of the parables in the different Gospels sharpens the lack of such a clear point of argument. Overall, even granting occasional exegetical references to Scripture in the Gospel parables, they still stand remarkably lacking in the clear, didactic *nimshal* which is central to all of our rabbinic examples.

IV. THE MEANING OF MĀŠĀL
IN THE OLD TESTAMENT

Efforts To Define a Mashal Before 1975

Various attempts to derive the meaning of the word māšāl from a root, *mšl* I, meaning "to rule,"[38] or "to stand,"[39] have been made. Neither has won many adherents among scholars, largely because there are seventeen verbal occurrences of *māšāl* and thirty nominal cases where the meaning of the word is clearly, "to be like" or "to compare." Thus, we must posit a *mšl* II, "to be like," as a second, independent root. This was first argued forcefully by Otto Eissfeldt in 1913,[40] and in recent years has won widespread consensus among those who have investigated the question.[41] This is especially evident in the occurrence of niphal forms of the verb, which can only be understood as direct comparisons, e.g. Psalm 49:13, *nimšal kabběhēmôt nidmû*, "He is *like* the beasts who cease to be (are cut off)." Interestingly, some manuscripts read *nidmâ* in the singular, and the LXX follows this reading with *kai ōmiốthē aùtoîs*, "and he is *like* them," as though from the verb *dmh*, "to be like." This particular line in Psalm 49 is repeated again at the end of the psalm in v. 21, so that it functions as a kind of refrain within the poem. This is significant because the psalmist announces at the very beginning that the entire poem is a *māšāl:*

> pî yĕdabbēr ḥokmôt   wĕhāgût libbî tĕbûnôt
> 'atteh lĕmāšāl °ozni   'eptah bĕkinnôr hîdatî
> My mouth will speak wisdom, and the reflection of my heart will be understanding; I will incline my ear to a *māšāl*, I will unlock my riddle on the lyre (vv. 4–5).

Is not the whole psalm then to be understood as a "likeness" or "comparison"?

It is generally agreed that the noun *māšāl* covered a wide range of different types of wisdom sayings. These include short proverbial statements such as that of 1 Samuel 24:14, *ka'ăšer yō' mar měšal haggadmōnî / mērěšā'îm yēşē' rešaʿ* "Just as the *mashal* of the ancients says, 'From the wicked comes wickedness.' " Or that of Ezekiel 18:2, "The fathers have eaten sour grapes, but the teeth of the children grate," where the saying is introduced by *mah lākem 'attem mōšělîm 'ethammāšāl hazzeh,* "Why is it that you people make this mashal . . . ?" But it also includes the description of long didactic psalms such as Psalm 49 above, and Psalm 78, which is also called both a *māšāl* and a *ḥîdâ* ("riddle"): *'eptěḥâ běmāšāl pî / 'abbî 'â ḥîdôt minnî-qedem,* "I will open my mouth in a *mashal,* and speak riddles from the ancient past." Still a third type of *māšāl* is the long story-like parable in Ezekiel 17 of the two eagles, which may have judged to be a strict allegory in form, and which opens with a description similar to that of Psalms 49 and 78: *ḥûd ḥîda ŭměšōl māšāl' el-bêt yiśrā' ēl,* "Tell a riddle and make a *mashal* for the house of Israel. . . ." Finally, in a few places, the term *māšāl* indicates a person who will be an example of shame for others: Ezekiel 14:8, *wahăšimōtîhû lě 'ôt wělimšālîm,* "And I will make him a sign and *měšālîm* (plural!).

When confronted by such a wide diversity in usage, it is both the challenge and duty of the interpreter to try to find some common threads that run among the known cases. Aubrey Johnson, in 1955,[42] investigated the body of texts using *māšāl* and decided that they all had in common the purpose of being a lesson for others. They served to illustrate the message of the preacher and make it more effective.

Otto Eissfeldt argued in his *The Old Testament: An Introduction* (1966) that the oldest uses of *māšāl* are for popular proverbs, often simple questions or observations such as "What has straw in common with wheat?" in Jeremiah 23:28 and "Is Saul also among the prophets?" in 1 Samuel 10:12 and 19:24.[43] These are usually single-line sayings in prose often with the use of assonance (cf Prov 13:3; 11:2) although it is not impossible that *parallelismus membrorum* played a role in some examples that may be found among the collections in the Book of Proverbs and elsewhere.[44] According to Eissfeldt, the more formal artistic wisdom saying in metrical form and parallel lines developed later under the influence of foreign wisdom literature. It was the product of the professional class of the "wise," teachers in the schools for scribes and other government officials, whose interests lay in collecting universal knowledge and in practical education for good prudent judgment among leaders.[45]

William McKane, in 1970,[46] followed Eissfeldt in maintaining that the basic meaning of a *māšāl* was the popular proverb, short and pithy and rooted in popular wisdom, and that all elaborate forms are really literary creations that are built up for theological reasons as "models" to be followed.

Recent Investigations of Māšāl

George Landes, in 1978,[47] made a major attempt to classify all the occurrences of *māšāl* under five categories: (1) *the popular proverb,* which he considers to be the basic sense, following McKane, because it provides insightful observations to help in making prudent decisions (1 Sam 10:11–12; 24:14; Jer 31:29; Ez 12:22: 16:44; 18:2; Job 13:12; Prov 1:6, 10:1; 25:1; 26:7,9; Eccl 12:9); (2) the *satirical taunt song,* which describes a divine judgment that should be a lesson to Israel (Num 21:27–30; Is 14:4–21; Mic 2:4; Hab 2:6–19, and those passages where a person becomes a *māšāl*—Dt 28:37: 1 Kgs 9:7; Jer 24:9; Ez 14:8; Pss 44:15; 69:12; Job 17:6); (3) the *prophetic oracle* type, found in the story of Balaam as paradigms for Israel's future (Num 23:7, 18; 24:3, 15, 20, 21, 23); (4) *didactic poems* which serve as historical lessons for Israel to discern the wisdom concerned with the right way and the wrong way to live (Pss 49; 78; Job 29–31); (5) the *allegorizing parable,* found uniquely in the Book of Ezekiel, where imagery from nature is used and then narrowly interpreted by the prophet as warning lessons for the people (Ez 17:3–10; 21:1–4; 24:3–5). Landes, as did both Johnson and McKane, opts for a basic sense of moral lesson for the meaning of *māšāl*. He would add the Book of Jonah to his list of category (5), the allegorizing parables, following a suggestion of George Mendenhall in 1974.[48] This also leads him to the insight that the association of *māšāl* with *ḥidâ* in Psalms 49 and 78 and Ezekiel 17 points to an enigmatic or mysterious side to the *māšāl*.

In 1981, David Suter applied the idea of the *māšāl* to the Similitudes in the Book of Enoch.[49] He concluded that Landes' definition of a "model" or "paradigm" was too narrow, for the *māšāl* leads to a network of relations that *becomes* the model by employing a series of comparisons and contrasts used broadly to describe differences in moral behavior between the just and wicked, and between the present and the future. Especially in the Similitudes of Enoch the concept of the *māšāl* connects eschatological and cosmological elements so that a comparison can be established between the proper order of the cosmos at present and of the righteous in the age to come. He puts a great deal of emphasis on the relation of the *māšāl* to the *ḥidâ* or riddle, an aspect that Landes had noted. The Enoch book's concern with eschatological and apocalyptic ends links naturally to this mysterious side of the *māšāl*.

Timothy Polk took up the question of the nature of the Old Testament *māšāl* in 1983.[50] Although he too agreed with the insights of earlier authors that the *māšāl* has the basic meaning of a comparison used as a model or paradigm, he lamented the loss of a noetic side of self-understanding when such strong stress is placed on its normative function for human behavior. He pursued many of the directions found in modern New Testament parable research that emphasize the performative and reader-involving quality of the parable. The *māšāl* shares the true parable's nature as behavior-affecting, cathetic and reader-involving which requires a judgment made by the hearer on his or her own actions as well as on those of the actors in the story of a *māšāl* or parable. He sees the *māšāl* as paradigmatic because it has an openness in its use of imagery toward new meanings, which force a judgment on the part of the reader or hearer that challenges dogmatic certitudes. It has a definite connection to the riddle in that there is some mystery to be unlocked in the *māšāl*, a mystery which opens the hearer or reader to new action and possible new readings and invites a decision which has any number of directions or applications. Polk then analyzes the individual examples of the *mashal* in Ezekiel to illustrate his point. These include 12:22–23; 16:44; 18:2; 21:5; 14:7–8 and, in great detail, 17:1–24. As to this last, he observes that the chapter functions as a *māšāl* at several levels within the text itself connecting fable and application, judgment oracle with salvation oracle, Israel condemned with Israel redeemed. These in turn serve as models for the reality that impinged on the readership. The metaphorical depiction of Israel's history as one of judgment and salvation becomes paradigmatic and transhistorical. No one can escape the metaphor of "all the trees" in the very last verse with its ultimate inclusiveness and unlimited applicability.[51]

Moshe Greenberg's treatment of the same parable in Ezekiel 17 sees a unified movement among the four parts and develops a corkscrew model of intensification, chiasmus, and spatial planes to indicate the elaborate interconnections of metaphor and possible meanings.[52] In this, he is in agreement with Polk, although their insights into the particular structure of the passage differ somewhat. It is also very compatible with the viewpoint on Christian parables expressed above by John R. Donahue about the multiple levels of the parable and its interpretation.[53]

Observations

The foregoing sketch of recent attempts to understand the nature of the *māšāl* shows both a number of common points of agreement and a trajectory toward a fuller sense of the term than was held by commentators twenty years ago. All agree that the *māšāl* is not a literary form as such but a general concept that can be realized in a wide range of specific literary forms (proverbs, taunt songs, allegories, etc.). They also agree that there is a fundamental element of the lesson and norm for the reader or hearer to grasp in any *māšāl*. And all agree that the *māšāl* involves a likeness or comparison between two things, and does not derive from the root *mšl*, I "to rule or stand firm."

Each successive writer, however, has also pushed the discussion of the *māšāl* further along the lines of the parable. Beginning with Landes, they often refer to the *māšāl* as a parable, and accent the performative and decision-making quality inherent in the story or saying. This is particularly true of all elaborate forms of *meshalim* beyond the simple proverb (categories (2) to (5) in Landes' listing). Thus the work done on the *meshalim* in the Hebrew Scriptures relates closely to the advances made in general biblical hermeneutical theory, and in parable study of both the New Testament and Rabbinic sources.

V. NARRATIVE THEOLOGY AND PARABLE

Shifts Away from Historical Critical Method

There has been extensive interest in Christian theology and biblical studies about the potential of a "narrative theology" approach to unlocking the meaning of sacred texts for contemporary readers. Fundamentally this stems from the shift in scholarly circles away from an historical-critical methodology as the only means of interpreting texts, and a growing awareness of the world of the reader as a central feature of the interpretive process.

Historical critical methodology was born in the double development of the Enlightenment's rational search for the observable, i.e., scientific, truth of history,[54] and of the vast explosion in knowledge of the past which began with the first excavations at Pompeii in 1748, and was fed by the seemingly unending archaeological finds in the Near East throughout the nineteenth century.[55] Although many other factors were at work, these two, at least, produced a growing conviction that we can know our past accurately enough to understand what ancients thought and did. This conviction has dominated biblical studies in the first half of the twentieth century.[56] At the same time, historical-critical method has brought forward the realization that ancients did not think like modern people, and that their interests and presuppositions were often substantially different from those of the modern interpreter. Indeed, investigation of major literary remains discovered during excavations in ancient sites has revealed that the biblical texts which themselves claim ancient origins were the products of changing interests and theological perceptions over centuries.

The text itself has a history of interpretation that is present not only in the communities which call it sacred and define its meaning for their traditions, but within the composition of the text itself by authors and editors who built on the work of their predecessors, whether they were individual authors (such as a prophet) or a tradition or school of thought (such as those who established the priestly legislation in the Pentateuch). This in turn has led to a strong emphasis within historical-critical research on the need for an "historical consciousness" on the part of the modern interpreter, i.e. on the necessary awareness in the interpreter of his or her own presuppositions and biases as a reader of the text.

Put in another way, this critical concentration on identification of the original authors and editors of the text in order to discover the earliest and most authentic levels of ancient thought eventually exposed the greatest weakness in the historical-critical work of the last 150 years: a naive supposition that the interpreters were objective discoverers of the real meaning of the text as the biblical writers intended. It raised the need for a theory of hermeneutics to the forefront of biblical study.[57] The emphasis, in the words of one of the foremost of modern philosophers of hermeneutics, Paul Ricoeur, moved from the world behind the text to the world in front of the text.[58] This is certainly a far different atmosphere than the one inhabited by historical criticism's search for the original meaning and purpose of biblical texts. Instead, there are many possible readings and many reading groups so that the *text* must mediate the written tradition to the contemporary readers in constantly new readings. There is a richness and power in texts, and especially sacred texts, which cannot be captured by only one interpretive analysis.

And this is where the interest in narrative theology is born. Language is much more than rational discourse or the exposition of the truth. In narrative particularly, the purposes of persuasion, entertainment, and expressiveness must be added to that of exposition. There is a world of meaning in the art of narrative that cannot be read on only one level. Since words are symbols, they stand for meaning, but what all symbols have in common, in the words of Philip Wheelwright, is that they are always "more in intention than they are in existence."[59] They point beyond themselves; they are "self-transcendent." They do not just point to an object, as a signal, but are used in talk *about* things that are not part of our immediate and actual surroundings.[60] And when used in story and discourse, the richness of the symbolization multiplies its ways of communicating. It shares in the quality of language that Wheelwright calls "depth-language," or full expressive language, rather than in "steno-language" the plain-sense communication of science.

Rediscovery of the Power of Narrative

Many significant religious thinkers have begun to explore the specifically narrative nature of the biblical texts. Martin Buber commented that "Scripture does not state its doctrine as doctrine, but by telling a story, and without exceeding the limits set by the nature of a story."[61] He associates the proper locus of revelation in the art of narrative about human experience and does not feel uncomfortable that it is not a source of propositional truths. Herbert Schneidau has recently echoed this when he understands the Bible not to define ultimate truth but something more contingent in human experience: the essence of the Bible is narrative, and narrative is the essence of human experience.[62]

The proponents of the parable as metaphorical language often cite the close connections between the role of language in myth and in the parable. This has been a cornerstone of the thought of Joseph Campbell, the famous mythologist, who sees the function of myth to help people realize the meaning of their experience, and the myth narrative is to be read as a metaphor touching that experience.[63] A myth, for Northrup Frye as a literary critic, is the ironic distancing through metaphor between experience and literature.[64] Here, parable, narrative and myth are treated as though all share similar qualities of disclosure about ordinary human experience as it comes into contact with the world of the divine.

Finally, studies on the poetics of biblical narrative have applied theories about multiple points of view,[65] and intentional gaps in narrative,[66] to show how extensive is the role of audience involvement in understanding the narrative text. They lay the groundwork for a development of story theology based on the biblical texts.

John Collins, writing on story theology in modern biblical studies, lists several qualities that are worth remembering:[67] (1) A story is not about a general law, but is a concrete, specific illustration; thus, Adam may be all humanity, but he is depicted as one individual. (2) Concrete figures are easier for readers to identify with. (3) A story never makes claim to universal truth, but remains faithful to the texture of experience so that each story illumines an area of human experience but does not give an exhaustive explanation of all experience. (4) Stories are indeterminate and evocative and so not interpretable on only one level. (5) Stories do not have the intention of proving theology or guaranteeing the propositions of truth. (6) The "history-like" quality of a story does not make it an historical record. (7) The power of the story comes from the reader's ability to identify with it.

The Example of a Narrative Christology

It can be argued, as it is by J. B. Metz, Walter Kaspar, and other modern Roman Catholic theologians, that Christian theology has become too tied to philosophical (i.e. steno or scientific) discourse and has overlooked the narrative story element intrinsic to the revelation that it explores. Metz holds that we cannot have the content, i.e. revelation, without its form, the story. Christian theology is based on memory and the experience of the first communities of faith. Idealism tried to define theology as the identification of universal ideas, but Metz argues that basic human experience does not fit into such theories, and the remedy is to recover the category of narrative.[68] This new narrative Christology would have three distinguishing characteristics: (a) it would have to rely on the biblical stories if it is to know the person it acknowledges in faith, Jesus; since Jesus is a "person," he must be known through stories; (b) it stresses the role of person as agent, and not as eternal relation; Metz speaks of "event," "act" etc. of God; (c) it must be self-involving—one's praxis is as important as one's knowledge, it demands acknowledgment and action on the part of the believer, it insists on nothing less than the imitation of Christ.

Like Metz, Frans Jozef van Beeck calls for a new narrative Christology. He understands the priority of the language of Christian theology as "activity, intersubjectivity and rhetoric."[69] Commitment is an essential note of this language because the narrator and hearer are seeking insight into a relationship much as lovers seek to learn about each other. Biblical narratives thus have a primary aim of testimony about and insight into a person and a relationship and are therefore more like metaphors than biographies.[70] Communal experience lies at the root of these stories and because of their metaphorical and self-involving nature call forth in turn the worship, the witness, and the theology of the believing community.[71] At this point, Van Beeck goes on to conclude that the Gospel stories of Jesus reveal him as the man for others (i.e. his interpersonalness), willing to be misunderstood and to accept inhuman conduct. His unique ability to live in this manner stems from his absolute relatedness to the Father as his modus of being-a-person. Here he goes beyond the revelatory power of story or metaphor to a level of "critical reflection" akin to the "existential-theological" level of Dan O. Via. Within Christian theology, this is a necessary and legitimate enterprise, but Van Beeck has left the level of narrative, and opened himself to the charges that David Stern brought against Ricoeur above, namely that the disclosure which is discovered through the metaphorical understanding of the text was in fact already predetermined by the belief of the reader or hearer. Indeed, Van Beeck relies heavily on the reconstruction of the underlying Gospel story in the Synoptics as presented by Hans Frei.[72]

Van Beeck and Metz and others who argue for recognition of the role of metaphor in narrative and story are not to be faulted at this level. It is a part of their theological task to connect the narratives of biblical revelation with the doctrines and philosophical formulations of the theological tradition. At the same time, however, they are rediscovering the important role of figurative speech in the language of revelation, and reversing three centuries of attempts to discard the nature of biblical language and express its message in conceptual discourse. By asserting the notion of person as agent in story, these theologians not only seek the knowing of Jesus in the narratives of what he did, but also define the response of the hearer as acting, proclaiming, and serving this personal agent, Jesus. That is, it is self-involving.[73] Many problems remain to be developed by these theologians. They use words like "story" or "narrative" very broadly and never completely clarify how knowledge of this sort fits their metaphysical view of person and knowledge. Nor do they answer entirely how the biblical story moves to critical reflection without betraying the open-ended quality of metaphor as revelational. And even in their use of Scripture, they are selective of which stories, parables or gospel they cite. Surely, the choice between Mark or John, for example, will have a dramatic effect not only on the identity of the Jesus spoken about, but the metaphysical conclusions linked to its narratives. Robert Krieg develops some of these difficulties at length in his study.[74]

Krieg, however, points to some other positive aspects of modern reflection on narrative interpretation of the self. He cites Alasdair MacIntyre's arguments that when we treat a person's life as a narrative, it brings out the unity and coherence of the whole in order to understand personal existence.[75] The narrative life-journey keeps in balance the tension between our being goal-oriented but yet unpredictable and inconsistent in given moments. MacIntyre does not accept the validity or usefulness for ethics of Locke and Hume's search for a permanent, immutable inner core of a person's psychological state. Krieg draws a lesson from this for the Christian understanding of Jesus. Since the story of Jesus as narrative brings his life, teaching, claims and setting into historical connection with first century Judaism, the Gentile world, and the world of the evangelists and New Testament communities, it avoids Gnosticism with its claims about the pre-existent Lord stripped of any real link to his human life, disciples, etc. For Krieg, this has important ramifications for Christian-Jewish dialogue in that it forces Christians to recognize that Judaism is in God's plan because of the rootedness of Jesus in that real world, and not in doctrinal statements of later theology. It links Christianity and Judaism concretely in the liturgy when the story is proclaimed as sacred memory.[76]

Krieg also notes approvingly Ricoeur's comments on the distinction between biography (or history) and fiction as two narrative strategies.[77] Fiction is history-like but includes an element of imagination. Yet both seek to communicate the truth about the basic historicity of human experience. Since Gospel narratives are not strictly biographies of Jesus, they share some of the qualities of fiction in which the listener is asked to suspend judgment from outside history and follow the logic of the narrative on its own terms. Ricoeur concludes that a scientific history cannot be written of the Gospel stories, but such a history can function in conjunction with the configurational structure of the narrative as it presents itself in its mix of biographical, historical and fictional techniques.

Krieg completes his study by summarizing the value of a narrative Christology as putting us back in touch with the historical, personal existence of Jesus alongside our highly developed theology of Christ beyond spatial and temporal categories. Narrative in the forms of Christian biography, historical account and gospel give us complementary views of the personal existence of Jesus Christ and contribute to the task of systematic theology by specifying how notional terms can function.[78] For Christians, this is a promising line of development since it can forcefully bring together the story narrative of Jesus with biographical aspects of the disciples' responses and our own discipleship in order to understand our lives today. The same lesson can be applied to the Hebrew Scriptures as narrative and story and paradigm for the Jew.

Some Observations on Narrative Theology for the Bible

In particular, the *mashal* in the Scriptures, both Old and New Testaments, can help us today understand how the prophets, or the teachers of Torah, or Jesus or the apostolic churches interpreted their religious life situation in its "essential reality." They extend the difficult task of knowing what actually happened to the possible ways it should be understood. In this, is there room for Christians and Jews to share the key stories and the understanding of their stories as an entrée into discovery of the key images and paradigms on which each faith bases its own understanding and development? And will we discover much closer understanding in turn of the God whom we both acknowledge and have learned about in these normative narratives? Because narrative theology has largely been a Christian enterprise, I have focused on what it says about Christology, but it has obvious ramifications for exploring the common Testament's narratives.

VI. CONCLUSIONS

Modern study of the genre of parable and the *meshalim* in Scripture, Midrash and Talmud have revealed a certain amount of convergence around the recognition of its polysemous nature, i.e., its many interlocking levels of signs to be decoded at different levels of meaning. As Alan Mintz points out so effectively below in his article on the religious dimensions of modern Hebrew literature, centuries of interpretation have blurred the sharp edges of even pointed stories. They are read in light of their own history of interpretation, and contain thereby a surplus of meaning that makes them worthy of intensive reading. They have become classics.[79] If this is true of the Bible as a whole, with its various genres of prophetic oracle, law, poem, creedal list, etc., it is all the more true of those genres such as the *mashal* (or the myth) that partake closely of the nature of metaphorical language.

Narrative texts, but especially parable, myth or allegory texts, provide the literary context for communicating personal encounter language and for eliciting a response of acceptance. It is always the address of one to another, speaker and listener in relationship. Language becomes the vehicle by which one accepts another and another's viewpoint.

Since both Judaism and Christianity at least accept one sacred Testament and its narrative about God and the community of faith, and both rely heavily on the remembering of those encounters with God expressed literarily by our ancestors, and both demand commitment to the word and to the community that articulated them, there is a stronger possibility of dialogue around the biblical texts than around doctrinal or legal issues.

Moreover, the developments in Catholic thinking on revisiting doctrinal issues through a narrative form of theology offer some hopeful leads for a return to the biblical text as the matrix of Christian theological language. The emphases of Johannes Metz and Robert Krieg on the three traits of a narrative theology as (1) the reliance on narrative, (2) the notion of person as agent, and (3) the use of self-involving language, invite Jewish thinkers to develop some similar paradigm that would make mutual exploration of the common Testament a stimulus for a new theological language that might foster better communication and less misunderstanding between the faiths.

Catechetical Developments

Already, there has been some fruit from the narrative approach to Christian understanding of its own Jewish origin. It has forced recognition of the rootedness of all Christian insight into Jesus and the work of God in the Jewish (and for later books, Hellenistic) world of thought. It has begun a renaissance in the study of Christian origins, fostered new appreciation of the riches of the Hebrew Scriptures and broken down the sharp break with Judaism that permitted "us" to oppose and reject "them," and which in turn led to a long and tragic history of antisemitism based on a faulty understanding of Scripture itself.

Much work will be needed to bring the literary theories of parable interpretation to bear on the biblical text in the classroom, but it can be done. Sofia Cavalletti, a prominent Italian catecheticist, already talks of the mystery disclosed by parables and the need to see them as challenging and provocative.[80] It is wrong, she says, to try to explain a parable's meaning catechetically; it is better to meditate and question, and seek the rich possibilities of understanding when we contemplate the bond between different levels of meaning.

As a kind of closing epilogue I am intrigued by the observations of an Indian priest, P. Ribes, S. J., on the power of the biblical parables and narratives to reach even an audience on the subcontinent.[81] He attributes to the parables eight characteristics that make them primary tools of catechesis to any people: Parables are (1) transcultural in experience; (2) culturally free from too much local conditioning; (3) timeless and always relevant; (4) symbolic, not tied to one level of word signs; (5) subversive in their challenge to the existing order; (6) provocative in their challenges to the hearers; (7) excellent sounding boards to elicit audience reaction; (8) prophetic and proclamatory in exhorting a change of heart. If the parable can do all that Reverend Ribes claims from his experience, then there should be some lively and fruitful encounters in the Jewish-Christian dialogue of the future.

NOTES

1. Throughout this article, the English transliteration *mashal* or *meshalim* will be used except where it is important to indicate the Hebrew form, *māšāl* (*mĕšālîm*). Greek *parabolé* is found in both the New Testament and in the Septuagint translation of the Old Testament. In the latter case, it renders Hebrew *mashal* in all cases: see Edwin Hatch and Henry Redpath, *A Concordance to the Septuagint* (Oxford: The Clarendon Press, 1895) vol. II, p. 1056.

2. John Dominic Crossan, *In Parables: The Challenge of the Historical Jesus* (New York: Harper and Row, 1973).

3. See Amos N. Wilder, *Early Christian Rhetoric* (New York: Harper and Row, 1964) 78–79.

4. This point is well made by Pheme Perkins, *Hearing the Parables of Jesus* (Mahwah: Paulist Press, 1981) 154–158.

5. See A. Jülicher, *Die Gleichnisreden Jesu* (second edition; Tübingen: J.C.B. Mohr, 1899), and Joachim Jeremias, *The Parables of Jesus* (revised edition; New York: Scribner's, 1963).

6. C.H. Dodd, *The Parables of the Kingdom* (revised edition; New York: Scribner's, 1961).

7. Wilder, *Early Christian Rhetoric*, p. 89.

8. *Ibid.*

9. Robert Funk, *Language, Hermeneutic and the Word of God* (New York: Harper and Row, 1966), 133–162.

10. Sallie TeSelle, *Speaking in Parables: A Study in Metaphor and Theology* (Philadelphia: Fortress Press, 1975) 92–118, draws the same basic insight when she goes through the power of modern metaphors to elicit new insight into life.

11. Dan Otto Via, *The Parables: Their Literary and Existential Dimension* (Philadelphia: Fortress Press, 1967).

12. Via, *The Parables*, pp. 70–108.

13. Crossan, *In Parables*, pp. 7–22.

14. *Ibid.*, p. 13.

15. *Ibid.*, pp. 35–36 and the structure of chapters 2–4.

16. Norman Perrin, *Jesus and the Language of the Kingdom: Symbol and Metaphor in New Testament Interpretation* (Philadelphia: Fortress Press, 1976). The title of Perrin's book tells all.

17. See Crossan's later article on "Structural Analysis and the Parables of Jesus," *Semeia* 1 (1974) 192–221.

18. John Dominic Crossan, "Parable, Allegory and Paradox," in *Semiology and Parables: An Exploration of the Possibilities Offered by Structuralism for Exegesis,* edited by Daniel Patte (Pittsburgh Theological Monographs 9; Pittsburgh: Pickwick Press, 1976) 247–281.

19. Claude Lévi-Strauss, *Structural Anthropology* (New York: Doubleday, 1967), in the chapter, "The Structural Study of Myth."

20. Pierre Maranda, editor, *Mythology* (Baltimore: Penguin, 1972).

21. Roman Jakobson and M. Halles, *Fundamentals of Language* (Janua Linguarum NR 1; 's-Gravenhage: Mouton, 1956).

22. Crossan, "Parable, Allegory and Paradox," p. 255.

23. John R. Donahue, "Response to John Dominic Crossan," in *Semiology and Parables,* pp. 282–289. See more recently his book, *The Gospel in Parable.* (Philadelphia: Fortress Press, 1988) 1–27.

24. Gunther Bornkamm, *Jesus of Nazareth* (New York: Harper & Row, 1960) 69.

25. John Dominic Crossan, *In Parables,* p. 20.

26. Clemens Thoma and Simon Lauer, editors, *Die Gleichnisse der Rabbinen, Erster Teil: Pesiqta deRav Kahana (PesK): Einleitung, Übersetzung, Parallelen, Kommentar, Texte* [Judaica et Christiana 10] (Bern: Peter Lang, 1986). See also the article by Clemens Thoma in this volume which explains these positions more fully.

27. Louis Isaac Rabinowitz, "Parable in the Talmud and Midrash," *Encyclopedia Judaica* 13 (Jerusalem: Keter Publishing House, 1972) cols. 73–77.

28. Clemens Thoma, "Literary and Theological Aspects of the Rabbinic Parables," in this volume.

29. *Ibid.*

30. *Ibid.*

31. David Flusser, *Die rabbinischen Gleichnisse und der Gleichniserzahler Jesus, 1. Teil* (Judaica et Christiana 4; Bern: Peter Lang, 1981). See also his approach witnessed in the article in this volume, "Aesop's Miser and the Parable of the Talents."

32. David Stern, "Jesus Parables from the Perspective of Rabbinic Literature: The Example of the Wicked Husbandmen," in this volume.

33. "Rhetoric and Midrash: The Case of the Mashal," *Prooftexts* 1 (Baltimore: Johns Hopkins University Press, 1981) 261–291.

34. Aaron Milavec, "A Fresh Analysis of the Parable of the Wicked Husbandmen in the Light of the Jewish-Catholic Dialogue," in this volume.

35. The texts are Jeremiah 2:21 and Hosea 10:1.

36. See Milavec, *art. cit.*

37. The weakness of this approach shows up the most in Milavec's argument for how Matthew's version of the parable actually reduces the allegorical elements that link the identity of the "son" to Jesus. This is strained by his attempts to rid the text of any rejection of Israel in the reading. It can be readily conceded that the original story in the parable could well have used two rounds of servants and then a son with only a natural allusion to the close connection of servant–son in various Hebrew Scripture contexts, and not require that Jesus pointed to himself. But it is very difficult to find any of this simplicity in the existing accounts of the parable.

38. A. Bentzen, *Introduction to the Old Testament,* vol. 1 (second edition; Copenhagen: G.E.C. Gad, 1952) 167.

39. J. Schmidt, *Studien zur Stilistik der Alttestamentlichen Sprachliteratur* (Alttestamentliche Abhandlungen 13:1, 1936) 1–2.

40. Otto Eissfeldt, *Der Mashal im Alten Testament* (BZAW 24; Giessen: Töpelmann, 1913).

41. So, for example, William McKane, "The Meaning of *māšāl,*" in his *Proverbs* (Old Testament Library; Philadelphia: Westminster Press, 1970) 22–33; Gerhard von Rad, *Wisdom in Israel* (Nashville: Abingdon Press, 1972) 25–34; James Crenshaw, "Wisdom," *Old Testament Form Criticism,* edited by John Hayes (San Antonio: Trinity University Press, 1974) 229–39.

42. Aubrey Johnson, "*māšāl,*" *SVT* III (Leiden: Brill, 1955) 162–69.

43. Otto Eissfeldt, *The Old Testament: An Introduction* (New York: Harper and Row, 1966) 81–84.

44. Other examples of popular proverbs cited by Eissfeldt include 1 Kings 20–21; Genesis 10:9; 1 Samuel 24:14; 2 Samuel 5:8. An example of a double line proverb in parallelism may be Jeremiah 31:29 (also in Ezekiel 18:2).

45. See Eissfeldt, pp. 86–87.

46. William McKane, *Proverbs;* see footnote 41 above.

47. George M. Lades, "Jonah: A *māšāl?*" *Israelite Wisdom: Theological and Literary Essays in Honor of Samuel Terrien,* edited by John Gammie, *et al.* (Missoula: Scholar's Press, 1978) 137–58.

48. George E. Mendenhall, "The Shady Side of Wisdom: The Date and Purpose of Genesis 3," *A Light unto My Path: Old Testament Essays in Honor of Jacob M. Myers,* edited by Howard Bream, *et al.* (Philadelphia: Temple University, 1974) 319–334.

49. David Winston Suter, "*Māšāl* in the Similitudes of Enoch," *JBL* 100 (1981) 193–212.

50. Timothy Polk, "Paradigms, Parables, and *Měšālîm:* On Reading the *māšāl* in Scripture," *CBQ* 45 (1983) 564–83.

51. *Ibid.,* 582–583.

52. Moshe Greenberg, *Ezekiel 1–20* (Anchor Bible 22; New York: Doubleday, 1983) 307–324.

53. John R. Donahue, "Semiology and Parables," 286–88. See note 23 above.

54. Hans Frei, *The Eclipse of Biblical Narrative* (New Haven: Yale University Press, 1974) and the passing remark of Frank Kermode, "New Ways with Bible Stories," in this volume.

55. See Keith Schoville, *Biblical Archaeology in Focus* (Grand Rapids: Baker Book House, 1973) 84–95, and Philip King, *American Archaeology in the Mideast: A History of the American Schools of Oriental Research* (Philadelphia: ASOR, 1983) 1–110, esp. 1–27.

56. See Edgar Krentz, *The Historical-Critical Method* (Guides to Biblical Scholarship; Philadelphia: Fortress Press, 1975) 22–41.

57. Frei, *The Eclipse of Biblical Narrative,* 1–16.

58. See Paul Ricoeur, "Toward a Hermeneutic of the Idea of Revelation," in *Essays on Biblical Interpretation,* edited by Lewis Mudge (Philadelphia: Fortress, 1980) 73–118, esp. 95–100; also his *Interpretation Theory: Discourse on the Surplus of Meaning* (Fort Worth: Texas Christian University Press, 1976), and *The Symbolism of Evil* (Boston: Beacon Press, 1967) 347–357 on hermeneutics and critical reflection of a "second naiveté."

59. Philip Wheelwright, *The Burning Fountain: A Study in the Language of Symbolism* (Bloomington: Indiana University, 1954) 19.

60. Susanne Langer, *Philosophy in a New Key* (Cambridge: Harvard University Press, 1942) 30–31.

61. Martin Buber, as quoted by Frank McConnell, *The Bible and the Narrative Tradition* (New York: Oxford University Press, 1986) 14.

62. Herbert N. Schneidau, "Biblical Narrative and Modern Consciousness," in *The Bible and the Narrative Tradition,* ed. Frank McConnell (New York: Oxford Unviersity Press, 1986) 132–50, esp. 132–34.

63. Joseph Campbell in an interview with Eugene Kennedy in the *National Catholic Reporter,* May 1, 1987, pp. 7–8.

64. Northrup Frye, "The Expanding World of Metaphor," *JAAR* 53 (1985) 585–98.

65. Adele Berlin, *Poetics and Interpretation of Biblical Narrative* (Sheffield: Almond Press, 1983) 43–47.

66. Meir Sternberg, *The Poetics of Biblical Narrative, Ideological Literature and the Drama of Reading* (Bloomington: Indiana University Press, 1985) 186–229, on the theory of "gaps."

67. John Collins, "The Rediscovery of Biblical Narrative," *Chicago Studies* 21 (1982) 45–58.

68. Johannes B. Metz, "An Identity Crisis in Christianity?" in William Kelly, ed., *Theology and Discovery* (Milwaukee: Marquette University Press, 1980) 169–178, esp. 172–77; and see his *Faith in History and Society,* translated by D. Smith (New York: Seabury, 1980).

69. Frans Jozef van Beeck, *Christ Proclaimed: Christology as Rhetoric* (New York: Paulist Press, 1979) 66.

70. *Ibid.*, 327. See also Ricoeur, *Biblical Hermeneutics,* 99–116, on revelation as testimony.

71. Van Beeck, *Christ Proclaimed,* 325–327.

72. See note 54 above.

73. See Robert Krieg, *Story-Shaped Christology: The Role of Narratives in Identifying Jesus Christ* (New York: Paulist Press, 1988) 34–110, who traces these concepts in Schillebeeckx, Küng, and Kaspar, as well as in van Beeck.

74. *Ibid.*

75. Alasdair MacIntyre, *After Virtue* (Notre Dame: University of Notre Dame Press, 1971) 191–203.

76. Krieg, *Story-Shaped Christology,* 145–148.

77. Paul Ricoeur, "The Narrative Function," in *Hermeneutics and the Human Sciences,* ed. John Thompson (Cambridge: Cambridge University Press, 1981) 274–96.

78. Krieg, *Story-Shaped Christology,* 163.

79. Alan Mintz, "Modern Hebrew Literature as a Source for Jewish Theology: Repositioning the Question," in this volume.

80. Sofia Cavalletti, "The Parables in Catechesis," *SIDIC* XIX, no. 1 (1987) 16–18.

81. P. Ribes, S.J. reported in *Word-Event* 60 (March 15, 1986) 19–20.

III.
STORY: ANCIENT AND MODERN

Narrative Aspects of the Epistle of St. Paul to the Romans

Romano Penna

I. STATUS QUAESTIONIS

For some time now and most fortunately, theological studies have recovered the narrative dimension.[1] It is indeed a question of true rediscovery. That which in the beginning had been a determining factor of the biblical way of talking about God and man gave way, little by little, to a type of abstract speculative argumentation in the Christian tradition. It so happened that, though in the frame of a faith in the incarnate Logos, "it was not the Logos that was to be narrative, but the biblical narrations which were to be rendered logical."[2]

The portion in the canon of the New Testament most suited to such treatment was the Epistle of Paul to the Romans, though even more frequently, at least up to the time of F. Christian Baur, it was considered a mine of systematic theological axioms. Significant examples of such an approach are the works of St. Augustine, *Expositio Quarumdam Propositionum Ex Epistola Ad Romanos,*[3] and of Philip Melancton, *Loci Communes Rerum Theologicarum Seu Hypotyposes Theologiae.*[4] Even most recently, attempts have not been lacking which, though not in themselves illegitimate, are conditioned by systematized pre-suppositions, either to consider the Epistle to the Romans as a mirror of all Pauline theology[5] or to attribute to that writing a structure of doctrinal character.[6] The Tuebingen professor, Ferdinand Christian Baur,[7] began in the last century to emphasize the fundamental value of the historical circumstances of the Epistle to the Romans and most especially its major theme concerning Paul's rapport with Judaism, thereby removing Romans from the dogmatic perspective in which it had been placed.

Having emphasized this rapport, Baur and his successors did not consider, however, the typical style of the epistle nor whether it dealt with questions from a purely argumentative point of view, and to what extent the epistle employed particular narrative techniques in the exposition of its message. Even contemporary specific studies are wanting in that respect. To my knowledge, there exists only a brief mention in an article by G. Lohfink on the narrative structure as a fundamental dimension of the New Testament.[8] He recognizes that in Romans the narrative texts, though much less numerous than the argumentative ones, "clearly take on a primary function."[9] But Lohfink does not make a detailed analysis of the narrative texts. Stower's study on the literary genre of the diatribe in Romans limits itself to indicate briefly the technique of the *Exemplum* in the history of Abraham, in chapter four of the Epistle.[10]

It would be worthwhile to attempt a wider and more detailed analysis of the text of Romans to explore if there may be other narrative passages, and to propose a scrutiny of their number and gender. However, let us premise some methodological observations.

II. EXACT DETERMINATION OF METHOD

In the first place, I want to prevent possible misunderstandings by stating clearly what I do *not* mean by "narrative":

(1) I do not mean *narratio* in the sense of the ancient rhetoric. This, when in the case of a continual discourse (according to its three genres: judicial, deliberative, and epideictic), usually consisted of six *partes orationis:* the *exordium,* the *narratio,* the *propositio,* the *argumentatio* or *probatio,* the *refutatio* or *reprehensio,* the *peroratio* or *conclusio.* Among these, the *narratio* constituted the entrance into the subject and bore the presentation of facts or data to be discussed.[11]

Some authors recommend subdividing Romans according to these categories. They propose to identify the *narratio* in the short initial section 1:13–15 (which is then resumed in the *peroratio* 15:14–33).[12] But such a position, apart from the fact that we have too weak a basis from which to attribute to Paul the schema appropriate to the rhetorical schools, does not correspond to our concept of narration, which is much more vast and flexible. In fact, we intend to verify in Romans the presence of narrative elements on the entire arch of the epistle. It is theoretically possible that we may find some of them in chapters five to eleven and vice versa, that not all of the section 1:18–4:25 is of the narrative type.

(2) I do not mean that kind of narration which is such only for us and not for the native readers. The Epistle to Romans offers an entire series of information on the situation of the Christian community in the years 50–60 C.E. From the exhortative part of the writing, for example, and most of all from 14:1 to 15:13, we can derive notions directly concerning the internal life of that church. From this point of view, the epistle "recounts" to us some aspects of the communitarian experience of the Christians in Rome. Furthermore, only this verification tells us that Paul did not compose a purely doctrinal writing but also makes reference to the concrete living conditions of those whom he addresses. Information of this kind, however, cannot be considered a type of narration because the original readers, being part of that community, did not perceive it as such. They would consider "narrative" only such information which the sender told them by way of a third person or which, though referring to them, involved their past.

At this point we encounter the problem of what should appropriately be termed narration or story. We cannot here discuss the theory of the entire question.[13] It is important, however, to realize that narrating has never been alien to man, right from the beginning. Some of the greatest literary expressions of humanity assumed the narrative form, from the epics of Homer and Virgil to the poems of Dante Alighieri, from the tragedies of Aeschylus to the plays of William Shakespeare, from the ancient Greek history writers to the romantic novels of F. Dostoevski and A. Manzoni.

Narration has always been a fundamental mode of communication among men and, therefore, in the religious sphere as well (cf. the concept of myth), from the ancient Mesopotamic poems to the Bible. Narration has also taken many different forms, as in prose or poetry. Between an historical account and a fable for children there is no other connection but that both narrate something. Narration can, therefore, be the common denominator of very diverse literary forms. There results, then, the essential element of narration, which absolutely implies that it refer to life, be it to characters or occurrences. It is secondary to the definition of narration whether those facts be real or fictitious. The important factor is that it proposes one or more actors to which one attributes an action or a series of actions.

It is in this broad sense that we want to single out in the Letter to the Romans the presence of the narrative aspects. Being various realizations of the concept of narration, we should anticipate that these narrative aspects are found on different levels in Romans. In effect, it is possible to ascertain diverse forms of narration in the Pauline Epistle, which we will now review without claiming to do a commentary on them.

III. FORMS OF NARRATION IN ROMANS

Let me present here a dissection of the narrative forms present in Romans, though I am fully aware that this is merely an attempt which does not hold a claim to perfection. The fundamental critical guide was to exclude propositions which have God as their grammatical and logical subject (i.e. a non-historical subject), or a theological abstract concept (e.g. the law in 3:19–20, or hope in 5:5), generically speaking, man in an axiomatic formulation (cf. 3:38). Positively speaking, I have included in the list all those texts which have varying human subjects, as well as those that may be dealing with similes.

(1) The literary form making the greatest impression in Romans is certainly the *biblical narrative,* that is, the repositioning of characters and events of the Sacred Scriptures.[14] There are two sections in which they are presented to the reader: chapter four and the block of chapters nine to eleven. Both have a place and a function of great importance for the treatment of the theme of justification by faith.

The character through whom the story has come to be most widely remembered is *Abraham,* in chapter 4:1–3, 10–11, 13, 17–22. In these texts reverberate various moments of the ancient story about the great biblical patriarch: from the promise of descendants, in Rom 4:13, 17–18 (cf. resp. Gn 12:7; 17:5; 15:5), to the announcement of the birth of Isaac, even though he was old, in Rom 4:19–21 (cf. Gn 1:1, 17), to the reception of the circumcision, in Rom 4:11 (cf. Gn 17:11). Most of all, there is the reference to Abraham's pure faith according to the passage of Gn 15:6, which is quoted a good three times in Rom 4:3, 9, 22. It is for this, his own attitude, that Abraham is proposed as a model of authentic faith and father of all true believers (cf. Rom 4:11b–12). The pivotal point of Paul's reasoning is the fact that, according to the biblical story, faith was accredited as justice to Abraham while he was still uncircumcised (cf. Rom 4:10f) and, therefore, anterior to every act of law, namely to prescind from every merit. The entire narration serves to explain that the same portrayal applies to the believer in Christ (cf. Rom 4:23–24), who therefore knows that he must conform not so much to some abstract principles, as to the lived history by the most genuine "homo biblicus."

There follow other related characters, even though they are treated but summarily. They are *Isaac* and *Jacob* in Rom 9:7–13, both with various references to the book of Genesis (cf. 21:12; 18:10; 25:23; and Malachi 1:2–3). They are placed opposite the respective brothers Ismael (even though not mentioned by name) and Esau, in order to emphasize the theological theme according to which the election is based not on works but on the free will of Him who calls (cf. Rom 9:11). The same comparison, but in a contrary sense, is valid for the *Pharaoh* in Rom 9:14–17 (cf. Ex 9:16), stating that God sovereignly "uses mercy with whom he wishes and hardens him whom he wants" (Rom 9:18).

This also explains that the obstinacy of Israel in regard to the Gospel belongs to a divine plan. As a parallel, the life of the prophet Elijah is recalled in Rom 11:2b–4 (with quotations from 1 Kings 19:10, 14, 18), especially in reference to the seven thousand men in Israel who did not bend their knee before Baal. The purpose was to highlight the existence of a "remnant people," even at the moment when all the rest of Israel persisted in unbelief.

Other Old Testament characters remembered by Paul are Moses (cf. Rom 10:5, 19), David (cf. Rom 4:6–8), Isaiah (cf. Rom 9:27, 29; 10:16–20; 15:12), Hosea (cf. Rom 9:25), yet not so much as protagonists of some story but as hagiographers, that is, authors of texts quoted by the Apostles. These names are explicitly mentioned instead of resorting to the most frequent and impersonal formula, "it is written" (cf. Rom 1:17; 2:14; 3:4; etc.). The respective texts quoted by Paul articulate a *particularly concrete and imaginative language:* like the two macarisms of Ps 32:1–2; the covert allusion to the singular matrimonial event in Hosea (cf. Hos 2:1–25); the metaphor of the sand on the seashore (cf. Is 10:22–23); the remembrance of Sodom and Gomorrah (cf. Is 28:16); the dual metaphor of ascent into heaven and descent into the abyss (cf. Deut 30:12f); the image of jealousy (cf. Deut 32:21); and the paradox of being found by those who do not seek (cf. Is 65:1f).

(2) Quite relevant for the discourse conducted by Paul in Romans is the *narrative dimension of the Christological Kerygma.* Not that this is a specific characteristic of Romans, given that the narrative dimension belongs instead to the Christian faith itself, as vouched for already by the old confessions of pre-Pauline faith in 1 Cor 15:3–5. Nevertheless, it is worth observing that the narrative dimension maintains itself and is repeatedly remembered in our epistle, where it is included in a dozen passages.

The first of these is immediately present in the address and offers a confession in truly original terms: "He was born of David's seed according to the flesh, and was appointed Son of God in power according to the Spirit of holiness from the resurrection of the dead" (Rom 1:3b–4a). We note here only that in the whole New Testament no other christological formula exists which hinges on the two extremes of Jesus' entire earthly life, his birth by Davidic descent and his resurrection from the dead (cf. 2 Tim 2:8). The commentaries will obviously be much more expansive; for the time being it is most interesting to observe that between these two extremes the entire history of Jesus is contained.

Other passages in Romans, instead, insist or at least always include the component of death or blood, which in this first text is absent. It is a question of the following passages: "God had pre-established that Jesus serve as an instrument of expiation . . . by his blood" (Rom 3:25); "Jesus was put to death for our sins and raised to life to justify us" (Rom 4:25); "Christ died for us . . . by the death of his Son" (Rom 5:6, 8, 10); "When he died he died once for all, to sin, so his life now is life with God" (Rom 6:10); "He not only died for us, he rose from the dead, and there, at God's right hand he stands and pleads for us" (Rom 8:34); "If your lips confess that Jesus is Lord and if you believe in your heart that God raised him from the dead" (Rom 10:9); "This explains why Christ died and came to life" (Rom 14:9); "Christ did not please himself but, as Scripture says, 'The reproaches of them that reproached thee fell upon me' " (Rom 15:3; cf. Ps 69:10); "Christ became the servant of circumcised Jews . . . to carry out the promise made to the patriarchs" (Rom 15:8); see also Rom 7:4; 8:3, 32.

It is evident that Paul does not narrate details, whether the events of Jesus' birth as do Matthew 1–2 and Luke 1–2, or the history of the passion, as in all four Gospels. His preoccupation is not biographical but kerygmatic or, better yet, he reflects on this kerygma. Its presence scattered throughout the Epistle to the Romans tells how much importance Paul accords to kerygma. In accord with modern sensibility it is, of course, debatable to what extent the Resurrection truly belongs to an historical or at least historiographical dimension. But that does not diminish the fact that Paul "recounts" it together with Jesus' death, nor that to his readers the two events are inseparably on the same level.

(3) In Romans, the *autobiographical elements of the sender* are not lacking. Here and there, in the course of the Letter, Paul also talks about himself. Beginning with the address, he is not satisfied to mention only his own name, as is customary in ancient epistolography, but he adds his specific apostolic qualification (cf. 1:1, "Apostle by vocation,

specially chosen to preach the Good News of God") and its origin from the Lord Jesus (cf. 1:5, "Through whom we have received grace and apostleship"), as well as its purpose (cf. *ibid.,* "To obtain the obedience of the faith on the part of all the Gentiles"). This last characteristic returns in 11:13b, where with a certain boldness, Paul asserts, "As Apostle of the Gentiles, I am proud of my ministry."

Yet, he does not forget but rather emphasizes his Jewish identity (cf. 11:1b, "Also I am an Israelite, descended from Abraham through the tribe of Benjamin"), as found elsewhere (cf. 2 Cor 11:21; Phil 3:5–6). But what is new and original in Romans is the explicitly professed anxiety regarding the salvation of his people: "I say the truth in Christ, I do not lie, and my conscience gives testimony to it in the Holy Spirit. I myself would wish to be condemned, separated from Christ to the advantage of my brothers and my blood relatives according to the flesh" (Rom 9:1–3; cf. 11:14: "With the hope of bringing forth the jealousy of those of my blood, and, thus, save some").

There emerges here overpoweringly an image not only of the apostle but of the man, conscious of his ethnic membership and his great inner sensibility, that is, a motive of suffering and of generous altruistic efforts.

A particular autobiographical note is supplied in 3:8, where Paul speaks of having been slandered, as if he had preached the need to do evil as a means to do good (cf. 6:1). But he refuses resolutely to acknowledge an accusation that denotes a great misunderstanding of his message, if not a deliberate detraction.[15]

The most extensive autobiographical sections in Romans, however, are those that constitute the framework in which the entire body of the Epistle is set, namely the introduction (cf. 1:8–13) and the conclusion (cf. 15:16–32). There, more than ever, the rapport with the reader is on a direct and conversational basis, personalized, i.e., narratively. Paul expresses the desire to meet with the Christians of Rome, his awareness of having already traveled through all of the regions from Jerusalem to Illyricum, the plan to reach Spain, his fears of the imminent voyage (from Corinth where Paul probably composed the Epistle) to Jerusalem, to deliver there a collection for the poor of that church, and the request, therefore, for supporting prayers for the trials awaiting him.

These two sections are certainly important, not merely from the historical point of view but also to establish the occasion that had conditioned the dispatch of the Epistle to the Romans. Together with this, other autobiographical fragments mentioned above contribute to make

Romans a writing altogether other than impersonal and theoretical, and to place it on a living and dynamic level.

(4) There follow some passages that may be called a *theological biography of the readers,* where, by means of pronouns of the first and second person plural, the sender describes a situation referring to or involving his readers from the point of view of their new identity as Christians.

Thus we read: "The fame of your faith expands throughout the world" (1:8b; cf. 16:19a: "Your fidelity to Christ, anyway, is famous everywhere"); "My brothers, I am quite certain that you are full of good intentions, perfectly well instructed and able to advise each other" (15:14). More specifically, Paul narrates elsewhere the itinerary or the spiritual aim to be pursued by his readers. In this case, the fundamental theme is that of faith; "We believe in him who raised Jesus our Lord from the dead" (4:24; cf. 10:9); "by faith we are justified and at peace with God . . . we have entered this state of grace in which we can boast . . . we can boast about our sufferings . . ." (5:1–4).

Baptism also is narrated as a decisive moment in a biographical turning point: "Do you not know that all of us who have been baptized into Christ Jesus were baptized into his death? We were buried therefore with him by baptism . . . so that . . . we too might walk in newness of life" (6:3–4; cf. 6:8, 11, 14, 17–18); "When you were slaves of sin . . . what return did you get from the things for which you are now ashamed? . . . but . . . the return you get is sanctification . . ." (6:20–22). Everything leads back, however, to the event of Christ's self-giving and the before and after baptism in the life of a Christian: "While we were in the flesh . . . but now we are discharged from the law . . ." (cf. 7:4–6). The same notion is found in 11:30: "Just as you were once disobedient to God but now have received mercy." Lastly, it is pointed out that the eschatological horizon has come closer: "For salvation is nearer to us now than when we first believed" (13:11b).

Thus, Paul does not talk abstractly about the Gospel and its theological content but refers frequently to the history of the Christians themselves who, based on their lived experience, have come not only to a better understanding of the Gospel but to its realization, so to speak, to an historicization of the Gospel in their existence.

(5) A good part of the material from the Epistle to the Romans could be labeled as *theological narration.* This refers to those pages in which the discourse is conducted in the third person plural, or with "you" or "I," but with universal value of an enallage.

In all of these cases, the Apostle, instead of reasoning abstractly or only proclaiming fundamental truths, describes and therefore "recounts" the situation of a moral or spiritual experience that has no reference to particular, well-defined persons (and therefore is not a biography), but to a general human condition.

There are five main sections. The first is 1:18–32, where Paul describes the situation of the "men who suppress the truth in their wickedness" (1:18b), that is, the humanity outside Christ and object of the anger of God. To tell the truth, this page is not entirely written in the narrative style, since we also find declarations of principle that space out the real and appropriate description. But the text of 1:21–22, 25, 26b–32 can be included very well in our classification; his intent is to say that all have sinned and are deprived of the glory of God (cf. 3:23).

A second section of theological narration is constituted by almost all of chapter two (with the exception of verses 6–11, 16), having also a stylistic variation corresponding to two different groups of persons. In 2:12–15, where the unwritten law observed by the pagans is treated, the discourse proceeds normally in the third person plural. Instead in 2:1–5, 17–29, where he deals with the law as a Jewish patrimony, Paul continues with the technique of direct allocution in the second person singular. In this case, the "you" does not refer to one singular interlocutor, but to Jews in general (cf. 2:17), according to the gender of the diatribe that tends to brighten up the discourse (but one can also hypothesize that, because of this literary device, the readers of Romans might be dominantly Christians coming from Judaism).

In the third place, we are able to include in this type of narration the passage of 5:12–19, when the Apostle opposes Adam and Christ as initiators of two qualitatively different moments in the history of humanity. Applying to these what 1QS 4:15 says about the two spirits, we can affirm that "in these two there is the history of all the sons of man." And effectively, instead of giving a theoretical discourse on sin and grace, Paul opposes the disobedience of Adam and Christ inasmuch as they both reverberate upon all those who adhere to their conduct, and lead respectively to death and life.

In the fourth place, there comes the famous passage of 7:7–25. In spite of his known difficulty, one thing is clear: it "recounts" an experience of life. This is confirmed by the frequent use of the first person singular (twenty-one times the pronoun, in the nominative, dative, accusative; and four times the possessive adjective "my"), which is a companion to the "you" of chapter two. Just as there, however, the "I" is not seen as autobiographical, unless in a very indirect way. On the first level, the writer gathers together facts from a very vast human experience, be they individualized as pagan or Jewish or Christian (or more than one).

Lastly, Paul recounts also the appropriate condition of Israel from the point of view of his inalienable religious patrimony (cf. 9:4–5: "They are Israelites and possess filial adoption, glory, alliance, legislation, the cult, the promise, the patriarchs; from them Christ comes according to the flesh"). Nevertheless, he makes known that Israel as a whole did not arrive at that which the law intended, that is, faith in Christ (cf. 9:30–10:4), other than the pagans, even though a remnant was converted (cf. 9:6b–7; 11:5–7).

Even the created world is personified and almost humanized while waiting for the eschatological redemption (cf. 8:20–21).

(6) In Romans there is also a type of narration that belongs to *similes*. They are not real parables, nor are they introduced by a special formula. Instead, they are examples which Paul introduces from everyday life in order to illustrate, with figurative language, particular points of his doctrine.

Here more than ever, the narration, even when dealing with short texts, appears mostly as such, since it is expressed through concrete and efficacious images which are easy to remember. They have the dual advantage of conferring plasticity to abstract concepts and incorporating the material of the discourse in the dimension of daily life. The passages in question are six. They offer an *imagery* treated by various spheres of the human experience.

First: Rom 4:4–5:

> Now to one who works, his wages are not reckoned as a gift but as his due. And to one who does not work but trusts him who justifies the ungodly, his faith is reckoned as righteousness.

As one can see, the example is not developed independently, but immediately passes to the theological lesson which it wishes to impart. Anyway, the comparison regarding the practices of workers is undoubtedly eloquent. We can therefore catch a glimpse of the thematic affinity to the parable of Jesus about the workers sent into the vineyard at different hours (cf. Mt 20:1–16).

Second: Rom 5:7f:

> With difficulty does one find one who might be disposed to die for a just man; maybe there can be one who has the courage to die for an

honest person. But God demonstrates his love for us because, while we were still sinners, Christ died for us.

In reality, here the example is imperfect; Paul says that what is retained as the greatest demonstration of brotherhood between friends (cf. 15:13) is surpassed by the comportment of God in Christ, who shows roads other than human ones. But truly the inadequateness of the comparison gives an enormous prominence to the fact and significance of the death of Christ.

Third: Rom 7:2–3:

> Thus a married woman is bound by law to her husband as long as he lives; but if her husband dies, she is discharged from the law concerning her husband. Accordingly, she will be called an adulteress if she lives with another man while her husband is alive. But if her husband dies, she is free from that law, and if she marries another man, she is not an adulteress. In the same way, my brothers, you also. . . .

Far from a matrimonial teaching of the catechism, Paul inserts this line in the form of comparison in the context of a reflection upon the failing of the validity of the Torah. The example is rich and appropriate and assumes the characteristics of an allegory, which is explained in the following verses 4–6: the spouse symbolizes the readers (Jewish-Christian?), the first husband is the Torah (or the old regime of the law), the second is Christ (or the new regime of the Spirit). This example does not say how the first husband might die; but in the explanation it is determined that this happened "through the body of Christ." We note nevertheless that while in the example he who dies is the husband (=Torah), in the explanation instead, those who die are the Christians themselves (v. 4: "died to the law in order to belong to another"; cf. v. 6). Here the comparison stumbles: regarding the historical-salvific plan, Paul does not say that it is the Torah which dies, but rather it is the Christian who dies for the Torah! The image however remains equally incisive.

Fourth: Rom 9:20–21:

> But who are you, a man, to answer back to God? Will what is molded say to its molder, 'Why have you made me thus?' Has the potter no right over the clay, to make out of the same lump one vessel for beauty and another for menial use?

The Apostle here is clearly inspired by the prophetic texts of Is 29:16; 45:9; Jer 18:6 and also Wis 15:7. He reformulates, however, the comparison in his own terms and applies it particularly to the new situation of Israel in confrontation with the Gospel. The examples conserve the same efficacious plasticity already inherent in the old biblical texts.

Fifth: Rom 11:16–24. We have here the longest simile and perhaps the most famous in all the epistle; but Paul is very conscious that he is dealing with an example "against nature" (v. 24). He deals with the image of the wild olive-tree grafted upon the good olive-tree, which outside of the metaphor alludes to the insertion of the converted pagans upon the trunk of Israel. The mere amplitude of the text indicates that the Apostle attributes to it a noteworthy importance. His purpose is twofold, theological and paraenetic. On one side, Paul wants to convince Christians of pagan origin that their new identity is intimately connected to the historical-salvific identity of the people of Israel. On the other side, Paul asks them not to boast before Jews, not even those who remain unbelievers, since "it is not you who support the root, but the root that supports you" (11:18). In addition, there is also a component of hope regarding non-believing Israel, which can always "be grafted back again upon the same olive tree, being of the same nature" (11:24). It is not an exaggeration to say that, as a whole, this simile recapitulates in itself, on an imaginative level, the entire dense subject of chapters 9–11.

Sixth: Rom 13:12:

> The night is far gone, the day is at hand. Let us then cast off the works of darkness and put on the armor of light.

The beautiful image used here (cf. also Eph 5:14; 1 Thes 5:6) continues the one already introduced in v. 11: "The time has come to wake yourselves up from sleep," which is also an image, very widespread throughout Hellenism (cf. the Commentaries). Night and day are here understood on an apocalyptic-conceptual background (=this world and the world to come; images of this kind are found for example in *Bar. syr.* 85:10). We can only note one more time the efficaciousness of this type of discourse which, upon the waves of the images, passes immediately from the announcement to the paraenesis.

IV. CONCLUSION

As we have seen in this analysis, Romans offers abundant narrative material which normally is not made evident. Far from being a speculative tract of theology, the Epistle loves to narrate. This genre is used on various levels according to different types. We have numbered six of them: the biblical narration, the narrative dimension of the christological kerygma, autobiographical elements of the sender, passages of theological biography of the readers, the theological narration, and the similes. The denomination of these types could vary, but between the one and the other of these there surely exists a formal distinction.

The concept of narration, then, is realized practically in an analogical fashion. It is an original dimension strongly attested to particularly in the more mature and most elaborate writings of the Apostle Paul. It confers upon the Epistle to the Romans (and indirectly to its author) a fresher and more concrete meaning; by making it more adherent to everyday life, narration renders the Epistle itself more vivid. The narrative dimension, moreover, inserts our Epistle more profoundly into the context of the Bible, which itself is of a substantially narrative type.[16] Finally, had both Jews and Christians not anything to narrate, they might not even have anything new to say. But if there is someone who has truly something original to communicate, he is Saint Paul in the Epistle to the Romans.

NOTES

1. The expression "narrative theology" dates back to H. Weinrich, in *Concilium* 9 (1973), 846–859. Here we cite only a few works under this title which are purely illustrative: D. Ritschl, H.O. Jones, *"Story" als Rohmaterial der Theologie* (München, 1976); J. Navone, Th. Cooper, *Tellers of the Word* (New York, 1981); R. Marlé "La Théologie, Un Art de Raconter? Le Projet de Théologie Narrative" *Etudes,* 358/1 (1983), 123–137; S. Lanza, *La Narrazione in Catechesi* (Roma, 1985).

2. Weinrich, p. 853.

3. Cf. *PL* 35, 2063–2088 (there are eighty-four propositions drawn especially from Romans 5–8); the work is of the year 394 C.E.

4. The work is of 1521, but enlarged in the 1535 and 1543 editions.

5. It is this way among Protestants; see, for example, R. Bultmann, *Theologie des N.T.* (Tübingen, ⁵1965), pp. 187–353; G. Eichholz, *Die Theologie des Paulus im Umriss* (Neukirchen-Vluyn, 1972).

6. This is how it is among Catholics; see, for example, the *Bible de Jérusalem* and specific studies like those of A. Feuillet, A. Descamps, J. Dupont, and K. Prümm.

7. Cf. "Ueber Zweck und Veranlassung des Roemerbriefs und die damit zusammenhaengenden Verhaeltnisse der Roemischen Gemeinde," *Tuebingen Zeitschrift fuer Theologie* III (1986), 59–178.

8. Cf. G. Lohfink, "Erzaehlung als Theologie. Zur sprachlichen Grundstruktur der Evangelien," *Stimmen der Zeit* 192 (1974), 521–532. On the Epistle to the Galatians, cf. R.B. Hays, "The Faith of Jesus Christ. An Investigation of the Narrative Substructure of Galatians 3:1–4," *SBL DS* 56 (Chico, 1983), 37–83, giving a status quaestionis on how the narrative dimension in Paul has been treated up to now.

9. Lohfink, *op. cit.*, p. 524, where he connects the dissertation of the first chapters of Romans with 3:21.

10. Cf. S.K. Stowers, "The Diatribe and Paul's Letter to the Romans," *SBL DS* 57 (Chico, 1981), 171–173. The presence of the *Exempla* among the stylistic characteristics of the diatribe had been noted by H. Weber, *De Senecae Philophi dicendi genere Bioneo* (Marburg, 1895), pp. 6–33.

11. Cf. H. Lausberg, *Handbuch der Literarischen Rhetorik. Eine Grundlegung der Literaturwissenschaft* (Munich, 1960), pp. 148f.

12. Thus think two scholars: W. Wuellner, "Paul's Rhetoric of Argumentation in Romans," *The Catholic Biblical Quarterly* 38 (1976), 330–351; R. Jewett, "Romans as an Ambassadorial Letter," *Interpretation* 36 (1982), 5–20.

13. We just refer to R. Barthes, "Introduzione all'analisi strutturale dei racconti," in *L'analisi del racconto* (Milan, 1969; Paris 1966); H. Weinrich, *Literatur fuer Leser: Essays und Aufsaetze zur Literaturwissenschaft* (Stuttgart, 1972); P. Ricoeur, *Temps et Récit*, I–III (Paris, 1983–1985).

14. We prefer this literary label to "Heilsgeschichte," which is more theological. This subject has already been widely studied: cf. especially J. Munck, *Paulus und die Heilsgeschichte,* (Copenhagen, 1954); O. Cullmann, *Heil als Geschichte, Heilsgeschichtliche Existenz im Neuen Testament* (Tuebingen, 1965); E. Kaesemann, *Paulinische Perspektiven* (Tuebingen, [2]1972), chaps. 3 and 4; O. Betz, "Die heilsgeschichtliche Rolle Israels bei Paulus," *Theologische Buecherei* 9 (1978), 1–21. We are therefore not interested here in the use of the Old Testament in Paul; cf. now D.A. Koch, "Die Schrift als Zeuge des Evangeliums. Untersuchungen zur Verwendung und zum Verstaendnis der Schrift bei Paulus," *BzHTh* 69, (Tuebingen, 1986), esp. 302–321.

15. Cf. R. Penna, "I diffamatori di Paolo in Rm 3,8," to be published.

16. Cf. N. Frye, *The Great Code. The Bible and Literature,* 1982.

Fear of Faith:
The Subordination of Prayer to Narrative in Modern Yiddish Poems

Kathryn Hellerstein

1. PRAYER AND NARRATIVE IN
THE TRADITIONAL LITURGY

At first glance, prayer and narrative would seem to be entirely unconnected to each other, so different as to be almost opposed. Prayer is a human being's address to God, either in petition, intercession, praise, thanks, or contemplation.[1] Narrative is a story and its discourse (or the way a story is conveyed) in the words of a speaker or speakers who relate to one or more listeners an event or series of events, arranged in the telling either temporally or causally.[2] Although both are human utterances, prayer assumes a hierarchy in which the speaker addresses the divine listener from a subordinate position, while narrative assumes no such hierarchy in situating its speaker or audience. Prayer is essentially a dramatic utterance, intended for a religious or spiritual purpose that is often ritualized; narrative may or may not have an explicit purpose, and if it does, it tends to teach, moralize, illustrate, or entertain.

Yet in the traditional Jewish liturgy, prayer and narrative, far from being unrelated, share a very close connection. In prescribed Jewish prayers of fixed times and seasons, narratives are often summoned and incorporated in the prayers in order to strengthen or to vary the petition. These narratives sometimes serve as examples which are rhetorically subordinated to the framing mode of the prayer; at other times narrative elements themselves become means of praying.

Consider the morning *Shema*, where the narrative serves to dramatize and reenact the statement of faith that the prayer offers. The Shema consists of three sections from the Torah—Deuteronomy 6:4–10, 11:13–22, and Numbers 15:37–41—enclosed within a framework of blessings that precede and follow the scriptural readings. In themselves, the scriptural passages do not constitute prayer in the strict sense, but at least from the Rabbinic period onwards, they were considered as a kind of Jewish credo. In the blessings following the last of these passages in the Shema, that credo is extended and dramatized through narrative. The first blessing following the Shema begins by affirming the truth of the preceding scriptural statements, particularly that God is "our King, the Rock of Jacob, the Shield of our salvation," and that "His words . . . are faithful and desirable for ever and to all eternity."[3] Following these affirmations and as proof of the fact that "besides Thee we have no King, Redeemer, and Deliverer," the blessing continues by narrating the story of the redemption from Egypt. That story, however, immediately culminates in the praise that the Children of Israel sang to God in the Song at the Sea, specifically Exodus 15:11 and 15:18, which are now recited by the congregants who reenact their ancestors' praise of God. That reenactment of praise itself issues now in a petition for redemption—for, in other words, a reenactment by God of the delivery from Egypt—with which the Shema concludes. Through these blessings, then, the narrative components in the Shema bring together the present moment of petition, the legendary past moments of praise, and the messianic future that the prayer anticipates.

In other prayers, narratives are atomized into rhetorical tropes which often describe the act of prayer. The resulting metonomy and synechdoche compound the speaker's prayer. One prays more intensely by telling of others praying. For example, in the *Nishmath,* which is recited in the Sabbath service before the *borkhu,* the congregation says:

> Were our mouth filled with song as the sea [is with water], and our tongue with ringing praise as the roaring waves; were our lips full of adoration as the wide expanse of heaven, and our eyes sparkling like the sun or the moon; were our hands spread out in prayer as the eagles of the sky, and our feet as swift as the deer—we should still be unable to thank thee and bless thy name, Lord our God and God of our fathers, for the one thousandth of the countless millions of favors which thou hast conferred on our fathers and on us.[4]

Following upon a declaration that the soul of every living being will bless and praise God, because the ever-waking God "guides his world with kindness," this catalogue of conditional comparisons emphasizes that it is impossible for mere human beings to praise God adequately. The tropes in this passage join the body parts as they are engaged in the act of praying to various elements of nature: thus, the mouth is compared to the sea, the tongue to the waves, the lips to the skies, the eyes to the heavenly bodies, the hands to eagles, the feet to deer. But these comparisons are negated by the conditional form of the syntax (were they/ *ilu*), so that we are made to understand that the congregation, indeed, the human body, is more unlike than like these elements of nature. At the same time, the language of praise emanating from these human parts enables all of nature to join in the praise of God. Like the Lord who, in the preceding passage, "rouses those who sleep . . . and enables the speechless to speak," the congregants rouse the sea, the skies, the heavenly bodies, and the animals from their speechlessness into an articulation of God's praise, even if such praise may be inadequate in comparison to its Divine object.

In contrast to such implicit narratives as those found in the *Nishmath,* the *piyyutim* (medieval liturgical poems) extend prayer to include full-fledged narratives.[5] For example, Yose ben Yose's *Avodah* for Yom Kippur narrates in poetry the holy service of the High Priest on the Day of Atonement. Yose ben Yose's *Avodah* is almost epic in scope, as though it intends to reenact in the words of recollection the Temple Service that can no longer be performed. In fact, by reciting this narrative as a prayer during the Yom Kippur service, the congregation symbolically performs the acts of worship that are historically obsolete. This concept, that reciting is akin to performing an act, is itself based on the rabbinic idea that, since the destruction of the Temple has made sacrifice impossible, Jews may substitute prayer for the deed of sacrifice. The recitation of narrative itself becomes a form of prayer. In other *piyyutim,* medieval poets recast biblical narratives into dramatic monologues or dialogues in verse in order to recount new versions of familiar stories, while in yet other genres of *piyyut,* the *kinnot* (lamentations for Tishe b'Av) and *selihot* (penitential prayers), contemporary narratives of the persecutions of the Jews during the Crusades are joined to biblical narratives in communal prayers of mourning and revenge. These prayers provide an occasion for the poet to rehearse the recent events; more significantly, the context of prayer elevates the historical and spiritual importance of these narratives into liturgy. In such poems as the anonymous "The Martyrs of Mainz" and David bar Meshullam of Speyer's "The Sacrifices," their authors frame the catalogue of murderous deeds against the Jews with an entreaty that God listen and avenge, but, with this frame of prayer, they also affirm the ultimate faith in God of the surviving "small congregation."[6]

In all these cases, narrative either comprises an essential part of prayer or serves as a kind of prayer. Narrative coexists with prayer, but always in a rhetorically subordinated way. In yet other classical liturgical poems, the poet compresses multiple narratives into a catalogue of God's deeds, with narratives of historical events turned into rhetorical devices. For example, "In the Middle of the Night," from a *kerovah*[7] by Yannai that was subsequently incorporated into the Ashkenazi Passover *Hagaddah*,[8] lists God's deeds of conquest over the enemies of Israel, all of which occurred, as the refrain reiterates, "in the middle of the night":

> It was then You worked many miracles   at night.
> At the beginning of the watches   on this night.
> You gave victory to the convert when divided was   the night.
> And so it came to pass in the middle of the night.
>
> You sentenced the king of Gerar in a dream   of night.
> You terrorized the Aramean in the yester   night.
> And Israel with an angel fought and he overcame him   at night.
> And so it came to pass in the middle of the night.[9]

This catalogue of narrated events compresses each narration into one verse. Each verse is bound into the poem first by its initial letter, which fits into the alphabetic acrostic, and second by its final word, *laylah* (night). As the acrostic orders the poem vertically, through the sequence of the alphabet, the repeated line endings bring each of the narrated acts into a relationship of unity: God made all these things happen at night. Paradoxically, this repetition of the word "night," signifying temporality, undermines the progress of time in the narrations by removing all these nights from their days, and the days from their years. In addition, this repeated word counteracts the reader's temporal movement through the poem, from beginning to end; as Shlomith Rimmon-Kenan has stated, ". . . although repetition can only exist in time it also destroys the very notion of time."[10] Yet, the final strophe of the poem breaks from the narration into a petition to God:

> O, bring near the day that is neither day nor   night.
> O, Most High, announce, yours the day is, yours   the night.
> Set watchmen to watch your city all the day and all   the night

Brighten, like the light of day, the dark   of night.
And so it came to pass in the middle of the night.[11]

This prayer asks God to reinstate the ultimate day of messianic redemption, at which time night's darkness, illuminated like the day, shall be obliterated, as shall be the need for God to vanquish the enemies of Israel, just as He has done throughout history, "in the middle of the night." The poetic device of repetition removes temporal order from the catalogue of narratives and prepares for the ultimate redemption from time, which is requested by the speaker at the end of the poem. In Yannai's *kerovah,* poetic form subordinates the narrative elements for the sake of the poem's purpose as a prayer.[12] Narrative is thus doubly yoked.

2. THE MODERN YIDDISH PRAYER-POEM: FIGURATIVE DEVOTION

From the classical Hebrew *piyyut* we now turn to the modern Yiddish poem. Through what is commonly thought to be the worldly, secular stream of this poetry runs a current of devotion.[13] In this body of literature, one finds many poems entitled "*tfile,*" which, although appearing to call themselves "prayers,"[14] are, in fact, prayer-poems that reverse the classical order in which narrative serves the end of prayer. In the modern Yiddish prayer-poem, narrative takes the place of prayer. When prayer itself no longer is possible, people tell stories about praying.

Yiddish prayer-poems may be either figuratively or literally devotional. The figuratively devotional prayer-poems tend to be blasphemous and idolatrous in theme. These poems use the apparent form of the prayer as a vehicle for some other tenor, which often has to do with the poet's dissociation from traditional Judaism and his or her orientation toward a secular aesthetics. An illustrious example of such a blasphemous prayer-poem is Moyshe-Leyb Halpern's persona poem, "*A tfile fun a lump*" (A Rogue's Prayer, 1919), in which a *lump,* a good-for-nothing rogue, prays for God's help to protect the lawless, loafing, independent life he has chosen to lead. With an ironic contrast between the persona and the situation in which this persona speaks, Halpern ensures that the poem will sabotage its own apparent intent. Since the speaker, the rogue, imposes anarchy on whatever convention he encounters, Halpern converts supplication into an attack on both the speaker and the God he addresses in the poem's last stanza:

Oh, help me, God,
Let me be the sickle blade
And let me be the stone that strayed
To break the blade. I shall spit
On You, on me, on the whole of it.
Oh, help me, help me, God.[15]

In the preceding stanza, the rogue paradoxically prayed to be cursed: "May they curse me roundly all their lives!" Now, at the end of the poem, he annihilates the very act of prayer in which he engages, through an equally paradoxical revision of the proverb of the stone that stops the reaping blade. With these paradoxes, the rogue blasphemes the God he beseeches.

An even subtly subversive poem is Yankev Glatshteyn's "*A tfile*" (A Prayer, 1921), which calls into question the very process by which a modern poem can become a Hebrew prayer:

You have imagined
Both me
And the puddle that mirror me,
In a foggy night.
You have sent me down into the world, a soap-bubble,
O Brama![16]

Whereas Halpern displaces a reader's expectations by writing a blasphemous prayer, Glatshteyn's poem introduces a whole new notion of deity, addressing the Hindu god "Brama" as the anthropomorphic inventor of the poet who invents the prayer of praise.

The figuratively devotional prayer-poem can also be narrative. Celia Dropkin's "*Dos lid fun a getsndinerin*" (The Song of a Woman Who Worships Idols, 1919)[17] makes false worship an ironic metaphor for a story of seduction. The persona begins and ends her lascivious narrative with a refrain that encloses her within the circular logic of her predicament:

Quietly, today before dawn,
I came into the temple.
Ah, how beautiful he is, my idol
Adorned with flowers.[18]

This woman brings alive the stone figure with her passionate actions. Her prayer is not words, but a deed that arouses inert matter to over-power her. Whereas Halpern's rogue curses the God to whom he prays, and Glatshteyn's poet persona figures himself as a mere figment of a capricious god's fancy, Dropkin's idol-worshiper invents her deity. But Dropkin lets it be understood that the poem's actual concern is not theological, but an ironic treatment of erotic infatuation. If, for Hal-pern, prayer is a rhetorical device to reveal the rogue's character, while for Glatshteyn it is a test of the poet's creative powers, for Dropkin prayer is a way of satirizing self-destructive sensuality. This figurative worship is a solitary, illicit act that both entraps and empowers the speaker of each poem. In all three poems, prayer is displaced from Jewish community and tradition and comes to represent figuratively what is private, foreign, or exotic.

Yet in the figurative prayer-poems, exotic worship can mask what is, for the poet, all-too-familiarly Jewish. Anna Margolin's "*Fargesene Geter*" (Forgotten Gods, 1920) inverts the order of worship, as it tells of the Greek gods' faith in those who pray:

When Zeus, and Pheobus, and Pan,
And Kyprid, silver-footed mistress,
World-intoxicateress, world-protectress,
Were veiled in silence
Down from Olympus,
They in their long and lucid going
Through flaming and slow self-extinguishing generations
Ignited torches and built temples
In the hearts of solitary ones,
Who still bring sacrifices and smoking incense.
The world is deep and bright,
The old winds rustle eternally through the young leaves.
With fear I hear in my soul
The heavy tread of forgotten gods.[19]

Deposed from the holy Mount Olympus, the gods and goddesses must hear prayers in order to remain gods. For this reason, lighting the torches and building the temples, they maintain their own worshipers, rather than the other way around. These new temples, though, are located not in the public realm of worship, on the heavenly mount, but in the private, within "the hearts of solitary ones/ Who still bring sacrifices and smoking incense." Attributing to the deities the roles of those who pray to them, Margolin disguises a subtextual analogy to the story of the Jews exiled from the Temple Mount. Margolin is a self-consciously modernist poet, ill-at-ease with explicit faith and messianic nationalism. Yet she calls forth recognizable tropes: the descent from the holy mountain (whether it is Olympus or Zion), the secretive, persistent faith, and the wandering of the exiled. Through these tropes, Margolin neatly displaces the Jews' traditional longing for their return to Zion onto an ambiguous nostalgia for the return of pagan gods to Olympus.

The ironic figures used to represent the act of devotion in these four prayer-poems we have just considered impose a distance between the stance of the Yiddish poet and that of traditional Jewish prayer. Yet as blasphemous or exotic as these figures may be, they cannot help but allude to the very models of devotion that the poets intend to subvert. While figurative prayer-poems rebel against Jewish conventions of prayer, literally devotional prayer-poems in Yiddish are explicitly Jewish in referent. Yet these literal prayer-poems, whether they address God directly or merely allude to Him, strangely avoid actual devotion. Ultimately they are not prayers. Rather, they narrate the act of praying. These literal prayer-poems reverse the pattern of Hebrew prayers, in which a subordinate narrative complements and strengthens the devotional address. Here, instead, the rhetorical mode of narrating subverts the initial rhetorical mode of praying. The rest of this essay will examine why, in the modern poems, the formerly harmonious factors of prayer and narration begin to work against each other, almost combatively, and why narration comes to dominate prayer.

3. LITERAL DEVOTION:
KADYA MOLODOWSKY AND MIRIAM ULINOVER

The first type of literally devotional prayer-poem is that in which the *siddur* (prayerbook) figures as a subject or central image. In poem number II of Kadya Molodowsky's sequence, "*Opgeshite bleter*" (Fallen Leaves, 1928), the speaker regards the prayerbook of *tkhines,* supplicatory prayers for women:

> Before me—an old prayerbook
> With yellowed pages bent at the corners,
> Marking *tkhines* (women's prayers) about dew and rain,
> Marking the Binding of Isaac

And Nimrod's fiery lime-kiln.
Tears fell quietly there
And made the pages soft;
Hearts softened with prayer.
Fingers that followed the prayers beginning
'May it be Thy will,'
Darkened those lines recited each seven times.
And who will now, God-fearing,
Carry the prayerbook under her arm?
And who will turn the yellowed leaves?[20]
                    (Fallen Leaves, II, lines 1–14)

Earlier in the sequence, the speaker has been established as a woman
lulled into forgetfulness and senselessness by the dark autumn night, yet
whose "white arms/ Will awaken, aroused." Now, her hands hold "an
old prayerbook/ With yellowed pages bent at the corners." The corners
of the pages have been bent to mark the women's petitions for dew and
rain, the prayers centered around the *akedah* and the ancient persecutions, the prayers of covenant. The pages of this prayerbook bear the
physical evidence of its use: the act of praying has changed these pages,
softening them with tears, darkening them with the traces of fingers
passing over the printed lines. In turn, the prayers have softened the
hearts and marked the lives of those who prayed.

The book this woman holds is a fossilized artifact that calls forth in
the speaker her memory of others praying. Yet the prayerbook records
ways of prayer no longer observed: "And who will now, God-fearing/
Carry the prayerbook under her arm?/ And who will turn the yellowed
leaves?" The question infers that there is no one left to pray from the
siddur. In answer, the speaker tentatively offers herself. She will not
keep the customs within the *siddur,* but rather will keep the book as an
object:

Perhaps I shall carry it to my green-covered table,
Place it in the middle,
And when my heart is arid,
Take the prayerbook to my burning lips.
                    (Fallen Leaves, II, lines 15–18)

She will carry the *siddur,* not to the synagogue, but to her own table. In
contrast to the yellowed leaves of the book, her table is a symbolic
green. Upon this green table, the *siddur* will remain closed until she lifts

it, according to the decree of her heart rather than of the law. At that time, she will not open the book to pray; rather, she will bring it to her lips.

This gesture is at once pious and iconoclastic. A traditional Jewish man or woman, having concluded praying, will in a gesture of farewell kiss the *siddur* upon closing it and before placing it on the shelf again. But the gesture of the speaker in Molodowsky's poem suggests a sensuous meaning as well, for she brings the book to her lips as though to quench her thirst; this is at once a thirst for spiritual comfort and for sensual satiation. If the "green covered table" suggests a table set for a meal, then the *siddur* is the sustenance. Yet the woman's arms, beneath which she will carry the prayerbook to the table, are the same "aroused" white arms mentioned earlier in the sequence. Her burning lips are the same as her ravenous, "blooming mouth" mentioned later. She raises the prayerbook not to her eyes or to her fingers, but to her lips. The kiss seals the distance between the modern secularist, "now," and those who "then," in the past, used to pray. Prayer is obsolete, the poem suggests. A symbolic kiss has replaced prayer.

Likewise, in the rhetoric of the poem, narrative has superseded prayer. The following summary of the poem's structure may clarify this statement. Lines 1–5 describe the prayerbook and the prayers within it. Lines 6–11 narrate the act of praying as an interaction between the person praying and the pages on which the prayers are written. The tears and fingers of these women marked the prayers as a record of the link between their emotions and the devotional rituals: their tears softened the pages; their fingers passing over the lines the prescribed seven times of recitation have darkened the very prayers. As the women have changed the physical representation of the prayers, so the prayers have changed the hearts of the women. Lines 12–14 pose questions that establish the difference between the previous time of prayer and the moment of speaking, between the past and the present. These questions interrupt the narration. They are asked because perhaps there is no one to continue the action of prayer, no one to carry the book, no one to turn the pages. Yet the last lines, 15–18, offering an answer to these questions, allow the narrative to continue. The poem ends with a tentative prophecy: the action of prayer has ceased and will be replaced by a sensual gesture.

Molodowsky's poem is deceptively devotional. Its subject—the old prayerbook, the women's prayers—and the apparently nostalgic treatment of that subject seem to herald a resurgence of praying. Yet, the action is at best tentative: "perhaps" the book will be brought to the lips. It is also impulsive. The former balance of emotion and ritual in the ways of prayer—the women's tears and sevenfold recitation—is now gone. This speaker will follow only the urge of her own emotions and not the measured practice of recitation.

Furthermore, the ambiguity of the symbolic adjectives at the end of the poem—"green," "burning," "arid"—make more uncertain than certain the renewal of prayer. Molodowsky sets up a correspondence between these adjectives and the three kinds of prayers listed in the opening lines. The *tkhines* for dew and rain (the poet seems to conflate women's supplicatory prayers and the line added to the standard Amidah between Sukkoth and Pesach, "Thou causest the wind to blow and the rain to fall")[21] correspond to the connations of nurture and growth in the table's green covering. The midrash of Abraham's miraculous rescue from death in the lime-kiln for refusing to worship Nimrod, already translated into Yiddish in the *Tsenerene,* corresponds to the speaker's arid heart and burning lips.[22] The speaker's connection to nature's cycles of seasons, disease, and growth stand in contrast to the prayers requesting dew and rain and the traditional story about rescue from a burning fire. But most tellingly, the dog-eared pages marking the story of the father bound by Covenant to bind his son Isaac for sacrifice correspond to the speaker's license whether or not to take up the prayerbook in the first place.

From these correspondences, the poem urges a reading of contrasts: in the presence of the old prayerbook, this modern speaker relies not upon the prayers of God's will (line 10), but upon her own will. Significantly, Molodowsky conflates into the poem's symbolic *"alter siddur"* a book of *tkhines* or Yiddish prayers for women, the standard Hebrew *siddur* for men, and the *Tsenerene* a volume of Biblical stories and midrashim translated into Yiddish for women. These prayers and sacred tales—all of a kind, from the speaker's point of view—stand in contrast to the new story of an individual's choice, the story of a woman's singular desire to appropriate tradition to her own ends. Significantly, in the final line of the poem, the old prayerbook remains closed, as do the lips of the woman who saves it.

In Miriam Ulinover's poem *"Der alte siddur"* (The Old Prayerbook, 1922), a prayerbook again figures as a symbol of the past.[23] Ulinover's poem removes the act of prayer even further from the speaker's rhetorical act of telling. Narrated by a granddaughter retelling her grandmother's story, this poem begins with an old prayerbook, clutched by a young girl that is the grandmother in her youth. This prayerbook serves as a link between the sexes and give the girl an uncustomary access to the traditional Jewish education in Hebrew, which was usually taught only to boys:

> In one hand the old prayerbook, tuition fee in her other,
> And hanging from its string, the dangling pointer,—
> As a child, my grandmother used to run quickly into the *kheder*
> To repeat the alphabet, with the boys, in order.
>
> (Der Alte Siddur, lines 1–4)

The girl's presence in the *kheder,* though, sets the normal order awry. Merely by reciting the alphabet, she disrupts the logic of sexual exclusion. Chaos results:

> Everything would have been fine; but the boys would hit her—
> A girl's voice yowling can carry high as heaven.
> Once long ago she nearly fainted, nearly perished
> From the blows and benevolent-slaps, what a horror!
>
> (Der Alte Siddur, lines 5–8)

Yet the poet presents these slaps or *mitsve-petshlekh* as a strangely logical cause for the grandmother's behavior as a young married woman. If, as a girl, the grandmother used the old prayerbook to try to join the boys in their learning, now, as a *naye vaybl,* a young woman, she uses it to distinguish herself from all the other women, and to join the men in their praying:

> But therefore a young wife is put in an ample chain,
> With the same old prayerbook, only now without a pointer,
> To lead the way through the entire *shtetl* to the yard of the *shul.*
> How the new wife proudly takes up marching!
> Wives stay mute, bashfully, silently, the women stare
> At her mouth that does not rest from the Sabbath-prayer,
> As she, together with the congregation and the cantor,
> Draws near the *Shekhine,* praying, chanting.
> In the *shul* an envious flurry, sweating, and brow-wiping,
> As wives, poor things, all engage in page-turning. . .
> She flares up and throws herself afresh into the prayer:
> For, of course, she is in her childhood home in the old *siddur!*
>
> (Der Alte Siddur, lines 9–20)

Whereas the girl's presence in *kheder* set awry the orderliness of the alphabet, now the young woman's presence as an active voice in *shul* sets awry the normal social order of prayer. In that order, women, amply bound to the prayerbook in the obligations of daily life, are in *shul* marginal, silent, without a pointer to keep their place. Because they are behind the screen of the *mekhitse,* separated from and invisible to the men, their presence is not felt, does not threaten. Yet this bold newly-wed, with her proud, active mouth reciting the prayers and her mind apprehending them, overthrows the *seder* of the *siddur,* the order of praying. Her enthusiastic voicing puts the other women to shame, and causes them enviously and confusedly to riffle the pages. Her voice crosses the curtain that divides the sexes, crosses the passive silence of the other women in order to approach the Holy Spirit with the congregation of men.

In this poem, as in Molodowsky's, the old prayerbook works as an amulet to conjure up the act of praying within a narrative. While Molodowsky's poem depicts a gesture of prayer that in the end is not a prayer at all, Ulinover's portrays a woman in the heat of devotion. Although these two depictions appear virtually opposed, in fact they both serve to distance the reader from the actual prayer by using the same strategy. The tentative statement of future action in Molodowsky's concluding lines and the vigorous description of present action in Ulinover's are both narratives. Whether the character in the poem—the "I" or the "she"—keeps the prayerbook closed or holds it open, whether her lips are sealed or rapidly moving, whether the tone is ambivalently nostalgic or vigorously comic, both poets keep the reader and themselves at a remove from the devotional words. The reader observes both the silent woman and the praying woman from the outside. Unlike the grandmother in her youth, neither poet enters "her childhood home in the old *siddur!*" Both these poems narrate the act of prayer through the artifact of the *siddur.* This liturgical volume, bound and frayed, is presented as a symbol of the archaic act of prayer. Although both poems were regarded as "religious" by their contemporary readers, they actually emphasize the remoteness of Jewish prayer from the modern Yiddish poet.

Yet some Yiddish prayer-poems address God literally and directly, or at least purport to. Molodowsky's "*Tfiles*" (Prayers, 1922) is a sequence of three poems. The first poem opens by addressing God in a negative supplication:

Don't let me fall
As a stone falls upon the hard ground.
And don't let my hands become dry
As the twigs of a tree
When the wind beats down the last leaves.
And when the storm raises dust from the earth
With anger and howling,
Don't let me become the last fly
Trembling terrified on a windowpane.
Don't let me fall.

(Tfiles, I, lines 1–10)[24]

The initial series of similes in lines 1–10 compares the speaker to what God should not let her become (a dropped stone, twigs stripped by the season, the last surviving fly). This catalogue of negated similes is enclosed by the twice-repeated line, *"nit loz mikh untergeyn"* (Don't let me fall). After this repetition, the poem unfolds in lines 11–16 what appears to be a positive request:

I have asked so much,
But as a blade of your grass in a distant wild field
Lets drop a seed in the earth's lap
And dies away,
Sow in me your living breath,
As you sow a seed in the earth.

(Tfiles, I, lines 11–16)

Yet this request qualifies itself in two ways. First, a narrative statement precedes it, *"kh'hob azoyfil gebet"* (I have asked so much), and this statement does not follow from the earlier lines, where the speaker has asked only that she be kept from falling, aging, and surviving too long, or, to state them positively, that she be sustained in a season of growth. Second, between this narrative statement and the actual request in the penultimate line, the poet unfolds the simile of the dying blade of grass. The syntactical complexity of this figure turns it back upon itself, so that it comes to signify God as much as the speaker. The action she asks God to take in line 15, to impart to her *"dayn lebedikn otem"* (your living breath), is enclosed by two clauses of similes. Initially, the act is likened to the dropping of a seed on the earth by a blade of grass. Although that blade of grass belongs to God (*a groz dayns*), the syntax alters the order of comparison. If the poem ended with the imperative request, it would seem as if the poet were likening God to the blade of grass, His living breath to the seed, and herself to the earth's lap:

> nor vi a groz dayns in vaytn vildn feld
> farlirt a kerndl in shoys fun dr'erd
> un shtarbt avek,
> farzay in mir dayn lebedikn otem,
>   (Tfiles, I, lines 12–15)

In this ordering of likeness, the poet, perhaps inadvertently, figures God as an ephemeral, dying aspect of nature and herself as the eternally receptive earth, ready to be replenished. Such a simile for God seems to diminish the One whose might and grandeur traditionally defy comparison, as in the *Shema:*

> Who is like thee, O Lord, among the mighty?
> Who is like thee, glorious in holiness,
> Awe-inspiring in renown, doing wonders?[25]

However, the final line of the poem corrects this reversal by restating the simile more clearly: *"vi du farzayst a kerndl in dr'erd"* (As you sow a seed in the earth). This line shifts from the figure of God as one of His own creations to the depiction of God as the power behind the perpetuation of life. This shift is subtle but essential. For in the initial simile, the poet has revealed her central doubt about the all-mightiness of God.

Such a doubt replaces the absolute authority of the God to whom the prayer is addressed with the uncertain authority of the prayer's author. We see this replacement of divine authority with human authorship in Part II of *"Tfiles"*:

> I still don't know whom,
> I still don't know why I ask, [.]
> A prayer lies bound to me,
> And asks of a God,
> And asks of a name.
>   (Tfiles, II, lines 1–5)

These lines amplify the doubt and uncertainty implied by the complex simile of the grass and the earth at the end of the previous poem. The first of the paired repetitions, *"ikh veys nokh nit"* (I still don't know, lines 1–2), urgently presses the speaker's wavering faith in prayer. The second of the paired repetitions, "*un bet zikh tsu*" (And asks of, lines 4–5), emphasizes the reversal in "*a tfile ligt bay mir gebundn*" (A prayer lies bound to me, line 3). The syntax of this line transforms the speaker into a passive object (*mir*) of the prayer (*a tfile*) that becomes an active subject of the verb *ligt* (lies). It is the prayer that binds the speaker as she addresses "*a got*" and "*a nomen.*" The prayer takes over the voice and the will of the speaker. In the first poem, the concluding simile reduced God to a tiny part of His own creation, and then reestablished His authority as the causal power of creation. Similarly, in the second poem, the figure of speech reverses the roles of speaker and verbal medium, transforming the prayer into the one asking and the "I" into the medium for the prayer.

As if the prayer speaks through her, the voice continues:

> I ask
> In the field,
> In the noise of the street,
> Together with the wind, when it runs before my lips,
> A prayer lies bound to me,
> And asks of a God,
> And asks of a name.
>
> (Tfiles, II, lines 6–12)

From the initial statements of not knowing, the poem has moved into a narration of the act of praying, which specifies the setting of the action, both the silent field and the noisy street. The catalogue of places where this supplication occurs culminates, as setting gives way to occasion: "*mit vint tsuzamen, ven er loyft mir far di lipn*" (Together with the wind, when it runs before my lips). The enclosing prepositions, *mit* and *tsuzamen,* couple the voice of prayer to the wind running before the lips of the speaker as the prayer's medium. This coupling makes the wind at once a force of nature outside of the speaker and the breath that originates within the speaker herself. Both breathings are unconsciously devout. The wind and the breath pray without deliberation or intention, but by dint of what they are. However, the repetition of lines 3–5 closes the poem on a note of doubt. The prayer has empowered the passive speaker only to address an unknown, almost arbitrary god, a deity that is itself an enigmatic aspect of language, a name.

This sequence of substitutions—of nature for God, of language for human spirit and nature, of language for God—leads to the ascendency of narrative over prayer in the third and final poem of the sequence:

> I lie on the earth,
> I kneel
> In the ring of my horizons,
> And stretch my hands
> With an entreaty
> To the west, when the sun sets,
> To the east, when it rises there,
> To each spark
> To show me the light
> And give light to my eyes [,]
> To each worm that glows in the darkness at night,
> That it shall bring its wonder before my heart
> And redeem the darkness that is enclosed in me.
> (Tfiles, III, lines 1–13)

In these lines, the speaker describes a physical act of worship. Significantly, she prays, not to God, but to the earth and its horizons. The image of the sun rising and setting at the edges of the speaker's world suggests that the earth, like her spirit, is permanently dark, despite the sun's departure and return. Yet conversely, if this synechdoche holds, then the speaker's spirit will, like the processes of nature, enlighten itself. The poem, which began as a direct entreaty in Part I, moves through doubt in Part II, and concludes by narrating the speaker's act in Part III. The divine listener, master of nature, has been replaced by nature itself, for the sun and the glowing worm, not God, will redeem her from her inner darkness (*oyslayzn di finsternish*). God's "living breath" (*lebedikn otem*) of Part I becomes "the wind running before my lips" in Part II. The poem changes in its course from a prayer to a narration, and thus writes God out.

4. NARRATIVES OF PRAYER: MALKA HEIFETZ TUSSMAN

In Malka Heifetz Tussman's prayer-poems, God remains firmly present, but these poems consistently turn mid-stride from supplicatory address to narrative. The untitled, dedicatory poem that opens *Haynt iz eybik* (Today Is Forever, 1977) is a case in point:

Lord, my God,
I—Your little garden—
Bring you the harvest of my soil—
My bounty
Ripe or not quite—
All the same your boon.
Accept it, my Lord, benignly
But not with fire.
No fire, my God.
It cannot be true that you delight
In the smoke of the fat offering—
Not true!
And see
How humble the years have
Made me:
That for each drop of mercy
I am thankful.
Thankful.[26]

In the initial lines, the speaker of this poem addresses God, "*mayn har*" (my Lord). Immediately we know that this is a self-conscious prayer, a prayer that reveals the boundaries of its genre, for the speaker undertakes to define herself through a metaphor that alludes to the prescribed ritual offerings in ancient Israel that were brought by individuals to the priests at the Tabernacle or at the Temple in Jerusalem. The figure makes the speaker herself into the little garden, offering God his boon, "*dayn gob,*" from her bountiful property, "*mayn farmeg.*" This metaphor of the garden does away with the necessity that Jewish culture, the priestly tribe, and organized religion mediate between the individual person making an offering and God.

As the figurative language of the poem transforms religious culture into an organic process, it also disrupts the harmony between ritual and season traditionally expressed in Jewish liturgy. The timely correspondence between God's will and the workings of nature is stated in a passage of *Birkat halevonoh* (New Moon Blessing) taken from Talmud Sanhedrin 42a:

> Blessed art thou, Lord our God, King of the universe, who didst created the heavens by thy command, and all their host by thy mere word. Thou hast subjected them to fixed laws and time, so that they might not deviate from their set function. They are glad and happy to do the will of their Creator, the true Author, whose achievement is

truth. He ordered the moon to renew itself as a glorious crown over those he sustained from birth, who likewise will be regenerated in the future, and will worship their Creator for his glorious majesty.[27]

The notion of the "fixed laws and time" of the moon is also implied in Eleazar ha-Kallir's *piyyut, Tefilat tal* (Prayer for Dew), recited on the first day of Pesach:

> Let dew sweeten the mountains;
> Let thy chosen taste thy wealth:
> Free thy people from exile,
> That we may sing and exult.
>
> Let our barns be filled with grain;
> Renew our days as of old;
> O God, uplift us by thy grace;
> Make us like a watered garden.[28]

Ha-Killir's simile of the watered garden, "*gan roveh simeynu, betol,*" exemplifies the timely complement of nature and Jewish ritual; the figure places the power of figuring upon God, whose grace transforms the petitioners, as the dew that they request in the prescribed season makes a garden fertile. In contrast, Tussman's speaker takes on the power of figuring by likening herself to a garden. In this figure-making, she is, rather than a petitioner, akin to God: one creator, she brings the fruits of her efforts to the Other. In turn, He bestows upon her the meager drops of mercy, unlike the generous dew in the *piyyut*. The offering, with which she approaches the deity, stands against the customary devotional declarations of the laws of ritual sacrifice, stated for example in the Kedushah for Hol Ha-mo'ed.[29] Unlike the ritual sacrifices that God commands Aaron, through Moses, to perform, her offering is neither timely nor seasonal. This speaker offers her sacrifice at the immediate moment, whether it is "*tsaytik tsi nit gor tsaytik*" (ripe or not quite ripe). To the point, the Yiddish adjective *tsaytik* (ripe) derives from the noun *tsayt* (time), and Tussman repeats the word allusively to establish the radical deviation of her prayer from the timeliness of traditional liturgy.

The poem calls into further question the traditional rituals of offering by dictating the terms in which God may receive the speaker's bounty. Significantly, in the only direct petition in the prayer, "*nem on, mayn har, mit gutvilikayt/ nor nit mit fayer,/ nit mit fayer*" (lines 7–9), the speaker requests control over the way God should receive her offering.

This plea for God's benign reception, "but not with fire./ Not with fire," stands in contrast to the commandments in Exodus and Leviticus which specify the burning of animal sacrifices, the very fire and "*roykh fun fetn korbn*" (smoke of the fat offering) that the speaker wishes to deny. In the rhetorical strategy of the poem, it is significant that the lines of petition give way immediately to the speaker's exclamatory denials of the truth of the entire Jewish legal tradition: "*s'iz dokh nit emes az du host lib/ dem roykh fun fetn korbn. . ./ se iz nit emes*" (It cannot be true that you delight/ In the smoke of the fat offering—/ Not true!). The urgency of these assertions, conveyed through the idiomatic syntax and the repetition of *nit emes* (not true), suggests the speaker's anxiety that God might be other than she believes, might be as His own words, quoted in the Torah and read aloud repeatedly in worship, imply. In these lines, the speaker redefines God according to the offering she believes appropriate to make, against the authority of the Torah.[30]

Tussman's prayer, then, becomes a narrative of prayer. As she prays, the speaker turns the prayer into the story of bringing an offering to God and of her entreaty that he accept it on her terms, thereby violating the definitions of offering made in the Torah and the cult of the priests. The poem closes with some lines that counteract the apparent arrogance in this redefinition of the nature of God:

> un ze
> vi hakhnoedik s'hobn mikh gemakht
> di yorn
> az far yedn tropn khesed
> zol ikh danken.
> danken.
>
> (And see
> How humble the years have
> Made me:
> That for each drop of mercy
> I am thankful.
> Thankful.)
>   (Untitled, lines 13–18)

The third of these lines reveals that the petitioner has been humbled by the cumulative timeliness of her years, not by any direct act or power of the deity. This speaker relies upon the passing of time, upon a most mortal awareness of temporality, to bring her to the point of being grateful. This subtle thematic emphasis on temporality presses forth the rhetorical presence of narration in the prayer. The narrative mode shapes the poem's closure in the repetion of the verb *danken* (to thank) in the lines that read "literally," "I shall thank./ Thank." The poet omits any explicit direct object for this verb, specifying no source for the mercy and no receiver of thanks. By refraining from naming the deity in these lines, the poet renders ambiguous the significance of her gratitudinous act. Rather than being a direct thanksgiving to the listening God, the poem ends as a narration of that act of thanks, addressed, it seems, to the equally human reader. Moving as it initially seems, this is a disingenuous humbleness, for the prayer-poem redefines both God and the rituals of interaction with God in human terms.

Another of Tussman's poems, "*Tate ziser*" (Sweet Father), recounts the difficulty of praying:

And I call Him
Sweet Father
Although I don't remember my father.

But I do remember
A thorn,   5
A fire,
A thunder,
A mountain
And something of a voice.

When I think   10
I hear His voice
I shout at once:
Here I am!
Here I am, Sweet Father!

When a father abandons,   15
He is still a father,
And I will not stop longing
And calling
"Here I am"
Until He hears me   20
Until he remembers me
And calls my name
And talks to me
Through fire./ [Through light.][31]

Like Margolin's "*Fargesene geter*," this poem addresses the phenomenon of an incomplete devotional amnesia, in which the worshiper's fragmented memories of the deity assert themselves. Whereas Margolin masks this devotional impulse by means of an impersonal narrator who speaks in the name of classical pagan deities, Tussman makes her speaker an identifiable first person who speaks of the Jewish God. This deity is identified through the images that serve as tokens of remembering—the thorn, fire, thunder, and mountain—alluding to the story of God speaking to Moses from the burning bush (Exodus 3:1–6), and especially through the Yiddish translation, repeated threefold in lines 13, 14, and 19, of Moses' words of response, the Hebrew *hinneyni*, "*do bin ikh*" (Here I am) (Exodus 3:4). This phrase recurs frequently throughout the *Tanakh,* but significantly, for this poem, in Genesis, Exodus, and First Samuel.[32] The phrase is repeated three times in the story of the Binding of Isaac (Genesis 22:1, 7, 11), where Abraham responds first in obedience to God's commanding voice, then in acknowledgment of Isaac's query, and finally in obedience to the angel of God who prevents the sacrifice from taking place. This phrase also recurs in the story of the boy Samuel's first vision of God, when, awakened in the night, he thrice mistakes the voice of God for the voice of Eli (1 Samuel 3:1–10).[33] In all three biblical episodes, the speaker responds to the initiating communication from God with the phrase *hinneyni,* and in all three, the speaker responds with his statement of presence without fully knowing what will ensue; for the phrase stating personal presence implies a trust in the summoner, a faith in the unknown. And, finally, all three who respond with *hinneyni*— Abraham, Moses, and Samuel—after recognizing the voice of God, obey what they know.

Tussman's poem contrasts itself by design with these moments of recognition by implying a faith not in the power of knowing, but in the power of remembering. Her poem opens *in medias res* with the speaker's assertion that she both calls God a name and calls out to Him, even though she says that she does not remember Him (lines 1–3). The poem ends with the reversal of this situation (lines 20–24), in which the speaker states that her calling will make God hear her, remember her and respond to her with His voice. Although it begins with the speaker's incomplete memory of the deity, the poem ends with the hope that God will complete his memory of the speaker.

Significantly, Tussman refers to this forgotten and forgetting God through the metaphor of *tate ziser,* the sweet father. The Yiddish phrase is a colloquial version of such traditional phrases of address in Hebrew prayers as *avinu malkeynu* (Our Father Our King) and *av harakhamim* (Merciful Father). Yet *tate ziser* connotes a familiar and familial father, not the powerful father of kingship who grants mercy. By addressing God intimately, Tussman establishes both God's emotional immediacy for this worshiper and the enormity of her estrangement from Him. The metaphorical filial sentiment strains against the fragmented abstractness of forgetting. Yet this tension enriches the familial metaphor, for even if God is like a father who willingly abandons his offspring (*az a tate farlozt/ iz er alts nokh a tate*), his fatherhood remains intact. The relationship of parent to child, of God to worshiper transcends either member's will or consciousness.

In depicting the reciprocal distancing and forgetting by both deity and worshiper, Tussman calls into question the entire structure of worship. Unlike the young Samuel, who mistakes the divine voice for that of his mentor Eli, this speaker takes as God's voice whatever voice she hears (*ven mir dakht zikh/ ikh her zayn kol bald shry ikh:/ do bin ikh!/ do bin ikh, tate ziser!* line 10–14). These lines dramatize the extent to which the incomplete communication is predicated on the speaker's desire and expectation. Not remembering God, the speaker does remember the symbols that figure in the essential stories of human communion with God, especially the exact response of others who did hear the divine voice. By quoting the biblical phrase repeatedly, the poet joins the individual speaker's voice with the archetypal voice of communal prayer. Yet rhetorically, this poem is not a prayer, but a narration of the mutual forgetting that explains why prayer is not possible at the present moment. The poem's only direct address to God, *do bin ikh,* is presented initially as a direct quotation within the narrative action as the speaker tries to remember (lines 13–14) and then repeated as the example of habitual action in the future, as the speaker awaits God's remembering (line 19). This direct address, then, is ensconced in a narrative context. Because the poem is a narration, it maintains praying in balance with forgetting as a device subordinate to the rhetoric of telling. Both prayer and forgetfulness share a tentative reciprocity between the deity and the worshiper. In contrast, the narration is the poet's surety of exchange, for it allows her to express what may come to pass: "Until he hears me/ Until he remembers me/ and calls my name . . ." As a narrative, this poem is true to its assertion of faith at a distance.[34]

Tussman's dramatic monologue *"Fargessen"* (Forgotten) offers a culminating example for this discussion of how narration subordinates prayer in the modern Yiddish poem:

Master of the world!
Creator,
I stand before You with bared head,
With eyes uncovered,
Stubbornly facing Your light.   5
Not a single hair
Trembles on my brow
Before Your greatness.
I place my Sabbath candles
In candlesticks   10
Tall and straight as a ruler
So they may flicker toward You
Without a drop of humbleness.
I rise to You
Without the slightest fear.   15
For a long time I've honed my daring
To stand before You
Face to face, Creator,
And to let my just complaints
Open out before You   20
From my mouth.

Woe is me: I've forgotten!
I can't remember
What I came to demand.
I've forgotten.   25
Woe is me.[35]

Although this entire poem is addressed directly to God in the conventional opening of a prayer, *har fun der velt!/ boyre-oylem,* the mode of address is neither supplication nor praise, but narration. The action narrated is the speaker's own stance, which, *mit opgedektn kop,/ mit oygn nit farshtelt*—explicitly challenges the traditional pious stance of a Jewish woman, who stands, her hair covered with a kerchief and her eyes covered by her hands, to carry out one of the three positive commandments for women, as she blesses the Sabbath candles.[36] Yet unlike a pious woman, who carefully ensures that her candles lean a little in the sockets, so as not to affront the deity, this speaker fixes her candles upright for the express purpose of confronting Him with her pride (lines 9–13).[37] The flames become a metaphor for the speaker rising arrogantly to face God (lines 14–15).

In lines 16–21, the speaker explains how she has personally prepared to confront God. Her confrontation should be read against the backdrop of the type of *tkhine,* a Yiddish supplicatory prayer, that accompanies the traditional blessing a pious woman makes over the Sabbath candles on Friday night. One of these *tkhines* is the following, composed in the early eighteenth century by one of the most popular authors of these Yiddish prayers, Sarah bas Tovim:[38]

BLESSED ARE YOU, LORD OUR GOD, RULER OF THE UNIVERSE, WHO HAS SANCTIFIED US BY YOUR COMMANDMENTS AND COMMANDED US TO KINDLE THE SABBATH LIGHT.

In honor of God, in honor of our commandment, in honor of the dear holy Sabbath; our Lord God has given us the dear holy Sabbath and has commanded us the dear commandment. May I be able to observe it properly, and may it carry as much weight as the entire 613 commandments performed by all Israel, AMEN, SO MAY IT BE HIS WILL.

MAY IT BE YOUR WILL, LORD OUR GOD AND GOD OF OUR FATHERS, THAT THE TEMPLE BE SPEEDILY REBUILT IN OUR DAYS, AND GRANT US A SHARE IN YOUR TORAH. AND THERE WE WILL SERVE YOU WITH REVERENCE, AS IN THE DAYS OF OLD AND AS IN FORMER YEARS. THEN THE OFFERING OF JUDAH AND JERUSALEM WILL BE PLEASING TO THE LORD, AS IN DAYS OF OLD AND IN FORMER YEARS.

Lord of the world, may my [observance of the] commandment of kindling the lights be accepted as the act of the High Priest when he kindled the lights in the dear Temple was accepted. "Thy word is a lamp to my feet and a light to my path." This means: Your speech is a light to my feet; may the feet of my children walk on God's path. May my kindling of the lights be accepted, so that my children's eyes may be enlightened in the dear Torah. I also pray over the candles that my [observance of the] commandment may be accepted by the dear God, may he be blessed, like the light [which] burned from olive oil in the Temple, and was not extinguished. By the merit of the lights, [may] the dear Sabbath guard [us], as the dear Sabbath guarded Adam. As he was protected from a prompt death, so may our merit of the lights guard that our children's light may shine in the Torah [and] their zodiac signs may shine in the heavens. May they be able to give generous sustenance to their wives and children. And may our [performance of the] commandments be accepted as were the [performance of the] commandments of our Fathers and Mothers and the holy tribes. May we be as pure as a child newborn from its mother, Amen.[39]

The Hebrew blessing (indicated by CAPITAL LETTERS) acknowledges God's ascendancy over the universe and the worshiper's obedience to

the divine commandments, while the Yiddish *tkhine* that follows acknowledges the blessedness of the Jew who is able to carry out God's
commandments by enacting either one of the three positive commandments decreed to women, or the 613 *mitsvot* prescribed to "all Israel."
Even when the author of the *tkhine* startlingly compares the kindling of
the Sabbath candles to the High Priest's kindling in the Temple, she
forestalls any hint of pride by quoting and interpreting a biblical verse:
all her words lead her and the future generations along the path of God.

In contrast, the history recalled by Tussman's narrator consists of her
personal plan to confront God face-to-face in accusation. Yet at the moment of uttering her counter-*tkhine,* the force of forgetting overcomes
Tussman's speaker: *vey mir, vey mir:/ ikh hob fargesn!/ ikh ken zikh nit
dermonen/ vos/ ikh bin gekumen monen./ ikh hob fargesn, vey mir* (lines
22–26). In the preceding lines, the gesture of lighting the candles implies
that the speaker recalls the women's commandment and obeys it, in her
own fashion. Yet the last lines, in which she exclaims her forgetting, make
a statement about prayer. The word play on *dermonen zikh* (remember)
and *monen* (demand) is significant, for to remember is to demand. Remembering calls forth responsibility. She who remembers knows to act
upon the reciprocal exchange of supplication (a human demand upon
God) and commandment (God's demand upon humans). The *vey mir*
repeated three times (like *hinneyni* in *Tate ziser*) is more than the ironic-
comic Yiddish idiom, more than the twofold irony of the human folly in
attempting to approach God. The wit of these lines extends beyond the
human error of memory to a larger loss—the loss of the ability to pray. For
this speaker, the *du* (you) exists only in the first part of the poem as an
indirect object, *dir,* the second person singular dative, as she narrates her
daring plot (lines 1–21). When the time arrives to address God directly,
the syntax eliminates the listener. God has disappeared from the poem.
The emphasis falls upon the speaker and her actions. This prayer becomes
a narrative about the futility of praying.

5. CONCLUSION

In Hebrew liturgy, narrative, when recited, becomes a form of
prayer, reiterating the Covenant between God and the Jews. Prayer,
including the covenantal narratives subordinate to it, assumes the authority of God. In contrast, the modern Yiddish prayer-poems assume the
authority of the individual author, who revises the covenantal narrative
in his or her own terms.[40] It would seem, then, that in the modern

prayer-poems, the human author must be in conflict with divine authority. Possibly this phenomenon can be explained by a fear of faith, an anxiety of writers just over the brink of modernity: unable to relinquish entirely the forms of Jewish prayer, they distance themselves from devotion by taking on and subverting these forms. The modern prayer-poems reflect the struggle of post-enlightenment Yiddish poetry to define itself aesthetically and politically against the precedent of religious tradition that had given Hebrew primacy.

The poems by Halpern, Glatshteyn, and Dropkin take on the *tfile* as a literary device to stand against in figurative blasphemy or idolatry. This figurative anti-devotion allows these poets to appropriate and conquer the devotional urges that perhaps arose unintentionally within their contemplations of character, creation, and desire. Different as they are, Halpern's, Glatshteyn's, and Dropkin's prayer-poems parody prayer by asserting its futility: they all present solipsistic systems, in which the worshiper invents and subverts a deity.

Margolin, Ulinover, Molodowsky, and Tussman present more complex versions of devotion. Molodowsky's and Ulinover's literally devotional prayer-poems place the prayerbook as an object within a narrative. This *siddur* is a token of prayer. It contains prayer safely within its frayed covers. Such narratives enable the modern poet to recall prayer with ease; for a story holding the symbolic image of the prayerbook at its center gives authority to the story's author, rather than to God. Margolin's narrative history of forgotten gods realizes the speaker's fear that she must acknowledge and reinstate worship. The footsteps of these pagan gods invoke the modernist's responsibility to remember the Jewish ways she is trying to forget. As Molodowsky's prayer-poem *Tfiles* substitutes nature for deity, the prayer shifts into narrative. Tussman's poems develop, as it were, Margolin's fear of remembering, and although they invoke a Jewish God, they too become narratives about praying.

Prayer asserts the authority of God. The modern Yiddish poets appear to be uncomfortable with an absolute acceptance of this authority. They test it by trying out various forms of prayer, but they also convert the deed of prayer into the safer form of story to justify their own authorship—and authority.

NOTES

1. Michael Fishbane, "Prayer," *Contemporary Jewish Religious Thought*, ed. Arthur A. Cohen and Paul Mendes-Flohr (New York: Charles Scribner's

Sons, 1987), pp. 723–729. Fishbane categorizes prayer as petition, intercession, praise, or contemplation. He includes "thanks" under the rubric of "praise," because it "is still marked by self-regard and regard for God's beneficence to his creatures" (p. 725).

2. By narrative, I mean the linguistic result of one or more narrators relating to one or more narratees, an event or series of events. Narrative can be divided into the elements of story (events ordered or structured by temporal and/or causal sequences of events) and discourse—the way the author controls or modulates the narrator(s)' transmission of the story to determine the response of the narratee(s). This definition is drawn from a lecture by Gerald Prince, Department of Comparative Literature, University of Pennsylvania, "On Narrative," February 1987.

3. I am quoting from the morning Shema: the words in the evening Shema differ somewhat, but bear much the same meaning. English translation quoted from Joseph Heinemann, with Jakob J. Petuchowski, ed., *Literature of the Synagogue* (New York: Behrman House, 1975), p. 25.

4. Philip Birnbaum, trans., annotator, intro., *Daily Prayerbook: Ha siddur ha shalem* (New York: Hebrew Publishing Company, 1977), reprinted 1985, pp. 331–332. All references and citations of prayers and translations from the traditional Hebrew liturgy in this essay are taken from Birnbaum, unless otherwise noted.

5. These devotional poems were probably written initially in Palestine, in an uncertain era beginning anywhere from the second to the sixth centuries C.E. and culminating in the eleventh century. Scholars speculate that they began as the somewhat rebellious variations by cantors on the monotonously repeated traditional prayers. However, the ones that have come down to us were eventually adapted into what has become the traditional liturgy. See Jakob J. Petuchowski, *Theology and Poetry: Studies in the Medieval Piyyut* (London: Routledge and Kegan Paul, 1978), pp. 11–19. Also see T. Carmi, ed. and trans., *The Penguin Book of Hebrew Verse* (New York: Viking and Penguin, 1981), "Introduction," pp. 14ff, 51–55. And see Ezra Fleischer, "Piyyut," in *Encyclopaedia Judaica*, Vol. 13, col. 574. Also see the following works in Hebrew, from which both Petuchowski and Carmi draw: Ezra Fleischer. *Shirat hakodesh ha'ivrit biyemei habeinayim* [Hebrew Liturgical Poetry in the Middle Ages] (Jerusalem: Keter Publishing House, 1975). Aaron Mirsky, *Reshith Hapiyyut* (Jerusalem, 5725). And in German: A. A. Wolff, *Die Stimmen der ältesten glaubwürdigsten Rabbinen über die Pijutim* (Leipzig, 1857). Fleischer's theory about the origins of the *piyyut* is summarized in English by David Stern, "New Directions in Medieval Hebrew Poetry," *Prooftexts*, Vol. 1, No. 1, January 1981, pp. 104–115.

6. Carmi, pp. 372–373, 374–375.

7. Carmi, p. 588: "*kerova* (pl. *kerovot*). A poem sequence related to the benedictions of the *Amida*."

8. Joseph Heinemann, with Jakob J. Petuchowski, ed., *Literature of the*

Synagogue (New York: Behrman House, 1975), pp. 223–227. And Nahum N. Glatzer, ed., E. D. Goldschmidt, commentary, Jacob Sloan, trans., *The Passover Haggadah* (New York: Schocken, 1969), pp. 86–89.

9. Glatzer, *Passover Hagaddah*, p. 87.

10. Shlomith Rimmon-Kenan, "The Paradoxical Status of Repetition," *Poetics Today: Narratology II: The Fictional Text and the Reader*, Vol. 1, No. 4, Summer 1980, p. 158.

11. Glatzer, *Passover Haggadah*, p. 89.

12. It is worth considering as related example Eleazar Ha-Kaliri's *piyyut* for the first recitation of the *gevurot geshamim*, "Remember the Patriarch," in which the poet petitions God to remember Abraham, Isaac, Jacob, Moses, Aaron, the Twelve Tribes and, finally, their offspring, the petitioners themselves. As in "The Middle of the Night," each line of this poem compresses a single narrative, and each line ends with the word *mayim* (water). The catalogue of narratives and the poetic repetition culminate in a request for redemption through rain—the seasonal resurrection of the individual and the eschatological restoration of the nation from Exile. Heinemann and Petuchowski, pp. 229–235.

13. The following four pages of discussion are drawn from a paper I presented at the 58th YIVO Conference, October 13, 1985, New York City, "Poems as Prayers: Devotion and Anti-Devotion in Modern Yiddish Poetry."

14. From the beginnings of post-exilic Judaism, liturgical prayers in Hebrew and Aramaic have traditionally been recited by a minyan or by an individual in the context of a minyan. Later, though, there developed a tradition of prayers, in the vernacular Yiddish, usually for women to recite individually, both inside and outside the synagogue. These *tkhines,* too, have narrative elements embedded within them. Sometimes they imply a narrative framing the situation of the person speaking them. ["Before you get married, go to the cemetery and say the following at the grave of your parents/grandparents/ancestors in order that you shall be fruitful" "To be said by a woman after she has emerged from the mikva and before she has intercourse with her husband, so that she will conceive." . . .] The situational narrative, implied by the instructions to the person about to pray, and the internal narrative elements in the *tkhines* deserve a study, which time and space do not allow for here. I hope to develop this topic on another occasion.

15. Moyshe-Leyb Halpern, "A tfile fun a lump," *In nyu york* (New York: Farlag Vinkl, 1919), pp. 41–43. Translation by the author of this paper, in *In New York: A Selection*. Trans., ed., intro., Kathryn Hellerstein (Philadelphia: Jewish Publication Society, 1982), pp. 28–31. All translations of the Yiddish are mine, unless otherwise noted.

16. Yankev Glatshteyn, "A tfile," *Yankev glatshteyn* (New York: Farlag Kultur, 1921), pp. 40–41.

17. Norma Fain Pratt notes the poems by Dropkin and Margolin in "Culture and Radical Politics: Yiddish Women Writers, 1890–1940," *American Jewish*

History, Vol. 70, No. 1, September 1980, p. 85, note 36. I found Margolin's "Fargesene geter" in *Di Naye Velt,* July 23, 1920, but could not find Dropkin's "Dos lid fun a getsndiner," in *Di Naye Velt,* May 16, 1919. The texts I am using here are from each poet's subsequent collection of poems.

18. Celia Dropkin, "Dos lid fun a getsndinerin," *In heysn vint* (New York, 1935), pp. 28–29.

19. Anna Margolin, "Fargesene geter," *Lider* (New York, 1929), p. 130.

20. Kadya Molodowsky, "Opgeshite bleter" II, in *Kheshvandike nekht* (Vilna: B. Kletskin, 1927), p. 21.

21. Birnbaum, pp. 83–84.

22. For the story of Abraham and Nimrod's lime-kiln, see Louis Ginzberg, *The Legends of the Jews,* trans. Henrietta Szold (Philadelphia: Jewish Publication Society, Reprint 1968, Copyright 1909, 1937), Vol. 1, pp. 175–176. See also Chava Weissler, "The Traditional Piety of Ashkenazic Women," in *A History of Jewish Spirituality,* Vol. 2, ed. Arthur Green (Crossroad, forthcoming), p. 88, note 68, typescript: *Sefer ha-Yashar, Noah; Bere'shit Rabba* 38:13.

23. Miriam Ulinover, "Der alte siddur," *Der bobes oytser* (Warsaw, 1922). Facsimile edition with facing page Hebrew translations, reissued by Mossad Harav Kook, Jerusalem, 1975, pp. 24–25.

24. Kadya Molodowsky, "*Tfiles*" in *Kheshvandike nekht* (Vilna: B. Kletskin, 1927), pp. 73–75.

25. Birnbaum, *Daily Prayerbook,* pp. 81–82.

26. Malka Heifetz Tussman, "[untitled]," *Haynt iz eybik* (Tel Aviv: Farlag Yisroel Bukh, 1977), p. 7. Translation originally published in *Journal for Reform Judaism* (Spring 1979) and again in *American Yiddish Poetry: A Bilingual Anthology,* ed. Benjamin and Barbara Harshav (Los Angeles: University of California Press, 1986), pp. 612–615.

27. Birnbaum, pp. 561–562.

28. Birnbaum, pp. 633–636.

29. Birnbaum, pp. 615–620. For example, for the Sabbath that falls in the middle of Pesach: "Our Father, our King, speedily reveal thy glorious majesty to us; shine forth and be exalted over us in the sight of all the living. Unite our scattered people from among the nations; gather our dispersed from the far ends of the earth. Bring us to Zion thy city with ringing song, to Jerusalem thy sanctuary with everlasting joy. There we will prepare in thy honor our obligatory offerings, the regular daily offerings and the additional offerings, according to rule. The Musaf of (this Sabbath and that of) this Feast of Unleavened Bread we will prepare and present in thy honor with love, according to thy command, as thou has prescribed for us in thy Torah through thy servant Moses, as it is said: [On Sabbath]: On the Sabbath day, two perfect yearling male lambs and two-tenths of an ephah of fine flour mixed with oil as a meal-offering, and the libation. This is the burnt-offering of each Sabbath, in addition to the daily burnt offering and its libation. [On all eight days of Pesah]: You shall present an

offering made by fire, a burnt-offering to the Lord: two young bullocks, one ram, and seven yearling male lambs; you shall have them perfect. Their meal-offering and their libations were as specified: three tenths of an ephah [of fine flour] for each bullock, two-tenths for the ram, one-tenth for each lamb; wine according to their requisite libations. Moreover, a he-goat was offered to make atonement in addition to the two regular daily offerings."

30. In numerous conversations that I held with Malka Heifetz Tussman in 1978 and 1979, the poet told me that after the atrocities of the Holocaust, she could not believe that God would any longer accept sacrifice by fire. This intention informs the poem, but from without.

31. Tussman, *"Tate ziser,"* in *Haynt iz eybik,* p. 14. Translation in *American Yiddish Poetry,* pp. 614–615.

32. Solomon Mandelkern, *Konkordentsye letanakh* (Tel Aviv: Schocken, 1974), Vol. 1, pp. 338–339. Also, Alexander Cruden, *Cruden's Complete Concordance,* ed. A.D. Adama, *et al.* (Grand Rapids: Zondervan, 1979), p. 299. The phrase recurs twice in the story of Jacob tricking Isaac for Esau's birthright (Genesis 27:1, 18)

33. Malka Heifetz Tussman told me that she intended the poem to allude to the story of Samuel, not of Moses. She claimed to feel it too presumptuous to compare herself to Moses. Conversation with the poet, October 29, 1979.

34. Note, the poet changed the last line of the poem after the book appeared in print, and communicated this change to me on November 29, 1979: from *durkh fayer* to *durkh likht.* I understood this change to be consistent with the denial of God's delight in fire sacrifice in "Mayn har," discussed above, for the God she conceived of after the Holocaust would not make his presence known through the same element, the fire, that destroyed his people. Also, Malka Heifetz Tussman's own diminishing eyesight (due to glaucoma) made light a powerful symbolic image.

35. Tussman, *"Fargessen,"* in *Haynt iz eybik,* pp. 30–31. Translation in *American Yiddish Poetry,* pp. 616–617.

36. The three commandments for women are *hallah, niddah,* and *hadlakat hanerot.*

37. Conversation with the author, Berkeley, California, November, 1979.

38. For the historical identity of Sarah bas Tovim, see Israel Zinberg, *A History of Jewish Literature: Old Yiddish Literature from its Origins to the Haskalah Period,* trans. Bernard Martin (Cincinnati and New York: Hebrew Union College Press and Ktav, 1975), Vol. 7, pp. 253–256.

39. Sarah bas Tovim, "The Tkhine of Three Gates," translated by Chava Weissler, p. 10, typescript. Cited, courtesy of the translator.

40. This tension of authority is by no means unique to modern Yiddish poems. It has a precedent in the Italian Hebrew poets of the seventeenth century, who assimilated the two distinct "medieval" traditions of *shirat hakodesh* [*piyyutim,* liturgical poetry] and *shirat hahol* [secular poetry]. As David Stern

points out, summarizing Dan Pagis' study: "Already in such compositions and more prominently in still later ones, Pagis shows how the distinction between *shirat hakodesh* and *shirat hahol* had not only broken down; in fact, these two traditions, so discrete in their respective functions, had also been assimilated to each other. To be certain, piyyut by this time was no longer being composed for authentic liturgical purposes. Instead, Italian-Hebrew poets, within the confines of *accademie* they founded along the models of their Italian counterparts, composed strikingly religious, even mystical, albeit non-liturgical poems, *sonneti spiritualli* that Pagis compares to John Donne's Holy Sonnets. The same phenomenon of integration is also evident in such cases Pagis cites as when a seventeenth century Italian/Jewish poet, Y. Y. Qarmi, entitled his collection of religious poems a *siddur,* and even added his own commentary to it!" David Stern, "New Directions in Medieval Hebrew Poetry: Ezra Fleischer, *S:Hirat hakodesh ha'ivrit biyemei habeinayim . . .* and Dan Pagis, *Hiddush umasoret beshirat hahol . . ." Prooftexts,* Vol. 1, No. 1, January 1981, p. 113.

Modern Hebrew Literature as a Source for Jewish Theology: Repositioning the Question

Alan Mintz

Once the world was contained by the Torah; now the Torah is contained by the world. Once the life of the Jew was regulated by the rhythm of chosen days and appointed times; now the flux of experience is shaped by different forces. Once Zion was an otherworldly ideal; now it is an exigent and complex actuality. Once the soul of the individual Jew was bound up in the collective life of the people; now the space of the self, subject to perpetual analysis, recedes inward away from the community.

This great transformation, which goes by many names, marks the experience of the Jewish people in the modern era. Although many peoples and cultures have undergone a similar crisis, the instance of the Jews is unique on two counts. In Western Europe the process of secularization unfolded over the course of several centuries; for most Jews the ordeal was accelerated and compressed into one or two generations. While for many third world cultures the exposure to modernity has been equally jolting, it is only in the case of the Jews that this confrontation has involved a highly literary and intellectual culture not in the possession of a hieratic class alone.

What happened? How did it happen? Differing and related answers to these questions are offered by the responses of the Jewish people to the crisis of tradition: modern Jewish history, politics, literature, and philosophy, and the branches of academic study which have arisen to interpret them. For the purposes of this essay I wish to concentrate on one of these responses, modern Hebrew literature, and make a case for its special powers in illuminating the great transformation in Jewish life. Moreover, it is my contention that this literature can serve not only as an explanatory account for the dilemmas of modern Jewish identity but as something much more: a resource for restoration. In its very secularity, modern Hebrew literature can be utilized as a source for Jewish theology.

HEBREW LANGUAGE

There is, to begin with, the mystery of the Hebrew language. Mystery is not a term that sits comfortably in Jewish theological discourse, and I use it for its strangeness and perhaps its aptness. That Hebrew *literature* should be revived and take on new forms is astonishing, but it is not beyond belief because of the continuous and creative employment of the literary language down through the ages. That the *spoken* language should be brought back to life and become a natural and ambient medium for a significant portion of the Jewish people, literate and nonliterate alike—this surpasses astonishment. If many of the original visions of Zionism have failed or been compromised, the revival of the Hebrew language succeeded beyond any imagining.

For any religiously sensitive person there are signals of hope to be picked up here. If the deep cleavages within the Jewish people are one day to be lessened, it will be due in part to the power of the Hebrew language. It is that language—and it seems sometimes that it is *only* that language—which constitutes an arc of continuity between the tradition and the culture of the modern Jewish state which has supplanted it. Lodged deep within the recesses of the Hebrew language are both the meanings that have been lost and the resources for their reappropriation and transformation. So, while most of the remarks that follow refer to Hebrew literature in the sense of the kinds of writing we conventionally understand as literature (poetry, fiction, drama, and essays), we must never lose sight of the fact that these creations are constructed out of the more fundamental material of language, and it remains the Hebrew language and its rebirth on which everything depends.

It is both the discontinuity and continuity of Hebrew that make it a special case. What is modern about modern Hebrew literature are the new ends for which Hebrew began to be written at the end of the eighteenth century and the new forms in which this program was realized. Make no mistake. Before this time Hebrew had had a vital and unbroken history as a compositional medium: not just in the chain of post-biblical interpretation, and not just in the vast corpus of liturgical poetry, and not just in the flowering of the Spanish Golden Age, but in many modes and genres less conspicuously sacred or secular: historical chronicles, romances, treatises on logic and on astronomy, essays in philosophical consolation, travel literature, ethical wills, and personal correspondence.

What changed at the beginning of the modern era was that Hebrew was made into the chief instrument of the Haskalah (Enlightenment) movement to modernize Jewish life. For the first time Hebrew was pressed into use (through parody and satire) as a medium for social criticism; and the novels, ballads, and lyric poems written in imitation of Western models claimed for themselves, beyond their didactic function, nothing less than the autonomous dignity of art itself. When the hopes of the Haskalah foundered on the realities of Russian antisemitism at the end of the nineteenth century, Hebrew became the language of romantic nationalism and embodied the vision of establishing a Jewish homeland. The revival of a people was inconceivable without the revival of its language. Yet once revived, Hebrew could not be limited to this proper civic mission.

A generation of intellectuals had been born into the world of faith only to be banished from it by the disintegration of Jewish life in Eastern Europe at the close of the century. The new Hebrew literature became the modernist medium through which their uprootedness and dislocation were explored. By the late 1920s, the venue of Hebrew literature—its writers, periodicals and publishing houses—had been transferred to Tel Aviv and Jerusalem. From that time forward Hebrew became, largely but not exclusively, the literary (as well as popular) culture of a particular society, the Yishuv (the Jewish settlement in Palestine) and then the State of Israel.

I have adduced the provenance of modern Hebrew literature in order to make an obvious but important point. In confronting the dilemmas of identity and belief, to write in Hebrew represented a choice *not* to write in a Western language. A language like German provided such Jewish writers as Freud, Kafka, and Walter Benjamin with a powerful lexicon of modernity and with immediate access to the advanced questions of culture. Their contributions to modern culture were truly awesome; yet to the degree to which they sought to address the crisis of Jews and Judaism, their linguistic medium kept them on the outside.

For Hebrew writers, on the other hand, no matter how cut off they felt from the world of piety from which Hebrew had emerged, and no matter how artificial and unsuitable Hebrew must have been at first for engaging issues of modernity, the choice of Hebrew was a choice to work from the inside. To write in Hebrew, especially before the success of the Jewish national enterprise, was itself a statement of faith and a declaration of where one stood within the hermeneutical circle of modern culture. But it was far more than a matter of allegiance. Because Hebrew literature had become both the repository of classical Judaism and the record of a reawakened people's adventure in modernity, Hebrew was thought to possess the internal resources to negotiate the mediation between old and new. Substitution, retrieval, containment, synthesis, reconciliation—all the dynamics of cultural change could take place *within* Hebrew liturature because in that medium alone did the new meanings and old meanings exist simultaneously.

MODELS OF HEBREW LITERATURE

Granted the importance of Hebrew literature, what account does it render about what happened and how it happened, about the great transformation of Jewish experience and consciousness? As befits the complexity of modern Jewish history, the explanation turns out to be not one but two. In literary history, the branch of criticism that studies literature diachronically, there have been until recently two principal models for explaining the origins and development of modern Hebrew literature. These explanatory accounts are important because they close certain options and open others in the endeavor of making literature "available" to Jewish thought and theology.

The first is the Rebirth Model associated with the ideas of Joseph Klausner and Simon Halkin. It views the appearance of the new forms of writing in modern Hebrew literature—novel, short story, essay, lyric, epic, idyll, ballad—not as an imitation of fallen Western models but as the expression of a newly expanded and invigorated national life, at the center of which stood the themes of love, nature, power and art. This argument holds that the Jewish soul, released from prolonged constriction, had been freed to appropriate the full reach of its humanity. This is to be understood as a rebirth rather than a modern creation *ex nihilo* because the new forms of the imagination were extensions or delayed outgrowths of ancient, biblical forces that had lain quiescent through the long night of exile.

There is a radical and a conservative version of this rebirth model. The aim of the new literature, according to the radical version (M. Y. Berdichevsky [1865–1921]), is to revolt against the old, usurp its place, and stop at nothing less than a total "transvaluation of values." In the conservative version (Ahad Ha'am [1856–1927]), the new culture can be made an evolutionary development from the old by translating the religious values of the past into usable spiritual and ethical ideals through a process of hermeneutical recovery. Common to both of these approaches to modern Hebrew literature is a conception of sectors of experience and imagination which have been newly appropriated or restored. A spatial image may help us. The "house" of the modern Jewish spirit, we might say, has been enlarged; new rooms have been built on and inhabited. In the meantime, the old rooms remain standing, esteemed but unused, and from them the objects deemed still valuable have been taken and installed in the new living space.

According to the second approach, the Catastrophe Model associated with the work of Baruch Kurzweil (1907–1972), the house of the Jewish spirit was destroyed, its foundations razed, and in its place was erected a totally new and flimsy structure whose claim to connection with what preceded it is a lie. The total usurpation envisioned welcomingly by the young Berdichevsky had, in Kurzweil's eyes, sadly come true. Modern Hebrew literature was the medium that documented and described the collapse of the world of Torah and the disinheriting of the Jewish mind. In the vacuum created by this disaster, eros had become demonic sexuality and belief self-deluding ideology. Modern Hebrew was a significant literature when it dramatized these transformations as acts of evasion and bad faith (Bialik and Agnon); it was a trivial literature when it represented the new life of the Jewish people in Israel as a healthy redemption from a benighted past (Palmah Generation writers).

Kurzweil's stance is neither reactionary nor nostalgic but tragic, with full awareness that the term tragedy is alien to the Jewish tradition. The wholeness of the world of Torah is irretrievably lost, and man's life in the aftermath can be nothing other than absurd. Signs from the past are, of course, not wholly absent in modern Hebrew literature: biblical motifs, allusions to classical texts, transformed religious symbols. According to the rebirth model, these are consoling survivals and markers of cohesion, which support the status of the new literature as the legitimate successor to the classical civilization of the Jewish people. According to the catastrophe model, however, these survivals are the flotsam of a great shipwreck which reveal both the hollowness of the victory and the impossibility of complete divestiture.

In the face of these two models, I wish to argue that the question of religion and literature can be put otherwise. To say that in the life of the modern Jewish imagination religion has been either tragically lost or absorbed and superseded is to miss some of the unexpected directions in which this transaction can move. Both approaches hew close to the bone of modern Jewish history and take literature as a record of the pathos of that history. This linkage is accomplished, it seems to me, at the expense of the literariness of literature. By this I mean the way in which literature, especially modern literature, in addition to holding up a mirror to reality, determines an autonomous space of its own, at the level of both the literary object and the literary system as a whole. In this space of its own, certain maneuvers become possible as well as certain experiments in the mimicking of transcendence—and this precisely because the grip of history is held at bay.

There are potential materials here for use in the construction of a modern Jewish theology, but that ambitious undertaking is hardly my purpose in the following pages. I wish to present an itinerary of locations, four in all, where such materials may be found and indicate what they might look like, and by so doing to support my claim for a repositioning of the question as a whole. The tack I shall not take is the one most commonly followed in such discussions: taking a motif like the *akedah* (the binding of Isaac) or a biblical figure like David, and tracing its persistence and transformation in modern literature. These are useful exercises, to be sure, but they often reflect more on the ironizing energies of modern texts than on an engagement with the theological meanings represented by the motifs and figures. In that sense, the issues I wish to raise are adjacent to but not part of the widely-discussed topic of modern Hebrew literature and the tradition.

THE TEXT AS SCRIPTURE/SCRIPTURE AS TEXT

I begin with a phenomenon which is admittedly not unique to Hebrew literature but which is nevertheless central to our theme. It has been commonly observed that the modern literary text has come more and more to resemble the Bible in the way in which it is read. What was once regarded simply as the object of appreciation and evaluation is now approached by contemporary literary critics as a hidden universe of infinite complexity and inexhaustible meanings.

The hallmark of the modern literary text—let us call it simply "the text"—is its polysemousness, its "many-signedness." Constructed of multiple intersecting sign systems, the text does not necessarily yield up its meaning to the tracing of the surface sequence of events and gestures. In ways which resemble the midrashic techniques of the Rabbis, the decoding of the text requires nonlinear procedures which make connections among different systems of signs at different levels of meaning. The very proliferation of meanings and the impossibility of fixing their number or containing the text's production of them are reasons why some strong texts we call classics seem to have something to say, often something different to say, in each generation.

The fact that the meanings of the text are not just *there,* but can be realized only through interpretation, has placed new emphasis on the role of the interpreter. Far from being an ancillary or subsidiary activity, interpretation and the aggregating body of discrete interpretations have enlarged the conception of the text and blurred the sharpness of its boundaries. If the text cannot be realized without interpretation, then the text must come to include within it the history of its interpretations. Not all texts possess the surplus of meaning that makes them worthy of this kind of intensive reading. Those that do are said to be part of a canon, and although the canon of modern literature is open to change in a way in which the biblical canon is not, the aura of canonization privileges the text in not dissimilar ways.

Finally, as an object the modern literary text has undergone changes in status that recall the vicissitudes of Scripture in the hands of its students. A period in which the text was regarded as the ineffable creation of genius was followed by a period in which the text's sources of influence were searched out and its philosophy elucidated. The focus next moved inside the text to discover there a complex organic unity, only to have that structure challenged by the claim that the text's meaning is produced by shifting codes of signification whose turbulence makes the idea of a single, stable organization impossible.

How are we to take this analogy between Scripture and text? I think we should be suspicious of those who would urge too close an historical tie between the two. This position takes the form of the argument that the new status and methods of interpretation represent either a secularization or a displacement of the ways in which the Rabbis of the midrash read the Bible. There is a necessary presumption here of historical influence or transmission which is simply not defensible. Even if the Rabbis could be claimed as precursors of the critics, and this is doubtful, to suggest their influence is to ignore the many, many cultural transformations that mediate between then and now. The Scripture/text analogy is evocative, moreover, precisely because its two terms are ontologically unassimilable one to the other. The modern work of art, no matter how mystified or demystified its metaphysics may be, is grounded in humanly produced meanings, whereas the Bible and some of its commentaries claim for themselves a different kind of sanction.

The Scripture/text analogy nevertheless remains interesting, but on other grounds. It is the nature of man as a sign-producing and meaning-generating creature to set apart certain beautiful and powerful artifacts, to reverence them, and to make their interpretation a guarantee of the continuity of culture. In an age in which God no longer speaks audibly to man, endowing texts with the authority of His utterance, it should not be surprising that the need persists to be in the possession of such texts and approach them in ways which mirror, even mimic, the ways the Bible was once approached.

The whole question, in fact, needs to be reversed. Rather than looking to the Rabbis to teach us how to read modern literature, we should look to modern literature to teach us how to read the Rabbis and *their* great text, the Bible. What could be more ironic and more wonderful than that the late fruits of secular humanism in the form of literary criticism should help us to recuperate our relationship to the founding texts of our religious tradition?

The phenomenon I speak of is not a speculative proposal but a fact that is being repeatedly demonstrated, with impressive results, in the current study of the Bible and midrash and being tentatively extended to other bodies of traditional material. The names that come to mind in this regard are Meir Sternberg, Robert Alter, James Kugel, and David Stern, among others. The application of these methods is more than a happy accident. It was because students read Eliot and Faulkner, Agnon and Zach, because they trained on the devices of the modernist text, because they learned about point-of-view, metaphor, allusion, gap filling, and analogical structure—in short, because of the creation of this new sensibility of reading, it became possible to take up the text of the Bible and rediscover in it a religious drama that had been missed for a very long time.

This is much more than a simple case in which "modern methods" have been usefully applied to ancient texts. Form criticism, archeology, and comparative semitics have in their time yielded much useful knowledge about the Bible and its world; but little has approached literary theory in recovering the primary inner excitement of the experience of reading the text of Scripture. To speak of excitement in this context is not out of place. The original source of this excitement for modern readers was not the Bible but modernist texts. It was in the deep analysis of the poem and the novel that the revelatory power of the text was first reexperienced.

The shimmering overdeterminacy of the text, the serious play of meanings, the significance and inseparability of interpretation, the drama of sequential reading—all of these were factors in reconditioning the faculty of wonder in the presence of the aura of the text. It was only then that this sense of discovery could be retrojected in a way which makes us into the kind of readers the Bible and midrash truly deserve. It is not my intention to demote the importance of studying modern literature by making it merely propaedeutic to the "divine sciences." Yet that function has, in fact, been served, perhaps incidentally, and it provides us with a suggestive illustration of how signals of transcendence may be embedded in the secularity of the modern text.

NEGATION AND CREATIVITY

Let us now return to modern Hebrew literature proper to ask what its complex history can tell us about the possibilities of belief and disbelief. A starting point is the fact that the emergence of modern Hebrew literature ineluctably presupposed a rejection at some level of the metaphysics of normative Jewish belief: the sovereignty of God, the covenant with Israel, the divine origin of the Torah, the authority of the commandments. Doctrine, to be sure, was not necessarily at the center of this movement, as befits its role in Jewish culture generally; the target of rejection was the whole fabric of traditional Jewish life in Eastern Europe. Yet the failure of belief was inseparably part of things, whether conceived of as a patrimony outgrown and pushed aside (the rebirth model) or as a structure of plausibility that collapsed and was lost (the catastrophe model). It is the *moment* and *process* of negation that need to be more finely examined; for, as it is represented in the life of Hebrew literature, apostasy is a complex experience in which negation and creativity are intimately entwined.

A good example is to be found in the very originating moment of modern Hebrew literary history. In 1819 a Galician maskil (a proponent of the Hebrew Enlightenment) named Joseph Perl published a satire of hasidic tales called *Megalleh temirin* (The Revealer of Secrets). The work is made up of imaginary letters circulating among hasidic leaders and adherents concerning frantic efforts (including bribery, blackmail and other reprehensible measures) to locate the whereabouts of the German manuscripts of a book revealing damaging information about the inner workings of the hasidic movement. The literary material being parodied, incidentally, was the writings of Nahman of Bratslav, whose parabolic tales are today so admired by students of literature. What for Perl was so ridiculous and discrediting about this material, in addition to its obvious distastefulness to Enlightenment principle, had to do with language: The Hebrew in which it was written was crude and vulgar and awkwardly translated from Yiddish speech with many Yiddishisms still intact.

Ironically, it turned out to be precisely the uncouth and graceless stylistic qualities of Perl's satire which, unbeknownst to him, made the work significant. The revival of Hebrew as a modern literary language at this time had been based on the purity of high biblical models and conducted according to the most elevated and ornate stylistic principles. The artificiality of this medium made it hardly suitable for dealing with the real business of life. Therefore Perl's parodying of the "fallen" models of hasidism infiltrated into Hebrew a vitality, resourcefulness, and raw humor which, though essential to the growth of the new literature, could not be acquired "legitimately."

A more thematic example comes from the late nineteenth century confessional novel *Le'an?* ("Whither"?) by M. Z. Feierberg. The work is set in the heart of pious Ukrainian Jewish society of that period and traces the intellectual coming-of-age of the young protagonist as he passes from the first inklings of childhood doubts to a tragic sense of permanent loss in young adulthood and, finally, to an impassioned affirmation of a nationalist rebirth in the East.

From a compositional viewpoint, what is striking about the novel is the disproportion between its main sections and the proto-Zionist declaration at the end. The sections describing the journey toward apostasy are marvelously realized; by focusing on the child's fantasies and day-dreams, Feierberg succeeds in presenting disbelief as a process which unfolds from within the tradition and which is linked to the development of the moral and spiritual imagination. These richly evoked reveries contrast sharply with the depleted rhetoric of the closing visionary passages. The difference is more than simply the difference between what is known and what is yet to be, and it characterizes the autobiographical genre in Hebrew as a whole. The story of the struggle to disengage from the toils of the tradition inevitably makes for better art than the life of disengagement that follows.

Rejection draws its strength from the power of the object rejected, and disbelief lives off the strength of the culture of faith. From the examples above and from many others that could be furnished, it becomes clear that although modern Hebrew literature is a secular literature of revolt, in its genesis and at crucial moments in its development it drew its creative force from the tradition it was revolting against. Victory did not come without costs; the emancipation of Hebrew literature from its embroilment with faith and tradition has at times left it perilously denuded of subject and vitality. The struggle between faith and apostasy is, then, an embrace in which a secret exchange of strengths takes place, an exchange which lasts, of course, only as long as the struggle is joined.

ALLEGORY AND THE THEOLOGICAL LIFE OF LITERARY FORMS

Literary genres possess their own theological suggestiveness. The lyric poem presupposes the possibility of presence represented in the fresh articulation of the human voice. Epic implies the cohesion of the created social world and its rapport with a transcendent order. Narrative guarantees temporal duration and the successiveness of experience, and the more self-conscious forms of the novel play continually on the analogy between God's providence and the flawed but protean authority of the narrator or implied author over the world of the novel.

Allegory, however, is a special case because, unlike lyric, epic, and novel, it is not a modern, Western genre but a literary form found throughout classical sources of Judaism, and, for that matter, of Christianity as well. From the prophetic and wisdom literature of the Bible, to the rabbinic *mashal,* to the rationalist hermeneutics of medieval philosophy, to the extravagant symbolizations of the Kabbalah, to the tales of Nahman of Bratslav mentioned earlier, allegory has provided a way of speaking otherwise about matters which do not lend themselves to being spoken about directly. The modern Hebrew tradition is a rich one as well: the verse dramas of S. D. Luzzatto, the satire of Erter, the long poems of Bialik, the existential fables of Agnon, the theater of Hanoch Levine, and the fiction in the 1960s and 1970s of Oz, Yehoshua, and Appelfeld.

It would be easy to take Agnon as an example, that great classicist-modernist who made such obvious use of the parabolic materials of the tradition. To demonstrate how deep this tendency goes, let us turn instead to the fiction of A. B. Yehoshua, whose work is fully domesticated into the milieu of secular Israeli society. In Yehoshua's short fiction of the 1960s the hero is typically a well-educated, often nameless, native-born Israeli male (a high school Bible teacher, a philosophy lecturer, an aging university student) who is isolated from family and friends even as he moves among them. Deprived for so long of confirmation by others, and unaware of his own desperation, he momentarily loosens the controls that bind him to civilization and longs to participate in and even precipitate a cataclysmic disaster, only in the end to recede back into his isolation unchanged.

Yet even though these figures seem to embody the quintessence of individual alienation, the stories manage at the same time to speak of much larger issues: the effects of perpetual war on Israeli society, the image of the Arab in the Israeli mind, the relationship to the Diaspora. In such stories as "Facing the Forest," "Early in the Summer of 1970," and "Missile Base 612," the connection is made through subtle devices of background detail and submerged systems of reference rather than through the one-to-one correspondences we are used to associating with allegory. The centrifugal forces of allegory, which point us in a direction beyond the story, are held in close balance with the centripetal forces of textuality, which focus our interest on the workings of the story itself. The reader becomes aware of the allegorical possibilities only after the first reading, and in contrast to classical allegory, there may be no single "solution" but rather an ambiguous set of alternative interpretations.

In good hands, allegory provides a defense against the solipsism of the modern work of art. It is a defense against nakedness as well. Nietzsche observed that it is in the nature of modern knowledge to seek to rip off the veils surrounding truth and lay it open to direct description. In permitting the possibility of speaking otherwise, allegory "clothes" its difficult truths in narrative forms whose textures make us want to touch and feel them and thereby draw close to what they encloak.

For the Israeli writer, allegory has proven itself to be an alternative to the techniques of social realism with its insistence on the representativeness of fictional characters. Through allegory the writer can keep faith with the great national themes without sacrificing fineness of focus and symbolic movement. In modern Hebrew literature the national focus inevitably takes the form of a critical assessment of the state of Israeli society and the Jewish people as a whole. This preoccupation with the commonweal is the most significant aspect of Israeli literature as a *Jewish* literature. The allegorical mode represents a strong link between this contemporary concern and the dominant themes of classical Hebrew literature. It may no longer be transcendental realities that are pointed to by the allegorical counters; nevertheless the "otherness" enforced by allegory, even as a modern device, cannot help performing a function which in the end is not so very different.

TRUTH-TELLING AND CRITICAL THEOLOGY

The eclipse of traditional faith in the late nineteenth century created a vacuum which a variety of ideologies rushed to fill, functioning in turn very much like religions. The devotion and enthusiasm with which Jews committed themselves to communism and socialism—and many other movements, Zionism among them—bear witness both to the internal weakness of Judaism in that moment and to the tenacious persistence of the need to believe. The nature of these "deconversions" from traditional religion to an ideological surrogate religion is complex, and it has been the role of the best literature written in the West to examine the phenomenon with particular reference to the deformations that result from this displacement.

In the case of modern Hebrew literature, it was of course Zionism which had to be submitted to scrutiny. In this context Zionism means not so much the Zionist *idea* of the establishment of a national homeland in Palestine as the potent blend of Zionist-Socialist *ideology* brought from Russia by the young settlers of the Second Aliyah in the years just before the First World War. It was according to this ideology that the kibbutzim were founded and the major political and educational institutions of the Yishuv were set up. Although much had changed by the time of Ben Gurion and the establishment of modern Israel, the originating impulse was still evident in nearly all sectors of the new society.

At the very beginnings of Zionist ideology, Hebrew fiction was already there and involved in preparing a critique of the hubris of Zionism. The critique was an internal one, conducted in Hebrew within a broad consensus on national goals, yet the fact that it took place within the family did not make it any less radical or acrimonious. At issue was the claim of Zionism to solve the problem of the modern Jew, both as Jew and as modern man, and to offer a framework of belief and action which effectively replaced the piety of "exilic" Judaism. The founding figure in this truth-telling tradition was Yosef Haim Brenner, whose magisterial novels from the period of the Second Aliyah present the soul of the Jew, in the extremity of its theological and existential dispossession, as untransformed by the experience of the new land. Brenner was prophetic about the dangers of acting as if man had already been redeemed; the actual consequences of this presumption could only be observed at a remove in time.

In the fiction of the 1960s Amos Oz examined the later life of this ideological inheritance as it was realized in that most rationalist of utopian experiments, the kibbutz. In *Elsewhere, Perhaps* and *Where the Jackal Howls and Other Stories,* Oz finds the kibbutz an endangered community, not only prey to the forces of hatred at large in the world, but, more significantly, vulnerable to the turbulent passions of the unreconstructed human material contained within. Oz's stories are particularly insightful regarding the costs paid by the sons for the ideological purity and romantic self-dramatization of the fathers. Although the kibbutz in Oz's fiction is intended to be a metonymy for the Zionist enterprise as a whole, it remains a special case.

Vividly presented in Yaakov Shabtai's novels of the 1970s, *Past Continuous* and *Aharit davar* ["Epilogue"], the cityscape of Tel Aviv cuts even closer to the bone. Although his characters may have fantasies of going off to a settlement to put themselves back together, they are mired in the degraded aimlessness of their urban lives. The psychological space occupied by these figures is a vacuum created, again, by the passions, ideological and otherwise, of the generation of the founders. The absence left behind becomes in turn entropic and in turn demonic.

To speak of these writers as having theological ambitions would be inappropriate if not ridiculous. Yet if we have learned anything from literary theory in recent years, it is that the significance of a text depends on the interpretive community that reads it. So while such writers as Oz and Shabtai may have no intentions in this direction, there is nothing illegitimate about a desire to make theological use of their work.

What I have in mind relates to the tradition of negative theology in medieval Jewish philosophy; this is the position which holds that because of God's transcendent otherness we are limited to making statements about what God is not rather than describing his positive attributes. One of the roles of modern literature, I would submit, is to tell us where in the world God is *not.* This is not simply a way of labeling all social criticism as essentially religious. It applies specifically to literature which investigates the consequences of systems that have usurped the role of religion and operated in its place. Hebrew literature makes wonderfully good reading in this regard. If the picture drawn of Israeli society is unpretty, it need not be depressing. The demystifying and truth-telling force of this literature is welcomed by all who believe that the future of the Jewish people depends on an honestly renegotiated relationship to the religious heritage of Judaism. In that endeavor, knowing where God is not is valuable intelligence.

CONCLUSION

In searching modern Hebrew literature for sources of theological insight I have not drawn upon the most obvious instances: the magisterial figures of Bialik, Agnon, and Uri Zvi Greenberg. In their writings the problem of tradition and the crisis of Judaism are directly engaged and made the explicit subject of their best art. There is much to be learned here, of course, and students of modern Jewish culture must return to their work over and over again. Yet the question I have sought to pose rests on a more severe base: What can we learn from modern Hebrew literature in the modernity of its detachment from the tradition? To seek this learning, that is, to view modern literature theologically is not the same as theologizing it. Beware the voices which declare the departures and rebellions of modernity to have all been anticipated by our sages! If Hebrew literature is to help us in shaping a vision of the Jewish spirit of the future, it will do so only from within its own stubborn secularity.

Notes on the Contributors

Lawrence Boadt, C.S.P.: Professor of Scripture at the Washington Theological Union in Washington, D.C. Editor of Paulist Press, coordinating Jewish-Christian publications. Author, among other books, of *Reading the Old Testament* (1984).

David Flusser: Professor of Religious Sciences at Hebrew University, Jerusalem. Special field: Second Temple Era. Numerous books and articles; most recent, *Die rabbinischen Gleichnisse und der Gleichniserzaehler Jesus* (1981). Visiting Professor at the Theological Faculty, Lucerne.

Kathryn Hellerstein: Visiting Assistant Professor of English at Haverford College. Fellow at Annenberg Research Institute, Philadelphia. Visiting Scholar at Hebrew University, Jerusalem. Translations from Yiddish, articles and readings on Yiddish poetry.

Frank Kermode: Professor of Literature at Kings College, Cambridge, England. Also held teaching positions at several other English universities, as well as at Harvard and Columbia. Has published widely. Most recent, *Forms of Attention,* on the interpretation of narrative (1985).

Paul Michel: Specializes in medieval literature. Publication "Alieniloquium," *Elemente einer Grammatik der Bildrede* (1987). Professor of Germanistics at the University of Zurich.

Aaron Milavec: Professor of New Testament at University of Cincinnati, Ohio.

Alan Mintz: Robert H. Smith Professor of Hebrew Literature at the University of Maryland. Co-editor of *Prooftexts,* A Journal of Jewish

Literary History. Most recent publication, "Banished from Their Father's Table," *Loss of Faith in Hebrew Autobiography* (1989).

Romano Penna: Professor of New Testament Exegesis at Pontifical University Lateranensis, Rome. Many publications; most recent: *Anonimia e pseudepigrafia nel Nuovo Testamento* (1985).

David Stern: Assistant Professor of Oriental Studies at the University of Pennsylvania. Many articles on medieval Hebrew literature, translator, editor. Author, most recently, of *Parables of Interpretation: The Mashal and Parabolic Narrative in Midrash* (1986).

Clemens Thoma: Professor of Biblical Sciences and Judaic Studies at Theological Faculty, Lucerne. Chairman of Institute of Judaeo-Christian Research, Lucerne. Author of many books and articles; most recent, *Die Gleichnisse der Rabbinen, 1. Teil: Pesiqta de Rav Kahana* (1986).

Index

DATE DUE